ABOUT THE AUTHORS

Ross Fitzgerald is a well-known writer and broadcaster, and regular columnist for *The Australian* newspaper and *Spectator Australia*. He is Emeritus Professor of History and Politics at Griffith University, part-time Professional Fellow at the Australian Catholic University and the author of thirty books. Professor Fitzgerald's most recent publications include *The Pope's Battalions: Santamaria, Catholicism and the Labor Split* (UQP), and *Growing Old (Dis)gracefully: 35 Australians Reflect on Life over 50*, co-edited with Lyndal Moor (ABC Books).

Trevor Jordan is a Senior Lecturer in Applied Ethics at the Queensland University of Technology. He was married in Brisbane in 1975 during the local beer strike.

UNDER THE INFLUENCE

A history of alcohol in Australia

Ross Fitzgerald and Trevor L. Jordan

with the assistance of
Anna E. Blainey and Christine Rakvin

ABC
Books

The ABC 'Wave' device is a trademark of the Australian Broadcasting Corporation and is used under licence by HarperCollins*Publishers* Australia.

First published in Australia in 2009
by HarperCollins*Publishers* Australia Pty Limited
ABN 36 009 913 517
www.harpercollins.com.au

HarperCollins*Publishers*
25 Ryde Road, Pymble, Sydney, NSW 2073, Australia
31 View Road, Glenfield, Auckland 0627, New Zealand
A 53, Sector 57, Noida, UP, India
77–85 Fulham Palace Road, London W6 8JB, United Kingdom
2 Bloor Street East, 20th floor, Toronto, Ontario M4W 1A8, Canada
10 East 53rd Street, New York NY 10022, USA

National Library of Australia Cataloguing-in-Publication data:

Fitzgerald, Ross, 1944–
 Under the influence : a history of alcohol in Australia / Ross Fitzgerald.
 ISBN: 978 0 7333 2301 0 (pbk.)
 Drinking of alcoholic beverages – Australia – History.
 Drinking of alcoholic beverages – Social aspects – Australia.
 Australians – Alcohol use.
 Australia – Social life and customs.
 Australian Broadcasting Corporation.
394.130994

Extract from *Never Trust a Man Who Doesn't Drink* reproduced by kind permission of Barry Humphries

While efforts have been made to trace and acknowledge all copyright holders, in some cases this has been unsuccessful. These copyright holders are very welcome to contact the authors care of HarperCollins*Publishers*.

Cover photograph by Gunnar Svanberg Skulesson/Getty Images
Cover design by Heath McCurdy
Typeset in 11.5/16pt Bembo by Kirby Jones

Contents

Foreword

by Mandy Sayer

Almost every day in the Australian media appears an article related to alcohol abuse, from glassing attacks to teenage binge drinking, 24-hour licensing laws to drink driving deaths. Some city councils are attempting to curb overindulgence by introducing 2am lockouts from clubs and hotels; increasingly, entertainment venues are offering free booze buses to assist their inebriated patrons home; and more and more pubs are removing glassware from their racks and replacing it with the plastic cup.

Only last year our Prime Minister, Kevin Rudd, with one or two stark exceptions an abstemious Christian, announced a $53 million dollar program to address the binge-drinking epidemic in teenage Australians, while also threatening to dramatically raise the tax on their preferred alcoholic drinks: Alcopops.

And when you consider that this year 70,000 Australians will be hospitalised due to the effects of alcohol abuse, whether through trauma, injuries, accidents, or diseases, 3,000 of whom will die, you'd be forgiven for assuming that we as a nation have suddenly become a republic of dipsomaniacs.

In fact, as the authors of this extremely readable and thoroughly researched book illustrate, the patterns and problems of alcohol use in Australia can be traced directly back to the first days of European settlement. A small colony without any form of monetary currency, the early settlers imported and traded cheap rum, so much so that strong alcohol became one of our first currencies, even for those who did not drink. Many officers would buy rum at fixed prices from docking ships and resell them at market prices. Labourers were often paid in units of alcohol rather than coins. And the harsh circumstances of the early colonial life contributed to excessive drinking. Moreover most of the fresh water of the settlement was contaminated and virtually undrinkable.

Diluting drinking water with alcohol — rather than the other way around — was a common practice among our forefathers and mothers. Little wonder we have inherited and developed a drinking culture that continues to celebrate excess.

As Ross Fitzgerald and Trevor Jordan point out, many Australians will tell you that they don't trust a person who doesn't drink. In fact, I remember my own father often remarking on his belief that a person who doesn't drink has something to hide. I myself come from a family of heavy drinkers on both sides (my parents' idea of a social outing would be a trip to the local pub; by the time I was eight I knew all the beer gardens in Sydney, including which ones had what on tap). Like most of my fellow countrymen, I was trained in Australian pub etiquette at an early age: always return (and consume) a shout, no matter how big or expensive the round; if you're drinking faster than everyone else, satisfy yourself with a 'wedgie' (a single middy of beer) until the others catch up, then return to the regular chronology of the shout. Failure to comply with these cultural rules would result, at best, in social ostrasisation and, at worse, physical pulverisation.

Many Australians still adopt these rules with unquestioning compliance, little realising that the historical events that initially created the binge culture — lack of currency, harsh conditions, contaminated water, isolation and, later, six o'clock closing — are no longer relevant. Even though the myth of the hardworking, hard drinking Aussie bush hero has faded as an icon of our national identity, contemporary beer ads still trade on this legend.

As actor John Mellion continues to spout through the decades (even though he's long-since died): 'A hard-earned thirst needs a big cold beer.'

There are plenty of stories in my family about the effects of overindulgence — some funny, some horrifying — but up until I read *Under the Influence*, I'd assumed these stories were unique to my ancestors and relatives, rather than being connected to a larger historical narrative.

Figures for arrests due to public drunkenness, collected in the late nineteenth century, suggest the average Australian boozer was a Catholic male in his 20s and 30s, living in New South Wales (my great grandfathers on both sides). The stigma attached to public houses was so severe that women bought grog in jugs to drink at home or had tradesmen deliver it secretly (my maternal grandmother used to send her sons down to the local pub daily to have her billy-can filled with beer). At the same time, however, alcohol was often prescribed as medicine; indeed, one of our first and most famous vitners, Christopher Rawson Penfold, was also a doctor and his first wines were for private medicinal prescription, never for public consumption.

When my Irish paternal grandmother, a staunch Catholic teetotaller, was suffering from nervousness and insomnia, her doctor prescribed her a brandy before bed. Initially horrified at having to imbibe the dreaded drink, she soon found that the cure worked so well that she began drinking earlier and earlier in the day, until the morning my grandfather discovered her dividing her time between the two tasks of chopping vegetables for a pot of soup and grating soap for the laundry. The only problem was that the soap ended up in the soup and the vegetables in the boiler. When my grandfather stormed down to the doctor's surgery and abused him for turning his wife into a drunk, the doctor replied, 'Mr Sayer, I told her to drink two fingers of brandy a day — not two bottles.'

Furthermore, according to the authors, drink driving was common in Australia right up until the 1960s, which explains why, after a booze-fuelled family picnic, when my father was too drunk to drive, he arranged for a family friend, Jeff, to drive us home, while he piled into the back with us kids. The car had only crawled a few feet, however, when Jeff suddenly realised he was too pissed to steer, but assured us he was able to manage the accelerator and brakes. And it was my twelve-year-old brother, sitting on Jeff's lap, knuckles white against the black wheel, following the sequence of instructions — 'Turn left here … change lanes after the lights …' as Jeff worked the pedals — who finally got us home.

In reading *Under the Influence*, I have not only discovered that alcohol has been integral to major events in Australian history, I have also found — as will many other readers — that it has also been integral to major events in the history of my own family. It's fascinating — even intoxicating — to read the story of our country through the bottom of a glass.

But remember — enjoy this book responsibly!

Introduction

In November 2008, Australian Prime Minister Kevin Rudd, promising to 'scare the living daylights' out of complacent young drinkers, introduced a series of TV advertisements targeting drinkers aged 15–35 and their parents.[1] Coinciding with schoolies week, the ads containing portrayals of fighting, traffic accidents and sexual assault were the initial offering in a two-year campaign aimed at showing the violence, injury and humiliation that can result from binge drinking. The wider campaign included ads in teen magazines, online, in cinemas and toilet stalls. The tag-line for the TV ads stated that one in two Australians aged 15–17 when they get drunk will do something they regret. According to the federal Health Minister Helen Roxon, the campaign was necessary given that four Australians under the age of twenty-five died in an average week due to alcohol-related injuries and that one in four hospitalisations of people aged 15–24 were due to alcohol.[2] The $20 million ad campaign was part of a three-step bid to curb dangerous drinking. Another $14.4 million would be allocated for sporting and community groups to promote responsible drinking, and $19.1 million for early intervention programs. The government would have no trouble funding the campaign as the 175 million standard drinks consumed by adolescents aged between twelve and seventeen generated sales of $218 million, which put $107 million of taxes into federal government coffers.[3]

Earlier in April 2008, Rudd's new federal Labor government had announced that it was increasing the excise on pre-mixed alcohol drinks by 70 per cent. According to Nicola Roxon, this measure was aimed at addressing a rise in teenage binge drinking, particularly among young women. She cited figures indicating that the percentage of young girls between the ages of 14 and 19 years consuming pre-mixed drinks had risen from 14 per cent in 2000 to 60 per cent in 2004.

The industry was quick to respond. The evidence of an increase in binge drinking among the young was not there, it claimed. Pre-mixed drinks had nothing to do with binge drinking, and the government was only gouging tax revenue from the pockets of hard-working Australians. The industry line was a familiar one: the research was inconclusive, and spending millions of dollars advertising pre-mixed drinks only encouraged people to change brands, not to take up drinking alcohol. The public had heard it all before from tobacco companies defending their products. What they hadn't heard so often were the unguarded admissions from industry insiders about the purpose of pre-mixed drinks. An advertising executive for Naked Communications, bemoaning the loss of the Absolut Cut 5.5% alcohol pre-mixed product, observed: 'The real area of growth ... is still at 7% with a sophisticated but affordable drink that will appeal to young people on a budget ... They want to buy three drinks and feel it rather than five at 5.5% for double the money.'[4]

Who were the public to believe? Was the Rudd government responding to a moral panic? Were Australians becoming a nation of wowsers? In late 2007, new draft guidelines for alcohol consumption were released for comment by the National Health and Medical Research Council. They downgraded the recommended daily intake of alcohol to no more than two standard drinks for both men and women, arguing that short-term and long-term risks increased proportionally as a person exceeded that level. Even senior researchers committed to reducing alcohol dependence in the community argued that these new recommendations were so low that they might be culturally unacceptable.

Despite the many rumblings of discontent that followed the increased excise on pre-mixed drinks, it is unlikely that any of Kevin Rudd's new measures for reducing binge drinking will result in a 21st-century Rum Rebellion. Despite claims that drinking is central to Australian cultural life, barely 50 per cent of Australians are motivated to drink an alcoholic beverage on a daily or weekly basis. One in ten Australians have never drunk a full serve of alcohol, another 7 per cent are ex-drinkers, and a third of the population enjoy a drink now and then but don't consume alcohol on either a weekly or daily basis.[5] In reality, when it comes to alcohol consumption, Australians are a diverse, if not divided, community. Still, though we are not as heavy drinkers as many of us often think we are, in 2004–05 the annual cost to the community of alcohol abuse was reported as being $15.3 billion, including $1.6 billion associated with crime, just under $2 billion on health costs, $3.5 billion in lost productivity and $2.2 billion on road accidents.[6]

These figures seriously challenge the harm principle at the heart of liberal democratic ethos — that an individual ought to be free to pursue his or her interests so long as they do not harm others. It is perhaps a symptom of modern life that public debate often ends up drowning in a sea of figures. Ultimately, however, our response to alcohol will be a question of morality rather than maths. Our attitude to alcohol will be shaped by our understanding of who we are, and who and what we care about and for.

In responding to the community's current needs in relation to the influence of alcohol it wouldn't hurt to reflect on our collective past. Finding a balance between individual freedom and regulation is not a new problem: it has been present ever since the British colonisers decided to establish a penal colony in New South Wales and to supply it with alcohol. It was an important issue in the nineteenth century when the temperance movement spread to Australia. Anti-drink sentiments weren't the isolated preserve of conservative Christians; many radical socialists also campaigned against the alcohol industry's role in exploiting the working class. Perceptions of what could be achieved through public policy were profoundly affected by the experience of Prohibition in the United States of America in the early twentieth century.

The trouble with history is that there's just so much of it. Studying the past must be a strategic exercise: we must decide what best suits our purpose — tree and leaf detail or mountain-top vistas. In surveying how alcohol has influenced life in Australia, we have chosen the latter. Not because it is an easier road — it is not — but because only such a synoptic view will yield the perspectives we need to assess future options in the light of past experience. If this seems too pragmatic for those who prefer to dip into history as a kind of holiday from the present — so be it.

All histories in various ways explore the influences that shape events, identities and values. At times, alcohol has directly influenced historical events in Australia. Most Australian children of high school age have heard of the infamous Rum Rebellion, not least because it involved the equally infamous Captain William Bligh, whose bullying and verbal abuse provoked a mutiny on the HMS *Bounty*. Not so many would know that in 1918 a beer boycott contributed to a bloodless

4

revolt by Northern Territorians against their administrator, the Scottish-born John Anderson Gilruth, who had to flee by boat.[7] Booze also played a big role at the Eureka Stockade. Vivid moments of individual drunkenness and collective debauchery also occasionally figure in descriptions of Australia life. In 1867, for example, when Prince Alfred, Queen Victoria's son, was a no show (for security reasons) at a picnic to honour his visit to Melbourne — the first royal tour in Australia's history — the *Argus* newspaper reported parched crowds stampeding in a 'bacchanalian picture of unbelievable horror', swarming over the food, champagne, and wine that had been provided for the volunteer workers.[8] Although John Kerr's drunken antics as Governor-General on Melbourne Cup day in 1977 occurred two years after the event, alcohol also played its part in the dismissal of the Whitlam government, still regarded by many Australian Labor Party faithful as a virtual coup. Gough Whitlam would not have recommended Kerr for the position of Governor-General if he had been aware of Kerr's galloping alcoholism.[9] However, a mere chronicling of events in which alcohol played a part would be a very short book, and would hardly meet the test of social significance required nowadays to justify responsible researchers' time.

Most of what the public knows about grog in Australia is caricature, and most caricatures are meant to amuse. Thus, from vaudeville to video, the drunk has been a classic part of comic performance. Every New Year's Eve, SBS television, Australia's multicultural broadcaster, programs a sketch, sourced from overseas, about a drunken butler.[10] But caricatures are also deployed as rhetorical devices in arguments. Arguably, the extreme negative images of the harmful effects of alcohol consumption used from time to time as shock tactics in alcohol education programs are seeking a practical benefit from caricatures. In its early days, the iconic journal *The Bulletin* perpetuated a caricature of the nation as divided between boozers and wowsers. In general it was on the side of the boozers.

The Australian satirical journal, *Humbug* (15 September 1869), featured Marcus Clarke's essay on 'The Curse of the Country', Henry Kendall's poem 'The Demon of Drink', and Thomas Carrington's illustration 'King Nobbler'. 'We are a nation of *Drunkards*,' wrote Clarke. 'King Nobbler rules over us, and all classes bow down before him.' Clarke's heartfelt conclusion was that 'No man can hope to succeed in business, profession, or society, unless he is prepared to take his chance of death in an asylum for inebriates.' Regarding the power of alcohol, Kendall agreed:

> Thou art devil and despot to men;
> Thy grip is on wise and on weak —
> On mighty of sword and of pen;
> On those who in council-halls speak.

According to Michael Wilding, Clarke and Kendall both wrote from experience. In his bankruptcy statement, Clarke mentioned a debt for £150 for wines and spirits, while in other Australian journals of that time there were numerous mentions of Kendall's frequent inebriation.[11]

While caricatures bear some resemblance to reality, the real story, as always, is more complex and prosaic: most Australians have been neither boozers nor wowsers but more or less soberly somewhere in between.

The common phrase 'under the influence' is apt, describing the effects of alcohol as a drug on human behaviour, in particular, diminished levels of control. Yet it also connotes at least a degree of responsibility — one is influenced, not dominated. The amount of influence alcohol has will depend on variables such as quantity, individual tolerance levels and context. It would be easy and obvious to describe the influence that alcohol has had on Australian society as straightforwardly analogous to its effects on the human body, but this would be a mistake. Decisions about the manufacture, supply, consumption and regulation of alcohol are almost never taken by people who are directly suffering its effects. Alcohol is a powerful drug, but not so powerful that its social effects can be as unambiguous as its physiological effects. A broader range of social, economic, cultural, religious and political variables always comes into play. To take one example, even the devastatingly destructive impacts of alcohol on Indigenous Australians have been mediated through structures of colonialism and colonisation, which systemically dispossessed, exploited and impoverished, and then blamed the victims for not coping.

As we look at Australian history through the bottom of the beer, wine and whisky glass, social and cultural realities are refracted. Primarily, alcohol has been more a reflector of Australian culture than a major determinant of cultural change; its patterns of use and abuse reflect other influences — social, economic and cultural. Consideration of the history of these influences, then, is potentially more enlightening than simply reviewing the scientific data on its physiological effects.

When focusing on factors that have influenced the consumption of alcohol, we will naturally be interested in how these factors differ from patterns elsewhere. Many of the attitudes and practices surrounding alcohol in Australia are not unique; they are the same as those in other western developed countries. Nevertheless, looking for significant differences may help us to identify what is uniquely Australian. Some readers will be disillusioned, and others encouraged, to find out that Australians are not and have not been the booziest people on the planet. The claim that our level of alcohol consumption is a unique feature of our national identity is a myth. Of course, the function of many myths is not to describe reality — myths construct images not of who we are but who we want to be. Exaggerating our collective alcohol consumption, then, may be an oblique symptom of some disappointment with our everyday selves.

The physiological effects of drink can themselves be a source of escape from such disappointments. It is hard not to think that many of the first European settlers in Australia drank out of a sense of despair and disappointment rather than celebration. The physiological effects of drink also refract the picture of who we are and who we want to be. Alcohol is a powerful tool for managing the effects of modern times. As with other drugs, it partakes in equal measure of the two great principles that have dominated the utilitarian ethos of modern life: pleasure and pain. Alcohol became a powerful part of the bourgeois, industrial world. The immiseration of workers, social dislocation and a moral order in transition, for example, have all contributed to making drunkenness a social symptom of modernity. Drink is never neutral. People with strong feelings are either for it or against it. Even fence-sitting requires some moral justification. Alcohol is a barometer of moral concerns not because it is disapproved of by some, but because even those who promote its use and benefits must necessarily draw on moral frameworks, such as personal liberty and social toleration, to do so. Even to assert that the pursuit of pleasure through drinking requires no moral justification is itself one kind of moral framework — hedonism — and hedonism, some have claimed, is one aspect of our national character.

The history of alcohol in Australia presents us with a unique opportunity for moral reflection. Morality is not something confined to churches and philosophers, it is something embedded in our policies and practices regarding trade and consumption and our use of everyday objects. A popular notion holds that whether an individual drinks is not the point; it is how he or she handles the drink that matters. Arguably, how a community or nation handles alcohol may also be a strong indicator of its collective character. It is worth stating again: our attitudes towards alcohol tell us something about who we are, who we care about, and what we care about. In learning when to consume alcohol and when not, for example, we are learning about moral responsibility.

There have been many fine articles and monographs written on aspects of alcohol in Australia. In this book we bring together insights from these works and other historical records to answer questions about the influence of alcohol on various aspects of Australian life, and the influences that have shaped our alcohol consumption. Hopefully, the approach we have taken tells a tale far more interesting than a mere chronicling of the opening and closing of local wineries and breweries.

Necessarily, such a tale starts by exploring the external influences on Australian alcohol consumption when Europeans settled here. Why was a penal colony provisioned with alcohol in the first place? Why did early New South Wales have so much trouble with spirits, when the use of spirits was in decline in Britain at the time the colony was founded? We move on to consider how social life was organised around alcohol consumption. How did alcohol become both a marker and maker of social class and ethnicity? Who drank what? How has alcohol shaped gender relationships in Australia? What part has it played in defining broader national identities?

Everyone drinks, but not everyone drinks alcohol. Some Australians have always been non-participants in the drinking culture, being either quietly abstemious or abstinent. John Macarthur, for example, the ruthless and vengeful instigator of the Rum Rebellion, was personally averse to consumption of alcohol but avidly traded in it.[12] Others have not been so accommodating and have actively campaigned against the perceived evils of the demon drink. We ask: who was opposed to alcohol consumption, why did they oppose it, and how did they do it? What has been their legacy on Australian society and culture?

Excessive alcohol consumption exacts a heavy toll on individuals and society. Manifestly, alcohol can be harmful, and even the tolerant frameworks of liberalism have always sought to ameliorate its negative effects. How was the interpretation of such harms influenced by the intellectual theories of the day? Why has drunkenness been variously viewed as moral degeneration, criminality, medical disease, psychopathology, or aberrant behaviour in need of modification through, for example, so-called 'controlled drinking'?

Finally, we will assess whether the social tolerance of alcohol consumption, the fine balance between freedom and regulation in a liberal democracy, is coming to an end. How will the future of alcohol consumption be affected by the relative demise of tobacco and the emerging politics of health?

In the history of alcohol consumption, vested interests necessarily play a major role. It takes no complicated theory to work out that those who benefit from the sale of alcohol promote its consumption and supposed benefits. We should expect them to be self-serving to some extent. Profit-making from alcohol does play its role in the long history of human greed; perhaps surprisingly, even more so in times of prohibition. Nevertheless, selling grog is, after all, simply one way to make a buck. Those like Macarthur, who controlled the rum trade in Australia's formative years, also controlled the general stores and made significant profits from the sale of other goods.

Since the beginnings of European settlement in Australia, there has not been a time in our history when those in authority did not recognise that alcohol consumption can be harmful and that its use ought to be subject to some regulation and control. The penal colony of New South Wales was established at a time when notions of liberalism were being explored in Europe. It was not only evangelicals and revivalists who opposed drunkenness; enlightened men and women of the day also saw the abuse of alcohol as a possible impediment to the full flowering of humanity and the potential of individuals to be reformed in attitude and behaviour. European Australia, we will find, has been under the influence from the jump.

CHAPTER 1

A Groggy Start

On 26 January 1788, Captain Arthur Phillip (1738–1814), a company of British marines and forty male convicts gathered around a flagpole after a hard day of cutting down trees, clearing land and erecting tents by the banks of a freshwater stream leading into a natural harbour. The officers drank a toast to the health of the royal family and the new colony: the first recorded alcoholic drink by European settlers on Australian soil. Twelve days later, the last of the fleet's eleven ships, carrying the female convicts, disembarked. It rained heavily, and a large tree struck by lightning fell and killed five sheep and a pig. A night of debauchery followed — a mixture of drunkenness, sexual excess and, in some cases, sexual assault.[1] Alcohol had begun playing its part in bringing European civilisation, with all its many contradictions, to Terra Australis.

Why had this settlement, whose purpose was to control and rehabilitate felons, fallen so swiftly under the influence? Ironically, the site of the debauchery — the cove with a freshwater spring and now the site of two of Australia's most famous icons, the Sydney Opera

House and the Sydney Harbour Bridge — had already been named after the man who had begrudgingly allowed alcohol to be taken to the colony. Lord Sydney (Thomas Townsend, 1732–1800), the secretary of state for the colonies, was in charge of the plans to colonise New South Wales. While responsible for transporting boatloads of convicts, he was more interested in exporting ideas of English liberty. He was a student of Enlightenment ideas and a one-time supporter of the American Revolution. In the right environment and with firm hands to guide them, human beings, he thought, were capable of moral reform. Supplying the convict fleet with wine and spirits could only inhibit such reform by importing vices, so initially he opposed it.[2] Although he finally relented, Sydney succeeded in preventing money (in the form of coinage) — that other source of corruption — from being sent. Unfortunately for the majority of the colonists, but to the great fortune of an avaricious minority, Sydney did not foresee that one vice would be destined to fill the vacuum left by the other.

Another reason for alcohol's arrival in New South Wales was that the penal colony was the latest addition to Britain's oceanic empire. It not only required the navy to get there, but also a navy man, Captain Arthur Phillip, to be in command. Largely due to the efforts of the many planters, bankers, slavers, shippers, refiners, grocers and people in government with interests in sugar, rum was already an entrenched part of naval culture.[3] The institutionalisation of a rum ration began after the capture of Jamaica in 1655. By 1731, the navy ration was already half a pint per day. In the late eighteenth century, it increased to a pint a day for adult sailors. Official allocations of sugar and treacle to the poorhouses in Britain in the late eighteenth century were similar government support measures for the sugar industry.[4] At the time, such assistance was vital because beer was more popular than spirits. Beer was supplied to the workhouses, and in the wider community was drunk at nearly every meal, even by children.[5]

However, the drawback of beer for the new colonists was the expense: it took up more space and spoiled much more easily than spirits.

Then, as now, alcoholic drinks were known by many names. 'Spirits' was a general term describing all alcoholic drinks except beer, implying a process of distillation in addition to natural fermentation. From about 1800, 'rum' was used as a generic term for spirits, particularly by its opponents. Sometimes made from fruits (and fish roe!), rum was primarily a sugar-based product distilled and fermented from sugar-cane juice or molasses, yielding a variety of dark, golden or colourless spirits depending on the type of casks in which they were stored. Rum was a significant item of mercantile commerce, figuring prominently in the triangle of trade between Britain, Africa and the New World. The background of the rum trade was as dark as the molasses from which it was often made: 'From New England went rum to Africa, whence slaves to the West Indies, whence molasses back to New England (with which to make rum).'[6] Ultimately, the profitability of rum was founded on the 'false commodity' of slaves; that is, not on raw materials as such but on human lives whose labour was forcibly appropriated.[7]

Blackstrap, a mixture of rum and treacle, was the basis for the British sailor's grog, which was mixed in varying proportions with water. Officers took theirs unwatered. As Captain Phillip's fleet had taken a supply on board at Rio de Janeiro, blackstrap constituted most of the spirits that initially reached the colony. The first shipment of beer, probably in its more stable form of porter, would not land in Botany Bay until four years later.[8]

The stern and abstemious Phillip ended up in charge of the colony because of his intellectual sympathies with Lord Sydney. Major Robert Ross, who commanded the Marine Corps sent to the new colony, was initially to be in charge, but Sydney preferred Phillip. Having spent time with him socially, he saw in Phillip a man sympathetic to humanitarian ideals who could shape the penal settlement into a free colony. Phillip was, for instance, adamant that slavery would have no place in the new colony: 'There can be no slavery in a free land, and consequently no slaves.'[9] Today, we may find it hard to understand how men such as Phillip could be enlightened and humanitarian in outlook while at the same time being stern disciplinarians who meted out cruel corporal and capital punishments. In fact, this kind of authoritarian liberalism, or enlightened despotism, was widespread in contemporary European political circles.

Those charged with the duty of colonising the non-European world approached their task with intellectual seriousness. In Lord Sydney's eyes, the terms of the convicts' sentences were clearly set out by courts of law; once served they would be free men and women, entitled to the same rights as citizens in England to be free from the exercise of tyranny. Convicts would be able to contribute to the common good. Having their own land would enable them to improve materially and morally. Rather than being a cruel punishment, transportation, in theory, offered opportunities for a new life: 'Transported convicts were all assumed to go abroad under pardon, and they took whatever property they liked with them.'[10] As Alan Atkinson has observed: 'In strict law the sentence of transportation involved nothing more than banishment. No Transportation Act made any reference to hard labour or other penalties.'[11] In American colonies, such as Virginia and Maryland, convicts were sold to colonists to serve out their sentences, advantaging both civic and economic life.[12] In New South Wales, initially, there was no one to purchase their labour, so it was put solely at the disposal of the governor. Phillip believed that convicts would not need great incentives; they could either work for the common good or starve.

The colony turned out not to be the paradise that Captain James Cook's great botanist Joseph Banks had said it would be. (Cook and Banks had seen Botany Bay in the autumn of 1770; the colonists arrived mid-summer 1788.) The new land was harsh and the rewards for effort meagre. Phillip's strong and steady hand was needed more often than his optimistic beliefs might have anticipated. Not only were most of the colonists agriculturally unskilled, past experience strongly indicated that they preferred the easy road of theft and fraud to hard work. Nevertheless, criminal reform remained a practical necessity: 94 per cent of the convicts were serving sentences of seven years or less. Many had already served a year by the time they had disembarked. Phillip applied his disciplined and disciplining hand not only to the convicts but also to the marines and soldiers who looked after them. They were subjected to the same disciplines, punishments and rations as the convicts.

British colonial efforts were always a balancing act of contradictions: civilising the world required acts of barbaric cruelty; extending liberties required disciplining wayward bodies; encouraging enterprise meant supporting monopolies; and virtue and morality were required to temper the preoccupation with utility and profitability. Such contradictions were not the result of a lazy hypocrisy; they were the by-product of often conflicting intellectual and practical commitments. The use and regulation of alcohol came to be a pivotal expression of this clash.

Economically, Britain supported and rewarded enterprise but it was hardly ever free or openly competitive. Establishing the new colony in New South Wales was a government initiative, yet after the First Fleet the convoys were contracted out to private enterprise: the East India Company. A series of royal charters from the time of Elizabeth I had already guaranteed the East India Company a virtual monopoly of British commercial operations in the Indian and Pacific Oceans. In his 'biography' of the city of Sydney, John Birmingham called it 'the Microsoft of its day'.[13]

A different sort of balancing act had emerged with regard to ethics. The virtues most widely prized in individuals in Britain and

15

Europe were determined by standards of behaviour that served the public good.[14] In 1780, for example, Sir Hugh Palliser (1722–96), naval officer and later governor of Newfoundland, erected a memorial to honour the memory of Captain Cook. Appealing to two virtues widely admired in the eighteenth century, Sir Hugh described Cook as possessing 'every useful and amiable quality'.[15] Usefulness or utility as a virtue was an essential ingredient in the emerging industrial culture, generating profits through enterprise and innovation. But at times, the drive to succeed could also produce arrogance and conflict, and agricultural and industrial innovations could lead to social dislocation and enforced idleness among large sections of the population. Usefulness, therefore, needed to be balanced with amiability; a quality which, to Jane Austen's (1775–1817) Christian eyes, was superior to mere agreeableness. As Alasdair MacIntyre put it in his discussion of the virtues of that era, amiability meant more than being socially agreeable; it involved the capacity to get along with others in 'a genuine loving regard for other people as such, and not only the impression of such regard embodied in manners'.[16]

These two virtues — usefulness and amiability — give us some perspective on eighteenth-century attitudes to alcohol. Without appreciating them, we might misconstrue seemingly contradictory attitudes, policies and behaviours as instances of hypocrisy, as M. H. Ellis did, for example, in his extended biographical defence of the colonial entrepreneur and rebel John Macarthur (1767–1834). Ellis mounts an adversarial case in favour of Macarthur that paints many of his detractors as hypocrites because they complained about drunkenness in the community while themselves imbibing and even trading in spirits.[17] Such an either/or reading misses the point. Even without a sophisticated understanding of the underlying physiological processes, the behavioural effects of alcohol consumption were well known. The obvious difference between drinking alcohol and drunkenness was widely recognised. For centuries, alcohol had been useful at celebrations for toasting the health and honour of a worthy recipient and generally promoting amiability between all who shared in the toast. Up to a point, drinking alcohol was widely accepted as useful, and alcohol was commonly used for medicinal and other social purposes. The sugar lobby had even promoted the view that rum was healthier than brandy.[18] Nonetheless, general experience proved that excessive consumption led to disagreeable and unruly behaviour that was not only potentially destructive of social relationships but could also lead to inefficiency and waste in the workplace.

By the time Australia was being settled by the British, there were many reasons to question the social usefulness of drinking. In England, social awareness of public drunkenness had dramatically increased in the late seventeenth century when the introduction of gin — a Dutch creation — not only increased the popularity of spirit drinking but also instigated a so-called 'gin craze'. The succession of the Dutchman William of Orange to the British throne in 1689 had ushered in the British gin industry, which was boosted by minimal taxes and a ban on foreign imports of gin. Being relatively new, widespread gin production was also not covered by the restrictive rules of a guild. Over the next sixty years, gin manufacturing, retail and consumption skyrocketed. With grain prices low, gin wasn't only cheap to produce but also cheap enough for the poor to consume in quantity. Testimony to the high rate of drunkenness and its social repercussions could be found in official reports and in publications such as Thomas Wilson's *Distilled Liquors: The Bane of the Nation* (1736). According to a magistrates report of 1726, in some parishes one in ten houses was a gin shop.[19]

For both the evangelical and the enlightened, the succession of the Hanovers to the throne had only hastened Britain's descent into a period of intellectual and moral laxity. By the mid-eighteenth century, this perception of moral degeneration in English society was depicted in the writings of the novelist, essayist and magistrate Henry Fielding (1707–54) and typified by his artist friend William Hogarth (1697–1764) in his contrasting prints, *Beer Street* and *Gin Lane* (1751). Beer Street is inhabited by happy (amiable) and hard-working (useful) folk, while Gin Lane's inhabitants are depicted as unhealthy, immoral and irresponsible. In Gin Lane only the pawnbroker is doing a roaring trade, whereas in Beer Street all the small businesses and street traders are thriving and only the pawnbroker is going bust.

Opposition to public drunkenness began to have political effect. In the 1750s, taxes and duties were increased and strict licensing laws introduced, ending the sale of gin by chandlers and street hawkers. Over the next thirty years, British gin production fell from 7 million gallons per year to a mere 1 million. Meanwhile, Britain's new-found saccharophilia — a love for sugar and its products — had upped the

In William Hogarth's *Beer Street* (1751) everyone is happy, except the pawn broker. Climatic conditions in Australia were not favourable to brewing beer in the new colony. (Public domain)

In contrast to Beer Street, the inhabitants of William Hogarth's *Gin Lane* (1751) are debauched, debased and poor. Only the pawn broker is thriving. Though the 'gin craze' had long passed in England, the new colony was described as 'floating on a sea of spirits'. (Public domain)

consumption of rum from 207 gallons in 1698 to an annual average of over 2 million gallons from 1771–75.[20] By 1788, however, the overall consumption of gin and spirits was again in serious decline. Consequently, it could be said that government support for rations of rum in the navy and in the workhouses had constituted a 'much needed creeping socialism for an infant industry'.[21]

The spirit-drinking habits of the new colonists went against the trends at home. By the time Phillip arrived in Botany Bay, the geography of booze in Europe was something like this. In Ireland, where beer was uncommon outside of the towns and taxes were imposed on malt and hops, whisky still dominated. It was legal to distil whisky in limited amounts at home. Irish whisky consumption continued to rise well into the nineteenth century, when Irish navvies working on the railway cuttings reintroduced it to the working classes in England.[22] The Scottish highlanders were also renowned as whisky drinkers, although the drink of the middle classes in the Scottish lowlands was imported claret.[23] Indeed, wines were generally drunk by the middle and upper classes, but due to the colder climate it was mostly imported. Beer had once again become the predominant drink in England and in other northern European countries such as Germany, Belgium and the Netherlands. Its new-found popularity in England had been aided by the introduction of a new beer called porter. Dark brown in colour with a bitter taste, porter was brewed from malt partly charred or browned by drying at a high temperature. It was more stable and long-lasting than earlier beers and thus more commercially viable.[24] Part of the attraction of beer was that it could be produced locally, and home brewing was still quite prevalent in some rural areas in England in the eighteenth century. Although widely consumed, beer had not yet become a source of great profit to individuals. Some farmers took their raw materials to the brewer, but brewing was only starting to become a commercial enterprise. This symbol of the useful and amiable consumption of alcohol would not be available in quantity in New South Wales for many years. Consequently, nearly every governor from Phillip onwards had to contend with his own local spirits craze in one form or another.

The planners back home had thought that the inherent demands of surviving in a new environment would eventually bend hearts, minds and bodies towards the pursuit of the common good. Nevertheless, they could not see how this spirit would arise naturally among those whose supposed moral inadequacies had already led them to prefer thieving and fraud to hard work. The rights and potentialities of men and women in this new society had to be protected and guided by a firm, authoritarian hand. One early event typifies the equivocal effects of Phillip's authoritarian liberalism. On the king's birthday in 1788, Phillip issued pardons for all those awaiting trial or punishment for offences in the colony and distributed grog to every convict, soldier and sailor to toast the king's health. There was a large bonfire in celebration. The convict response to this largesse was to raid the officers' tents while they dined with the governor.[25]

Other than such special occasions and medicinal use, the first store of rum in the new colony was meant strictly for officers and officials. The convicts were forbidden to drink it under penalty of flogging. On 11 February 1788, just over two weeks after landing, the first flogging of a seaman for bringing spirits ashore had the distinction of being the colony's first judicial sentence. Another seaman was given fifty lashes for the same offence on 22 February. The next day, for a similar offence, a seaman received 100 lashes.[26] Despite such efforts, drunkenness in New South Wales remained common. The settlement was effectively an open prison and the rules were continually broken.

Supplies, however, were intermittent. In the early years, when no supply ships came, the colonists were starved not only of food but also of alcohol. Later, visiting whalers brought supplies of rum from Brazil while other ships brought it from Bengal. With profits to be made, it wasn't long before every available space, even on the convict ships, was loaded with goods for trade. Spirits and tobacco, both relatively imperishable, were the most popular, and they were conveniently available en route at Rio de Janeiro. To stem a disruptive flow of grog, Phillip proposed that all spirits required a permit to be landed, and all spirits without permit were to be seized. He wrote home suggesting that a duty placed on spirits would help the infant colony. The British government saw no benefit in this request, as only convict ships (they mistakenly thought) would visit the colony. They agreed, instead, to send 'a certain quantity of port wine and tobacco' to be distributed at cost price to civil and military officers, along with 'an allowance of rum for non-commissioned officers and privates'.[27] The British secretary of state also agreed to allow each convict a ration of half a gallon of rum per annum in addition to their other rations.[28] These were centrally stored and distributed as required. To supplement this meagre ration, convicts would band together and combine a tenth of their other rations to buy rum or sugar for illegal stills from their officers.[29]

Such supply initiatives only exacerbated the problem of drunkenness in the colony. The ability of the officers to purchase spirits at fixed prices and then to re-sell them at market rates encouraged private trade. As the first to board the ships, officers were also able to control and monopolise the amount of spirits landed beyond that supplied as rations. Trade in spirits was also boosted by the fact that even those who did not imbibe received a rum ration. Consequently, even a moralistic officer like Lieutenant William Dawes, engineer and surveyor on the First Fleet and a disciple of the prominent English evangelical reformer William Wilberforce, would trade what he did not need to those who wanted it.[30] Reverend Richard Johnson, the first Church of England chaplain in the colony, tired of waiting for the authorities to assist him, built his own church for £67 and was reputed to have paid his labourers in rum. His assistant, Reverend Samuel Marsden, who arrived six years later and became known as the 'flogging parson' for his severity on the magistrate's bench, was also willing to either sell or drink a bottle himself. Given the absence of any currency of exchange in New South Wales, it is hard to be overly critical of such behaviour.

The rapidly emerging rage for trade dampened Governor Phillip's vision of building a commonwealth of souls working towards a common good. The vision was further dampened with the arrival on the Second Fleet in 1790 of the first detachment of the New South Wales Corps, who replaced the marines as the convicts' supervisors. Generally, soldiers were not thought of highly, even by their superiors. Sometime later, for example, the Duke of Wellington would refer to his men as 'scum of the earth — the mere scum of the earth', who had 'enlisted for drink — that is a plain fact'.[31] Indeed, some of the New

South Wales Corps were military convicts from the Savoy military prison, who had enlisted to avoid punishment. The majority of the Corps were men who, one way or another, did not fit: 'ordinary wage-earners unable to find employment; skilled men in trades rendered redundant by technological change; poor Irish rural and urban labourers; the dispossessed of the Scottish highlands; and men unwilling to tie themselves down to unwanted parental responsibilities'.[32]

However, against all evidence to the contrary, the members of the Corps thought themselves a cut above the rest.

Many of the officers in the Corps were also marginal men in their own way, who, like the young John Macarthur, felt perpetually excluded from the English upper classes and saw a military commission as a stepping stone to status and social acceptance. Macarthur was an archetypal careerist — someone who uses public avenues to reach private destinations. He had paid for a succession of commissions, culminating in a transfer to the 68th Regiment at the Rock of Gibraltar. However, he quickly changed commissions to take advantage of opportunities in New South Wales. On their departure from England, Macarthur's wife, Elizabeth, wrote to her parents: 'We have a very reasonable expectation of reaping the most material advantages.'[33]

After their years of privation, the colonists expected relief with the arrival of the privately contracted Second Fleet. When it finally arrived, the hopeful locals were horrified to find an emaciated human cargo starved of their rightful rations by captains who had loaded their ships with articles of trade.[34] It became known as the Death Fleet, with 273 convicts dying en route from England. First Fleeter Captain Watkin Tench (1758–1833) observed that the ships' captains 'immediately opened stores, and exposed large quantities of goods to sale, which, though at exorbitant prices, were bought up'.[35] Among those goods was porter, the first beer in the colony. Seizing an opportunity to at least channel the flow of spirits, Phillip granted the colony's first liquor licence to the fleet's commander, Captain E. H.

Bond. Bond and his first officer, Thomas Reibey, set up shops in Sydney and Parramatta, selling both spirits and porter.[36]

With the Second Fleet came news that any marines who chose to settle in New Holland (as the colony was called at the time) would be eligible for generous grants of land and support from government stores for one year. While most left the colony, sixty-three stayed. The Third Fleet's arrival in July 1791 brought the news that expired convicts would also be granted land to encourage them to stay in the colony. This was the beginning of civil society in New South Wales. That the colony was to be a joint-stock endeavour provided no joy for the members of the NSW Corps who wanted to accrue benefits to themselves. From the outset, the officers of the Corps didn't envisage sharing either the burdens or the advantages of life in the new colony. Upon his arrival, the commander of the Corps, Major Francis Grose, complained to Phillip that Corps members received the same rations as convicts. Phillip told him he needed no reminding of how frugal the rations were; he saw the same amount on his own plate each night.

Grose appointed John Macarthur to the influential position of Corps paymaster, which he held from 1792 until 1799. Macarthur was able to invest Corps funds in trading enterprises. One of the Corps' first investments was to charter the ship *Britannia* to bring merchandise to the colony from Cape Town.[37] Macarthur arranged eleven shares of £200 each from among the officers. In October 1792, Grose wrote to Phillip for permission for this undertaking, having already encountered difficulties when they had chartered the *Pitt* without Phillip's permission. Phillip was sensitive to the East India Company's official monopoly over supply to the colony, but with a sense of increasing urgency over the delay of these official supplies he came to accept private enterprises. Yet even as these arrangements were being made, the *Royal Admiral* arrived with a cargo of porter, which was distributed to the licensed houses. The attempt to control the amount of alcohol in the colony through licensed premises had a limited impact on unruly behaviour. David Collins, the judge-advocate and later administrator of the colony in Van Diemen's Land, observed that some settlers shamefully abused the privilege of access to licensed premises, 'beating their wives, destroying their crops in the ground and destroying each other's property'.[38]

In November 1792, the *Philadelphia* arrived with beef, wine, rum, tobacco, pitch and tar. Phillip purchased £2929 worth of goods and the remainder was sold to civil and military officers, the only other source of customers in the colony. The next year, the captain of the *Hope* brought 7600 gallons of spirits to the colony. He flatly refused to sell food unless the spirits were also purchased. Phillip had returned to England and Major Grose was in charge of the colony. Grose purchased the spirits and distributed them to the officers — 'to defeat the shameful imposition of trading Sea Captains' he claimed.[39] Rum to the rescue! Buying rum had saved the colony from starvation.

On taking control, Grose immediately increased the rations of civil and military officers. He also replaced the civil magistrates with Corps officers. Under Grose, and later fellow Corps officer William Paterson (1755–1810), Governor Phillip's disciplinary policies were reversed and extensive land grants were made to officers of the Corps and their friends. Many, however, lacked the skills and finances to take advantage of them — they also had their normal military duties to perform, which meant labour was gradually diverted from public farms to these private concerns. As the government was the only reliable purchaser in the colony, it both provided labour for private use and paid for the fruits of that labour, adding considerable leverage to some of the more competent officers' enterprises. Further advantage was obtained by paying the convicts with goods, including rum.

It was not an original idea; many planters in the West Indies already used rum to avoid their legislated responsibilities to feed their slaves, 'fobbing them off with payments of rum wherewith to buy food'.[40] No doubt, such a cynical use of alcohol was enhanced by the inequalities of power between slaves and owners. In those colonies founded by free settlers, however, such as Georgia, established in 1732, alcohol consumption was restricted. To encourage hard work and reward enterprise, 'no Drunkards, or other notoriously vicious Persons' would be taken, and the drinking and sale of rum was to be prohibited.[41]

The NSW Corps has often been described as a monopoly, but it can be better described as a cartel. Its officers were not the only ones supplying the colony with alcohol, but being first to board incoming ships they had considerable control over the flow of alcohol. And being paid in treasury bills via regimental accounts, the officers were, for a time, the only colonists with ready access to the large amounts of money required to finance imports. As paymaster, John Macarthur made use of these funds in highly profitable enterprises that benefited both himself and his fellow officers. By borrowing from various common accounts, individual officers were able to invest amounts far beyond what was in their personal accounts. Ship captains were happy to be paid in treasury bills. The key part of the whole arrangement was that the officers did not compete against each other when purchasing goods, agreeing on purchase prices beforehand. In theory, these business enterprises did not interfere with their military duties, as they did not have to buy and sell goods themselves. Paymasters arranged the charters and the other officers selected convicts — often women not already co-opted as personal companions — to re-sell their goods. Prior to Governor Hunter's arrival, the chaplain Reverend Richard Johnson claimed that the mark-up on spirits was 1200 per cent. According to George Bond, an ensign in the Corps: 'Rum and brandy — which cost 10 shillings a gallon, are sold to soldiers and convicts from 10 to 20 shillings per bottle which will not contain a quart. Tea purchased at 10 shillings per pound sold at 5 guineas; coffee and other articles in proportion.'[42]

In the absence of competition, genuine commercial enterprise was unsustainable.

It is revealing to note an ensign of the Corps complaining about the prices. Unlike the officers, the troops do not appear to have received the paymaster's treasury notes until Governor William Bligh arrived in 1806. Most rank-and-file Corps members, civil authorities and convicts relied on the government store, which paid them in goods rather than cash. To take full advantage of their buying power and price fixing, Corps officers used purchased goods such as spirits as payment for direct labour and barter for locally produced products such as wheat. Only in the absence of true market forces could significant profit be made from the demand on spirits; without the forced use of consumables such as spirits and other goods for barter and pay, oversupply would be a problem. As far as future prospects were concerned, taking long-term advantage of bartering required the establishment of significant land holdings and enterprises in which free convict labour could be profitably employed to generate further profits. The acquisition of land holdings became as important as controlling goods and prices, with the most enterprising minority of Corps officers benefiting. Only Macarthur, his successor as paymaster, Captain Anthony Fenn Kemp, and the civil officer Garnham Blaxcell, a partner of Macarthur's, persisted with large-scale commercial activity in the face of serious competition.[43]

Formal control of the colony by officers of the Corps came to an end in 1795 with the arrival of Governor John Hunter (1737–1821). Hunter was alarmed at the unrestricted trade in spirits and its negative impact on useful activity. While he conceded that a small amount was useful and sufficient to entice men to labour 'which money could not purchase', he tried to limit the trade in spirits 'from which the destructions of health and the ruin of industry may be expected'. He tried to combat idleness by withdrawing government support for settlers who had occupied land for more than two years.

He decried 'the frequent state of inebriation in which great numbers of the lower order of people in these settlements have for some time past been seen'.[44] Hunter also forbade licensed premises to exchange spirits for crops to no avail. Grog was already entrenched in the new settlement. By 1796, Hunter could still lament to the Duke of Portland, the colonial secretary, that because of spirits 'all is confusion, disorder and licentiousness'.[45] Though Hunter's orders became increasingly strict, they were not carried out. Without the cooperation of the officers, nothing would happen. To the authorities back in England, the limited amount of commerce in the colony justified neither the expense nor the enforcement of customs regulations and so Hunter lacked a force of independent customs officers to carry out his orders.[46]

In 1798, Hunter received further orders from England to prevent the landing of any spirits for which permission had not been sought and obtained. Captains of supply ships would be advised of this order so they would not load up with spirits on speculation. Supply from India, which had already surpassed that from Rio de Janeiro, was to be restricted from that end. The number of licensed premises in New South Wales was to be reduced and officers were to confine themselves to their military duties and no longer be involved in retail.

These restrictions, although frustrating for the officers, did not prevent them trading. A more direct threat to their enterprises was economic competition. In 1798, Robert Campbell (1769–1846) from the Calcutta trading house Campbell, Clarke & Company sailed into Sydney Harbour aboard the *Hunter*. It was his second attempt to bring supplies of merchandise and spirits to the colony. The first attempt, a year before, had ended in shipwreck in Bass Strait. Like others before him, Campbell was forced to sell to the officers, but he quickly ascertained that Governor Hunter would have preferred to allow small settlers equal access to the goods. Campbell asked Hunter for permission to establish a trading house in Sydney, and bought a property on the shore of the cove in anticipation that London would approve. He returned to New South Wales in February 1800 with goods including 13,000 gallons of Bengal rum.

Authorities in London had already received complaints about the trading practices of the Corps officers, so they viewed Campbell favourably. A register was to be kept of all ships entering the colony and was to be sent twice a year to London. The governor would be responsible for granting permission for goods to be landed 'in such a manner as to prevent all monopoly, and afford the inhabitants an opportunity of purchasing that same at fair and reasonable price'.[47] Hunter appointed Richard Atkins — a civil magistrate critical of the officers, personally antagonistic to John Macarthur, and a heavy drinker — to be keeper of the shipping register.

Hunter tried to restrict harbour traffic, threatening to scuttle any boat found moving at night. Without the support of the Corps he had to rely on ex-convicts to spy on shipping in the harbour. One such spy, John Rycroft, intercepted a party transferring casks of spirits from the *Walker*. The perpetrators threatened to blow his brains out. In court, the judge-advocate and six officers, including John Macarthur, decided an attempt had been made to smuggle, but did not convict the prisoners. Instead, they challenged whether Rycroft, as an ex-convict, was authorised to make such interceptions.

Macarthur and his fellow officers maintained an attitude of almost permanent opposition to those seeking to thwart their interests. Those below them were often threatened with direct force. A different strategy was employed against superiors: any magistrate or governor deigning to censure them was accused of tyrannical motives and subjected to constant appeals regarding legal minutiae. Macarthur's philosophy was that attack was always the best defence, and he forcibly, if not always artfully, employed tactics of unrelenting pressure, verbal harassment and manipulation of popular resentment against authority. His greatest shortcoming was that common to all arch-manipulators: he deluded himself into thinking that those he successfully manipulated actually liked him. His sense of self-regard was so large that there was scarcely room for anyone else, except perhaps his wife, Elizabeth, who in effect ran the farming enterprises that eventually made his name.

In January 1800, Macarthur asked Hunter for permission to land 'a small supply of clothing, spirits, tea, sugar, and other necessaries' from a ship chartered by the officers. The charter party, he informed the governor, 'included almost every officer in the settlement and Norfolk Island'.[48] The total quantity of spirits on board was 9000 gallons. On the day the officers' ship arrived, another convict transport turned up bearing Irish rebels and a cargo of goods that included 3000 gallons of spirits. The total arriving that day was equivalent to four gallons for every man, woman and child in the colony.[49] Hunter had continued to write to the Duke of Portland informing him that opposing the officers 'will be vain on my part, for the want of proper officers to execute such Orders as I might on occasion give'.[50] This time, however, he took the opportunity to allow free settlers to buy directly from the convict transport rather than through the cartel.

Historian M. H. Ellis portrayed Macarthur and the other officers as true visionaries who established private enterprise in Australia.[51] Yet these entrepreneurs conducted a trade in which profits were easily made through a lazy system of price gouging and bartering. Until the Macarthurs' later success with wool growing they produced nothing; the benefits to the community were at best negligible, and at worst destructive to individual lives and a sense of common cause. Small landholders resented them. To control trade and counter this public deficit, Hunter proposed an 'assessment of condition', a kind of tax, for the landing of alcohol, which would help fund emerging needs, such as a new gaol and facilities for the hundreds of children in the colony. The officers met this threat by disingenuously implicating Hunter himself in the monopoly of spirits and having him replaced as governor. John Macarthur, the arch-manipulator — often described in the language of the day as a 'perturbator' — wrote to the Duke of Portland complaining about the licentiousness in the colony and Hunter's inability to deal with the grog trade. Due to lack of cooperation from the NSW Corps, Hunter had been so spectacularly unsuccessful in stopping the spirits trade that he was removed. It was not a complete victory for the Corps officers, however. The new governor was given orders to end their monopoly.

Philip Gidley King (1758–1808) had been Phillip's second lieutenant on the *Sirius*. He had also established the colony at Norfolk Island. There, King demonstrated that he understood the role of discipline in maintaining a commonwealth of souls under marginal conditions. On Norfolk Island, as in Phillip's Sydney, convicts, ex-convicts and soldiers alike were subject to the same rules and discipline: 'The lash was resorted to as a means of stemming drunken behaviour, both among the convicts and the soldiers of the newly arrived New South Wales Corps.'[52] Even so, King too had problems restricting the sale of spirits. Without legal authority he imposed a tax on alcohol imported to Norfolk Island, the money going to the chaplain for the use of the school. Effectively, it was the first customs duty in the antipodes. This strategy had little effect on supply; it simply raised prices and encouraged illicit distilling to take advantage of the new profit margins.

To those who thought themselves a cut above the rest, King's disciplinary egalitarianism was felt to be unfair. In 1794, he sent twenty members of the Corps to Sydney for trial by court-martial. Predictably, Grose, who was then in charge, sided with the Corps members and censured King. Going far beyond his mandate, Grose issued orders giving the military legal authority over the civilian population. Given these past encounters with the NSW Corps, King's eventual appointment as governor of New South Wales in 1799 must have seemed a direct challenge to the power of the NSW Corps.

Soon after he arrived again in Sydney, but several months before taking up his position as governor in 1800, King conveyed his impressions to Joseph Banks: 'This colony has been destroyed by the wonderful sea of spirits which have flowed into it; its salvation will depend on its being totally done away with.'[53] (King is not being contradictory here; at that time, the word 'wonderful' could mean astonishing rather than praiseworthy.) Between September 1800 and December 1801, 42,816 gallons of spirits had entered the colony. The average annual consumption has been calculated at about 4 gallons per person.[54] There was some irony in King's description of the sea of spirits as 'wonderful' for he himself was a heavy drinker. Still, he could write: 'Vice, dissipation, and a strange relaxation seems to pervade all descriptions [of men] … Cellars from the better sort of people to the blackest characters among the convicts are full of that fiery poison.'[55]

As governor, King introduced several new measures in an attempt to control the trade in spirits. Rum could not be landed without a permit, but a 5 per cent duty was also introduced. Private retailers were to be limited to 20 per cent profit margins, and civil and military officers were forbidden to continue trading in spirits.[56] King also restricted the number of treasury bills available in the colony — a move that had a general deflationary effect. It also directly affected the Corps' highly leveraged activities, funded by heavy borrowings from the common Corps accounts. If the economic foundations of the Corps' enterprises were not already beginning to unravel, King no doubt would have faced the same fate as Hunter.

Some of the convicts in the Corps' network of retailers had been emancipated and they set up their own profitable businesses. They worked their money harder and were willing to take more commercial risks than their counterparts in the Corps. Simeon Lord, for example, attracted business away from the officers by helping visiting captains to sell their goods by auction. Henry Kable and

James Underwood joined with Lord to invest in sealing. Kable also built ships locally. Andrew Thompson set up a general store and inn in the Hawkesbury district, where small settlers had long resented having to deal with the Sydney traders. In 1805, he established the first salt manufacturing plant and later had interests in a tannery and a brewery.[57] Unlike their Corps counterparts, who merely exploited their control over resources, these businessmen were creating genuine enterprises. Robert Campbell established his warehousing business in Sydney, investing sums far in excess of what the Corps could manage from their paymaster bills. Strategically, he sided with the free settlers and emancipists, offering them long terms of credit and readily accepting the products of their labour, such as grain, in return for goods. In 1804, 200 appreciative settlers presented him with a memorial: 'But for you, we would still be prey to the mercenary unsparing hand of avarice and extortion.'[58]

Ultimately, Governor King did not stem the flow of spirits. His tariffs merely stimulated illegal stills, home-brewing and smuggling. If he could not effectively control the spirits trade, he nevertheless effectively disrupted the ability of the Corps to control it by sporadically allowing in large quantities. Spirits became so abundant in the colony that they could be put to other uses. In 1802, Pemulwuy, an Eora man who had for a number of years led the resistance against the colonial invaders, was shot. His head was shipped to Joseph Banks in England in a barrel of spirits.[59] Equally sensational, but decidedly less gruesome, was a keg containing a strange animal with a body of fur and a duck-like bill — the unbelievable platypus.[60]

The Corps' capacity to deal with King in the same ruthless way it had Hunter was severely handicapped when it lost the services of the chief perturbator, John Macarthur. In a flagrant demonstration of the pathological level of his status anxiety, Macarthur wounded his commanding officer, William Paterson, in a duel. As Michael Duffy contends, Macarthur, in the spirit of the times, considered himself to be a man of honour. [61] As Alain de Botton observes: 'Entire societies have made the maintenance of status, and more particularly of "honour", a primary task of every male.' One of its manifestations was duelling. 'In the dueller's psyche, other people's opinions were the *only* factor in forming a sense of self. The dueller could not remain acceptable in his own eyes if those around him judged him to be evil or dishonourable, a coward or a failure, foolish or effeminate. So dependent was his self-image on the views of others that he would sooner die of a bullet or stab wound than allow unfavourable assessments of him to go unanswered.'[62]

As usual, Macarthur's offence against Paterson was the outcome of a convoluted series of other conflicts. Macarthur accused Lieutenant John Marshall, a naval officer, of stealing a deceased Corps officer's belongings and challenged him to a duel. Marshall willingly accepted. However, Macarthur and his second, Lieutenant Edward Abbott, felt that Marshall's second — a shop assistant — was beneath their station and refused to proceed with the duel. Marshall later confronted them and was charged with assault. He was found guilty of the assault, fined and given a one-year term of imprisonment. Governor King remitted the sentence and ordered him to report to the secretary of state in England. Macarthur objected to this action and organised a social boycott of the governor by the officers. When Paterson refused to join in, Macarthur threatened to embarrass him by releasing letters in which he had been critical of King. Paterson challenged Macarthur to a duel and was wounded. King intended to exile Macarthur to Norfolk Island, but Macarthur demanded a court-martial. In attacking Paterson, Macarthur had deeply divided the Corps. King was able to send Macarthur back to England to answer for his conduct. In a last act of defiance, Macarthur, although himself a teetotaller due to chronic dyspepsia, issued an invitation to the enlisted men to a dinner at which he would supply the grog. King refused Macarthur access to the spirits. The men almost rioted and were ordered back to their barracks. King's assessment of Macarthur was scarifying: 'Experience has convinced every man in this colony that there are no resources which art, cunning, impudence and a pair of basilisk eyes can afford that he does not put in practice to obtain any point he undertakes.'[63] Presciently, he added: 'If Captain Macarthur returns here in any official character it should be that of Governor, as one half of the colony already belongs to him, and it will not be long before he gets the other half.'[64] Macarthur escaped possible military punishment for his actions and a definite transfer to the less enterprising Norfolk Island by resigning his commission and later returning to New South Wales as an entrepreneur, attempting to produce high-quality wool from merino sheep.

Scarcely a child in Australia ends his or her basic schooling without having heard of the Rum Rebellion and, naturally, one would expect it to feature prominently in a treatment of the history of alcohol in Australia. Yet, like Ned Kelly and the Eureka Stockade, the Rum Rebellion has become a contested symbol of our past. The usual story is that the autocratic Governor William Bligh threatened the Corps' monopoly over the rum trade and they rebelled in response. But was this rebellion really over rum? As Alan Atkinson has observed, we owe the perception that this was the case to Bligh himself. At the opening of the trial of George Johnston, the Corps officer who led the rebellion, 'Bligh had told a simple story of enemies created by his own successes. But he named only one achievement, his banning of the barter in spirits and, as his own witnesses testified, very few had complained about that.'[65] After hearing extensive evidence, the members of the bench at Johnston's court-martial were thoroughly confused as to why there had been a rebellion at all. David Day makes the case that it was not so much a rum rebellion as it was a 'peach putsch'.[66] With successive governors establishing control and tariff policies, and with competitors emerging who could challenge the Corps cartel, high profit margins could only be sustained through local manufacture. Small illegal stills had been omnipresent in the colony, but most of their owners lacked the capacity necessary to corner the illegal trade. The temperate climate was not conducive to growing sugar cane. Large-scale distilling efforts were literally fruitless until peaches were planted and harvested in quantity. Governor King himself had already encouraged the production of cider and beer to counteract the pernicious spirits trade. At the end of 1805, after a bumper peach crop, settlers petitioned King, claiming that the amount of cider likely to be produced would spoil and seeking permission to distil the juice into spirits. Governor King was facing the continual conundrum faced by all legislators who seek to ban or restrict articles that are widely used by the public: 'By restricting the official flow of spirits, he simply created a black market that was supplied by smuggling and illegal distillation.'[67] King laid blame for the number of illegal stills on the 'number of Irish' in the colony, but he also knew that legitimate spirits production based on peaches would advantage large landholders — mainly Corps officers and other colony officials — over small landholders. In 1806, as a further encouragement to resist the pressure to distil spirits, King offered a prize to encourage the production of peach cider. To the person producing two hogsheads of peach cider judged to be the best, a cow would be awarded.

Bligh's methods would be more direct. Like previous governors, William Bligh had arrived in the colony with explicit instructions to halt the trade in spirits. He was ordered to limit the power of the Corps officers and to reassert civil rule — a sure path to alienating all those in the colony who had been advantaged by previous arrangements. Bligh had strong and influential supporters. In England, Joseph Banks had been flattering and fulsome in assessing the virtues that would stand Bligh in good stead. He was, Banks remarked, one 'who has integrity unimpeached, a mind capable of providing its own resources in difficulties without leening [sic] on others for advice, firm in discipline, civil in deportment and not subject to whimper and whine when severity of discipline is wanted'.[68]

Bligh's assessment of the colonial situation was similar to that of his predecessors. On touring the Hawkesbury settlement, for example, he observed that 'a pernicious fondness for spirituous liquors was gaining ground, to the destruction of public morals and happiness'.[69] The Reverend Samuel Marsden had also complained to Bligh about the deleterious effects of the barter of spirits, leading to 'Jealousies, Misunderstandings and many unhappy differences amongst the Officers and of Litigations, Bankruptcies, Robberies, Gaming & Murder amongst the lower orders of the Community'.[70] Bligh had been ordered to continue King's system of prohibition, except where premises were licensed. He added a total ban on barter. Yet this restriction on trade only made local distillation all the more attractive.

In today's parlance, John Macarthur would be described as 'oppositional' — he seemed implacably opposed to taking orders. Having already arranged the importation of two stills, the teetotal Macarthur, along with his business partner, Captain Edward Abbott, directly challenged the ban on local distilling. Holding to the fanciful and thoroughly self-serving belief that no order was binding unless backed by an Act of British Parliament, Macarthur claimed that any ban on distilling was illegal. Within a month of Bligh's orders against distilling, the *Dart* arrived with Macarthur's and Abbott's stills. Bligh had them impounded until they could be returned to England. Meanwhile, the copper bodies were separated from the other apparatus, filled with goods and stored in a warehouse belonging to Macarthur and Garnham Blaxcell, former secretary to Governor King and another of Macarthur's business partners. In direct contravention of Bligh's instructions that the still be returned to England on the next available ship, Macarthur claimed rights to possess the copper components and challenged Bligh in court, claiming that Bligh had no right to seize property in such a fashion.

Macarthur's challenge was provocative. Since Governor Bligh's arrival, security of property had become a contentious issue. To restore Arthur Phillip's original plans for the layout of the town, and to reinstate the land around Sydney Cove for the use of the Crown, Bligh was organising the removal of homes and businesses whose owners had been inappropriately granted leases on Crown land by previous administrators and governors. Consequently, Bligh not only alienated colonists by evicting lessees and demolishing their homes, he generated a profound sense of insecurity among virtually everyone who had accumulated wealth, property and advantage in the colony. On the other hand, Bligh's actions garnered significant support among the smaller landholders, particularly in the Hawkesbury. He had provided quick assistance following disastrous floods, and was seen as responding to their complaints about exorbitant prices and goods being charged by Sydney traders.

In the end, the events directly precipitating the rebellion had nothing to do with rum at all. A ship, the *Parramatta*, of which Macarthur was a co-owner, had arrived in Sydney. Breaching port regulations, the ship had taken a convict to Tahiti when it was last in port. Three convicts had also stowed away previously on another of Macarthur's ships. Macarthur and Blaxcell were called on to forfeit a £900 bond, an insurance premium against unscrupulous and careless captains who helped convicts escape. Macarthur appealed against the impost, but had to continue supporting the crew at his own expense while the appeal was being considered. To avoid these costs, he abandoned the ship, disengaged the crew and sent them to shore, advising them to seek assistance from the naval officer. Bligh ordered the judge-advocate, Richard Atkins, to gather evidence as to why the crew had come ashore in breach of port regulations. Dutifully, Atkins asked Macarthur to account for his actions, but Macarthur, oppositional as ever, refused to cooperate. A warrant was issued for his arrest, but Macarthur refused to submit to Francis Oakes, the chief constable at Parramatta. When Oakes arrived at his door, Macarthur gave him a note stating that he would 'never submit to the horrid tyranny that is attempted until I am forced; that I consider it with scorn and contempt, as I do the persons who have directed it'.[71] As usual, Macarthur had deflected wrongdoing on his part into a personal attack on the alleged impropriety and tyranny of those in authority.

Macarthur was brought to trial on 25 January 1808. True to form, he started throwing spanners into the works. He refused to recognise the authority of the judge-advocate, claiming that Atkins owed him a debt. Technically, Atkins did, but he had not borrowed money from Macarthur, but from another man whose creditors Macarthur had taken over. Macarthur was manoeuvring for the trial to be heard by the remaining panel of Corps officers, who were guaranteed to be sympathetic to his cause. In something of a rare event, many of them had dined together the evening before the trial. George Johnston, lieutenant-governor and Corps commander, had drunk so much at the dinner that he fell out of his carriage on the way home and injured his leg — an incident that was to affect the course of Australian history.

Bligh placed no faith in Richard Atkins to mount a creditable case. He considered him to be not only an alcoholic but also largely ignorant of the law. Bligh had complained to the Home Office that Atkins was 'the ridicule of the community; sentences of death have been pronounced in moments of intoxication; his determination is weak; his opinion floating and infirm; his knowledge of the law insignificant and subservient to private inclination'.[72] Bligh had George Crossley, a London solicitor and ex-convict convicted of perjury, prepare an indictment against Macarthur. The charges he drafted referred to several occasions on which Macarthur's behaviour had amounted to libel and sedition against the governor: Macarthur had several times publicly alleged tyrannical behaviour on Bligh's part; he had defied Bligh's orders to return the still parts to England; he had denied responsibility for the fate of the *Parramatta*; and he had defied Atkins's warrant and abused Bligh in both the letter he had handed to Francis Oakes and in comments to Oakes when he came to arrest him.

At the trial, Macarthur's Corps colleagues on the bench agreed to remove Atkins, but Atkins refused to step aside. Atkins consulted Bligh, who advised the Corps officers that as Atkins was the only legitimate judge-advocate the trial ought to proceed. Macarthur's colleagues refused to continue. Bligh's last expression of power was to issue a warrant for Macarthur to be restored to custody, which he was, but not until 9 a.m. the next day.

Bligh attempted to regain control by summoning George Johnston, as Corps commander, to discuss the matter. Apparently still suffering the effects of his inebriated fall the night before, Johnston claimed to be too ill to attend. We can only speculate that events may have turned out somewhat differently had Johnston been fit enough to respond to Bligh's concerns in person. Instead, Bligh prodded Johnston into action with correspondence. He wrote to Johnston advising him that the judge-advocate believed his fellow judges to be guilty of treason and their presence would be required before a panel of magistrates the following day. The alarmed Johnston promptly recovered from his injuries and sprang into action, fearing that an insurrection was about to occur. However, instead of calming the insurrectionists he sided with them. Later, he would claim in his defence that he had acted to prevent the colony from becoming ungovernable — the imprisoning of the Corps officers being a more serious threat to good order in the colony than the imprisonment of Governor Bligh.

Johnston ordered that Macarthur be released into the custody of his colleagues Garnham Blaxcell and Nicholas Bayley. Macarthur then almost single-handedly orchestrated the events that followed. He drafted a letter calling for Johnston to arrest Bligh. Although it eventually included about a hundred signatures, most of them were added well after the event. In the early evening of 26 January 1808 — twenty years to the day since the colony was founded — Johnston took 400 soldiers up Bridge Street to Government House to arrest the governor. Macarthur even advised them what music to play: 'The British Grenadiers'. At the governor's house, they were verbally abused by Bligh's daughter, Mary Putnam. Still grieving the recent death of her consumptive husband, she accused them of walking over his grave and coming to murder her father. Despite the pomp and seriousness of the occasion, there seems to have been a lackadaisical air to the proceedings: it took Johnston's men two hours to locate Bligh in the house. They claimed he had been hiding. Indeed, to the amusement of many of the colonists, Sergeant Major Whittle later posted up his drawing of a cowardly Bligh being retrieved from under a bed in the servants' quarters. This was almost certainly a propaganda piece, crudely justifying what had been a monumentally slow and inefficient show of force.

The party celebrating the insurrection was another debauched affair. George Caley, botanist, explorer and no fan of the new rebels, wrote an open letter to Johnston in which he described the new regime's birth in a 'phrensy [sic] of party bigotry' which 'blazed forth in illuminations, bonfires, burning effigies, roasting sheep, and all manner of riotous dissipation'. He complained that the prejudices of the ruling faction were now spread without fear of contradiction. 'This scene of wild extravagance, sanctioned by such usurpation, is a sure forerunner of oppression, decay of public credit, the unprotection of individuals and their property.' Not holding back, he added: 'It also betrays an imbecile mind, and leaves a remarkable and odious stigma upon your conduct.'[73]

Such criticism notwithstanding, those who had been slighted by Bligh — and there were many — were encouraged by the turn of

Governor William Bligh was arrested on 26 January 1808, the twentieth anniversary of the founding of the colony. Having survived the HMS *Bounty* mutiny by a combination of intelligence and courage, it is unlikely that Governor Bligh hid under a bed. This propaganda cartoon from the days following the rebellion is more likely a feeble attempt to justify why it took the lackadaisical rebels two hours to find Bligh in the upstairs rooms of Government House. (National Library of Australia)

events. A meeting of town citizens was called on 8 February 1808 to reinforce the notion that Johnston was a law-abiding guardian of British rights and liberties, which had been seriously curtailed by Bligh's edicts, and also to discuss their next steps. John Macarthur freely supplied wine and spirits to those gathered before the meeting commenced. The meeting agreed that a sword worth no less than 100 guineas should be presented to Johnston in appreciation. Confirming what was common knowledge, Macarthur was also officially thanked, 'having been chiefly instrumental in bringing about the happy change which took place on the said day'.[74] Subscriptions were taken to send Macarthur to England to explain the colonists' grievances. Although

£1000 was promised, no money was collected. Macarthur quickly found that he wasn't as widely admired or supported as he'd thought, particularly among the wider body of settlers and the poorer sections of the community. They despised the officers as a class who would do everything to maintain their own privileges and sense of superiority, but they especially disliked Macarthur. Settlers wrote to Johnston asking for Macarthur to be removed from his virtually self-appointed position as colonial secretary: 'His monopoly and extortion have been highly injurious to the inhabitants of every description.'[75] In the following months, particularly among the Hawkesbury farmers, there were many signed expressions of support for Governor Bligh.

In the days following the rebellion, it became clear that Johnston, though amiable and likeable, was not a useful or effective colonial leader — an assessment with which he himself concurred. Perhaps if he hadn't been laid up with his injury caused by alcoholic over-indulgence, Johnston may have been able to form an independent view of what was happening, rather than deferring to Macarthur in all matters relating to Bligh. Instead of immediately returning to England with Bligh to explain the overthrow, Johnston indulged Macarthur, following his advice and appointing him to the newly created position of colonial secretary. With the combination of Johnston's lack of ability and Macarthur's impetuousness, things quickly began to unravel. To the dissatisfaction of many, the opening night of frolicking celebrations was not the harbinger of new freedoms. Johnston was obliged to restore Bligh's restrictions on trade and barter of spirits; they were, after all, orders from England. Those who had felt personally slighted by Bligh, offended by his harsh manner and fearful of their property being seized, soon found that he had been carrying out orders from elsewhere. Johnston, though more amiable, was no more likely to grant them their wishes.

While Johnston was duty-bound to maintain an ordered and useful settlement, Macarthur could indulge himself in the benefits and privileges of power. He had always revelled in power and multiplied opportunities to aggravate others, but his irrational desire for total victory over Bligh soon alienated many of his closest colleagues. His one-time partner and rebellion supporter Captain Abbott, for example, decried the wholesale removal of Bligh's appointees from official positions and observed with derision that in Macarthur's resumed 'mock trial', Macarthur had all the advantages. Not only Bligh, but also many of his supporters, had been detained as the rebels endeavoured to mount a case to prove their bold assertions that Bligh was a direct and tyrannical threat to the rights of person and property in the colony. Ingloriously, they pillaged Bligh's papers, both official and private, in search of material to further foment discontent. Macarthur, the trader John Blaxland, and fellow Corps member turned settler Nicholas Bayly enjoyed reading titbits aloud to others from Bligh's private papers, but their colleagues cringed at such excess. When the trial against Macarthur was reconvened, it had turned into a trial against Bligh. Unsurprisingly, Macarthur was acquitted — a great victory, if not a particularly moral one. Bligh's officials were replaced by those sympathetic to the rebels.

Eventually Johnston, Macarthur and Bligh returned to England to justify their actions. Bligh voyaged to England after having made himself a nuisance to the various administrators in Sydney and Van Diemen's Land by refusing to accept his fate. Johnston and Macarthur left before the new governor, Lachlan Macquarie, arrived in 1809 to take control, having both already relinquished control to Joseph Foveaux, yet another Corps officer, who had been in charge of the colony at Norfolk Island. Always the manipulator, on his way back to England Macarthur lingered in Rio de Janeiro hoping to meet with Macquarie on his outward journey to apprise him of his version of events. But this never happened, and it was fortuitous for Macarthur that he had left the colony. Lachlan Macquarie arrived with a note of support for Bligh and instructions for him to return to England.

Johnston was to be arrested and sent back to England, and Macarthur was to be arrested and tried for conspiracy in the criminal court of New South Wales.

Macarthur and his mainly Whig supporters in England held the view that government was always required to justify itself to the people. However, in the aftermath of the revolution in France and the continuing war with that nation, those conducting Major George Johnston's court-martial saw no need to justify the due exercise of governmental authority. The burden of proof was on Johnston to prove that Bligh had committed such crimes as to justify the usurping of power. Macarthur erroneously believed that the rights and procedures operable in the colony closely paralleled those in England. He clung to the view, advocated in a pamphlet by Jeremy Bentham but untested, that the powers of colonial governors (usually granted by royal patents) were invalid as they had not been underwritten by an Act of Parliament, as they should be in a parliamentary democracy.[76] It was a moral and legal argument too fine and impractical to ground the plethora of tiny complaints Macarthur presented against Bligh in his attempt to support Johnston. The members of the bench, adjudicating the validity or not of a violent overthrow of government, were more concerned with who actually held authority in the colony, rather than who ought to hold that authority. To explain the situation in New South Wales, Richard Atkins produced his own commission, which made it clear that officials were 'all placed under the Governor, according to the rules and discipline of war'.[77] Members of the bench in London asked Macarthur directly why he had not obeyed Bligh's orders to go from his home to Sydney in response to the *Parramatta* matter. Rather disingenuously given the fact that the civil courts in New South Wales were stacked with Corps officers, Macarthur presented the view that the colony was governed by civil rather than military law as his justification for not following Bligh's orders. However, Charles Sutton commented from the bench: 'It is every man's duty to obey the laws of his country; the governor sent for you, and you should have gone.'[78] Yet another member of the bench observed:'I was once at the head of a colony myself, and if the orders which I sent were disobeyed, how would I govern the colony?'[79] Perhaps it began to dawn on Macarthur that no one was interested in his feelings of being affronted nor the manner in which orders were given; they were only interested in one fact: had Bligh exceeded the bounds of his legitimate authority such that a rebellion could be justified? Underlining the colonial governor's unique authority, Sutton referred to the royal patent of 1787, which established the two principal courts of law in New South Wales. He observed that the laws of England were only to apply 'as nearly as may be' and that the governor was empowered to overturn the judgments of the civil courts. The document was, he observed, effectively the Constitution of New South Wales. Macarthur's assumption that the colony should be governed as a civil community, with civil bodies limiting the authority of its governor, just as parliament limited the powers of the king, was an illusion.

As Johnston's trial proceeded it became crystal clear that the instigation and shaping of and the justificatory rhetoric for the rebellion were all Macarthur's — a view reinforced by Macarthur's volubility. His usual tendency to justify his always exaggerated sense of grievance by the multiplication of small grievances worked against himself and the hapless Johnston. This emphasis on quantity of argument over quality did nothing to sway the members of the bench, who wanted to get quickly to the point of the matter. Macarthur, as an overwhelmer rather than a reasoner, never understood that, over time, five leaky buckets held no more water than one leaky bucket. His tactic of creating impediments by multiplying legal issues only confused matters when clarity was demanded. Ultimately, the members of the bench were not clear why Macarthur had been tried in New South Wales in the first place, though he clearly seemed to have been 'the main-spring of everything'.[80] Macarthur played the part of the offended gentleman and preserver of English liberties so well that it appeared to the bench that he had been the focal point of a disturbance without any substance. This very lack of substance was disastrous for Johnston; it undermined his justifications for acting as forcefully and urgently as he did. He was found guilty, stripped of his rank and cast out of the army. He would have been hanged if the bench had not agreed that there had at least been some sort of vague crisis to prompt his misguided intervention. None of those who had pledged to support Johnston had done so. 'Every person that promised has risen upon my ruin. I alone am the sufferer, having lost my commission, and upward of £6,000 from conceding to their requests.'[81] Johnston eventually returned to Sydney with his de facto wife, whom the upright Governor Lachlan Macquarie forced him to marry. He lived comfortably on his estate in Annandale, Sydney, until 1823, when he died from alcoholic overindulgence.

Bligh never felt himself fully vindicated. He had the comfort of routine promotions to rear-admiral and then vice-admiral, but never commanded another ship.

For Macarthur, it had not turned out to be the glorious victory and vindication that he had expected. The threat of a conspiracy trial hanging over his head if he returned kept him in exile from New South Wales for another eight years, during which both his material fortunes and health began to suffer. He felt neglected by those in New South Wales who been beneficiaries of his favours, and found himself a man of little influence in England, lamenting: 'Men feel very differently towards each other in this bustling place to what they do in the solitude of N. S. Wales.'[82] In truth, the liberties John Macarthur had supposedly been protecting had been entirely his own. On his eventual return to New South Wales, he became an inveterate opponent of the emerging democratic spirit in the colony, championing instead the privileges of the 'really respectable settlers' who would become as 'powerful as an

Aristocracy'.[83] Macarthur did become rich and powerful again when his and Elizabeth's schemes to supply wool to England came to fruition — not because of superior science or entrepreneurial flair, but because for fine wool the 'wool manufacturers in England currently relied on Spain and Germany and they were attracted by the possibility, however remote, of finding a source of supply which would be safe in wartime'.[84] Macarthur's merinos supplied England with a familiar product that was no longer undercut in price by European rivals. Macarthur didn't enjoy the full benefits of his turn of good fortune, however. His mind had begun to deteriorate and he became increasingly erratic in public and at home brooded like a child. Even his devoted and long-suffering wife was accused of conspiring against him. Macarthur was appointed to the Legislative Council, but removed and declared insane in 1832. He died two years later.

It is interesting to compare Australia's first coup with later acts of rebellion. For example, in 1918 a beer boycott contributed to a bloodless revolt by Northern Territorians against their administrator, John Anderson Gilruth.[85] Like Bligh, Gilruth developed a reputation for being arrogant and insensitive.[86] A veterinary scientist by training, and the Territory's first administrator, he combined a confident bluntness of style with an open distrust of organised labour. Following the nationalisation of liquor supply in the Northern Territory in 1915, the price of beer rose and several hotels closed as a result of Gilruth's heavy-handed restrictions, which included no alcohol being served by territory hotels 'except on production of an affidavit made before a police officer that it was required for medical use only, and for personal consumption by the undersigned'.[87] The unions declared the territory hotels 'black' as part of a six-week strike. Matters came to a head when Gilruth refused a request for leave on Saturday 14 November 1918 by the women working in territory hotels so that they could celebrate the end of the World War I. With the approval of their regular customers, the women took time off anyway, but the next day Gilruth locked them out. It was a petty act by Gilruth that not only epitomised his arbitrary and unreasonable exercise of power, but also solidified opposition to his administration in ever wider sections of the community. Stop-work meetings and marches were held in the following weeks to protest the increasing cost of alcohol and the closure of hotels.

When a shipment of 700 cases of Melbourne Bitter arrived for the Christmas season, Gilruth refused permission for it to be unloaded. Rumour was that he planned to depart south and leave the Territory without beer for Christmas and the New Year. On 17 December 1918, a thousand men walked to Government House. A deputation presented Gilruth with a motion asking him to either address 'the citizens of Darwin' and justify his policies or immediately leave Darwin by steamer. Safe passage was assured. Gilruth who stood six feet and 3 inches tall, refused and bravely confronted the crowd. He was answerable only to the minister for territories, not the citizens of Darwin, he claimed. The swelling crowd broke through a picket fence and entered the garden of Government House and Gilruth was roughly handled. An effigy of him was set alight.

Gilruth later claimed that he could have resolved the matter there and then by agreeing to reduce the price of beer, but he doubted his superiors in the federal government would think it acceptable. Indeed, the government was concerned enough to send a gunboat to Darwin within a week. Gilruth and his family remained virtual prisoners in Government House and left on 16 February 1919 on the cruiser HMAS *Encounter*. A royal commissioner was appointed to investigate the events. Mr Justice N. K. Ewing concluded that Gilruth was not fitted 'to rule a democratic people'. [88]

Though some regarded the Darwin Rebellion, as it came to be called, as the nearest thing to a revolution since the Eureka Stockade in Ballarat in 1854, in style it was probably closer to the Rum Rebellion. Certainly, Gilruth's mode of administration was reminiscent of Bligh's in its autocratic approach if not its personal style. Gilruth was, perhaps, more urbane. The Darwin Rebellion also had its John Macarthur, of sorts, in the figure of Harold Nelson, an energetic and passionate union leader with the Australian Workers' Union, who was able to turn the alcohol shortage and price rises to the advantage of his members, arguing that behind the issue of Gilruth's tyrannical style was the broader fundamental principle of 'no taxation without representation'. Territory historian Ernestine Hill dubbed those who marched to Government House 'Nelson's Warriors, men of mettle, ready to die for the Cause and the Working Man's Beer'.[89] Nelson was later asked by Justice Ewing to assist the royal commission, in a paid capacity, as a 'representative of the citizens of the Northern Territory'.[90] Later, in 1921, Nelson was briefly imprisoned in Fanny Bay Gaol for refusing to

The Darwin Rebellion, December 1918. After a procession through the streets of Darwin and the burning of an effigy, protesters broke through a fence, forcing the Northern Territory Administrator, Dr John Gilruth, to retreat inside Government House. The final straw had been the autocratic Gilruth's refusal to allow a visiting ship to unload Christmas supplies of beer. (Rodgers Collection, Northern Territory Library)

pay his 'taxes without representation'. In 1922, he became the first Northern Territory member in the House of Representatives, holding the position for the next twelve years.

The story of a rebellion leader who later enters parliament does have an echo of the Eureka Stockade: Peter Lalor, its rebel leader, did the same. Alcohol also played a part in that rebellion, which again occurred in December, but in 1854, and the rebels also spoke of 'no taxation without representation', for they resented the imposition of monthly licence fees that were becoming increasingly burdensome. On 8 October 1854, a drunken miner named James Scobie was murdered by James Bentley, the publican of the Eureka Hotel. Scobie and a friend, Peter Martin, had attempted to enter the hotel after midnight, but Bentley refused them access then went after them with a spade, to the apparent delight of his wife and some other dinner guests. Martin was hit, but fled; Scobie died of his wounds. Tempers in the mining camp ran high when John D'Ewes, the police magistrate at Ballarat and a suspected silent partner of Bentley's, discharged him. An angry mob burnt down the Eureka Hotel on 17 October. Within the month, Bentley was re-tried and found guilty. However, far from being a victory for the miners, these incidents increased government concerns that order needed to be maintained and more troops were sent to Ballarat. In late November 1854, the Ballarat Reform League was formed under the leadership of Peter Lalor. Diggers were armed and a stockade was built on a hilltop commanding a view of the road to Melbourne. They were prepared to fight to defend their 'rights and liberties' against the gathering forces of tyranny.

One of the rebels, Raffaello Carboni, a red-haired Italian, provided a written account of the formation of the Ballarat Reform League and the events at the Eureka Stockade. At meetings of the Reform League he observed what he called 'a peculiar colonial habit'. On the platform there was 'a sly-grog seller, who plied with the black-bottle all the folks there, and the day was very hot, and the sun almost burning'.[91] According to Carboni, sly-grog sellers also 'got a little profit' out of the Eureka Stockade. 'A fellow was selling nobblers out of a keg of brandy hanging from his neck. It required Peter Lalor in person to order the devil-send out of the stockade.'[92]

On the afternoon of Saturday 2 December many of the diggers left the stockade to go to the hotels for drinks as usual. The locals knew that no licence hunts had been conducted on Saturday afternoons. Some of the diggers from other areas, however, who had come to lend their support, had it in mind to take the opportunity to get free supplies of food and alcohol from the town's proprietors. Carboni was appalled by the behaviour of these would-be 'bushrangers'. As he observed, there were many for whom 'grog is pluck, and the more they swallow the more they count on success'.[93] He gives an account of ten Vandemonians 'armed to the teeth with revolvers, swords, pikes

Site of Bentley's Hotel, Eureka, after it had been burnt down by an angry mob, after a magistrate acquitted the hotel owner of murder. He had beaten the intoxicated John Scobie to death with a spade for disturbing his late-night dinner. Such incidences increased the presence of troops at the diggings, and fuelled dissatisfaction among the miners, who later rebelled at the Eureka Stockade. (National Library of Australia)

and knives' demanding free drinks from hotel proprietor Carl Wiesenhavern, who agreed to give them one free drink each. When they boisterously demanded more, he went to the back room and returned with a pitcher of brandy, two fully loaded pistols and his partner, John Brandt, who carried a double-barrelled shotgun. Wiesenhavern placed the brandy on the table and cocked his weapons. 'Touch it if you dare; if any one among you got the pluck to put in his tumbler one drop out of the bottle there, he is a dead man.'[94]

Only those with tents in the stockade returned for the night, leaving barely 120 men to protect the Southern Cross flag. Historian Geoffrey Blainey has stated that on 1.50 a.m. on the Sunday morning whisky was freely given to the rebels, and some were intoxicated on their last night.[95] He adds: 'A few captains were suspicious that the issue of whiskey was a government plot, so they led their armed miners from the stockade.'[96] John Molony, on the other hand, argues that 'no reliable, contemporary evidence' justifies the allegation that many of the diggers in the stockade were drunk.[97] The mood in the stockade was relaxed, he claims, because most participants suspected authorities to respond with increased licence hunts rather than a direct attack. It is unlikely that either sobriety or inebriation would have played any significant role in what followed in the half-light of dawn the next day. It only took a few minutes for a force of 300 soldiers to take the Eureka Stockade and quash the rebellion.

Alcohol also played a part in what became known as 'Kerr's coup' — the removal of Prime Minister Gough Whitlam from office in 1975 by the Governor-General Sir John Kerr. With Kerr's help, the Opposition, led by Malcolm Fraser, blocked supply and triggered a double dissolution, which led to elections in both Houses and victory for the Coalition. Giving an account of the events in 2002, Gough Whitlam observed that he would never have appointed Sir John Kerr as governor-general had he known Kerr had a drinking problem: 'It is my fault that I didn't check on his background because if I had asked

any of the judges of the New South Wales Supreme Court, of which
he was the chief justice, or any senior counsel that I knew, about him,
they would have told me he had a drink problem. He never told me,
but while he was governor-general under me, he twice went to the
Prince of Wales Hospital in Sydney to be dried out.'[98]

When Lachlan Macquarie arrived in the colony in late 1809 to take
the reins from the alcoholic William Paterson, he brought with him
his own regiment to completely replace the NSW Corps. He also
brought a young lawyer, Ellis Bent, to be deputy judge-advocate.

To break up the trade monopolies, Macquarie had been instructed
to encourage free trade. Control measures were to be replaced by
high import tariffs. As if by natural forces, these new tariff measures
actually increased the number of illegal stills in the colony. Macquarie
put forward the case for a licensed distillery, but his superiors in
England saw no benefits in the idea.

The proceeds from the tariffs went to fund an ambitious building
program, which was not only of direct practical benefit but also
materially and symbolically promoted the common good over the
interests of particular individuals. A graceful Georgian building,
known to the locals as the Rum Hospital, was completed in 1814, the
remains of which today flank the Sydney Hospital and house a
section of the New South Wales Parliament and the Mint, a museum
and office building for the Historic Houses Trust. It was funded by
the proceeds of an officially sanctioned, limited monopoly in spirits
imports (the right to import 45,000 gallons of spirits over the next
three years) granted to three contractors: the colony's principal
surgeon D'Arcy Wentworth, merchant and pastoralist Alexander
Riley (later, one of the founders of the Bank of New South Wales),
and Garnham Blaxcell, a former business partner of John Macarthur.

Macquarie promoted and consolidated the effort to build the
common infrastructure in the spirit of the original founders' vision of

Governor-General Sir John Kerr delivers an inebriated speech when he presented the Melbourne Cup in 1977. (© Newspix/News Ltd)

a self-sufficient colony of those who had paid their debt to society, under the moral and administrative guidance of a wise governor. Much to the chagrin of the colony's retired civil and military officers, who regarded themselves as a kind of native ruling class, Macquarie favoured the emancipists. In fact, Macquarie's program was so successful that exclusivist interests complained that transportation to New South Wales could no longer be said to instil sufficient fear to act as a deterrent to crime.

By the time of Macquarie's rule, the worst of the colonial version of the spirits craze was over. Sanity had been restored by establishing a balance between freedom and regulation. The colonial government would protect the community from monopolists. The populace would no longer be driven to extremes by the threat of prohibition. People could have their freedom, but at a price that compensated the community for any negative impacts. Tariffs and licensing, already features of the regulatory scene, became the prominent tools for managing alcohol in the colony. Licences to produce alcoholic beverages were often given by patronage, which tended to entrench class distinctions, as only those with sufficient wealth and connections, or both, could acquire them. Many small-scale efforts therefore failed. Licences relating to distribution, on the other hand, were granted on the basis of personal character. In the past, officers had crudely selected unwanted but talented women convicts to retail their wares, or literate men with rudimentary book-keeping skills. Many had become independent traders whose wealth challenged the privileges of the officers and free settlers. Indeed, it was the inevitability of convicts completing their sentences and being emancipated that would give the Enlightenment ideals of usefulness and amiability a foothold in the colony. Alcohol was already shaping Australian society in none too subtle ways.

The S.S. *Walrus* was a travelling sugar refinery and distillery on the Albert and Logan Rivers, near Brisbane. It ceased being a distillery in 1871 because it was difficult for licensing authorities to police. (State Library Queensland)

CHAPTER 2

A Mass of Immovable Men

Beer and wine met at Waterloo; wine, red with fury, boiling over with enthusiasm, mad with audacity, rose thrice against that hill on which stood a mass of immovable men — the sons of beer. You have read history; beer gained the day.

English and Australian Cookery Book: Cookery for the many as well as the 'Upper Ten Thousand', Edward Abbott, 1864[1]

Beer, once touted by Carlton breweries as being as Australian as 'football, meat pies, kangaroos and Holden cars', is not in fact an unambiguous icon of Australianness. This is not to say that beer is not central to the images of Australian maleness; it's just that any claim to uniqueness is questionable. In a perceptive analysis of beer advertising in the 1970s and 1980s, the images used were found to be not uniquely Australian but based on 'transnational archetypes' rooted in patriotism.[2] Advertising agency George Patterson, for example, who developed the football, meat pies, kangaroos and Holden cars commercial for Carlton breweries borrowed it from General Motors in the US, whose advertisements featured baseball, hot dogs, apple pie and Chevrolet.[3] Other countries are equally notorious for beer drinking, including the Czech Republic, Ireland, Germany and the United Kingdom, home of the notorious 'lager lout'. Even the brand most recognised overseas as Australian, Fosters, was created by two American brothers, W. M. & R. Foster.[4]

Peter Burn, the first European recorded as killed by the local Aborigines in New South Wales, had been transported for stealing a barrel of beer.[5] By the time a colony had been founded in Australia, beer was already part of British identity and continued to expand its influence. Australian nationalist Edward Abbott, the author of Australia's first cookbook, published in 1864, recognised and respected the indebtedness of Australian culinary life to the traditions of England. Although himself an enthusiast for local wines, he borrowed a colourful phrase summing up the place of beer in British identity, indeed British maleness: 'the mass of immovable men — the sons of beer'.[6] Barriers of distance and climate, however, meant that it would take until the 1890s for a beer-drinking tradition to gain hold in the fledgling colony.

Beer's ambiguity as an Australian icon also has something to do with the nature of the product itself. Australians respond to beer, for example, differently from the way that the French respond to wine. Roland Barthes observed that in France 'to believe in wine is a collective coercive act'.[7] For a Frenchman not to believe in wine would be to risk social exclusion. Jonathan Dawson, who analysed beer advertising in Queensland in the 1970s and 1980s, observed that beer-drinking does not hold such definitive cultural power in Australia.[8] While wine might denote Frenchness, beer and Australianness are not so naturally suited to each other, otherwise breweries would not have had to work so hard and spend sizable sums to associate their products with patriotism (local or national), masculinity, sport and health.

Despite these efforts to promote their product widely, Australian breweries can sometimes be curiously protective of their product's image. Queensland author Andrew McGahan, writing about some of the problems encountered in turning his bestselling book *Praise* into a film, bemoaned: 'We couldn't even squeeze a stubbie of Fourex into the picture. The brewery refused us permission to use their product (as did all major breweries) and we had to resort to a fictional ale.'[9] As he pointed out, breweries prefer their product associated with sport, beaches and sunshine rather than alcoholic lowlifes in boarding houses. The company that produces the board game Scrabble felt the same way, but eventually relented. On the other hand, according to McGahan, tobacco companies, if they had been allowed, 'would have still thrown bucket-loads of money our way, just to feature the smoking of their brands', even though the main character, 'the chronically asthmatic Gordon is slowing suiciding with nicotine'.[10]

Paddling the beer to safety during the 1974 Brisbane floods.
(© Newspix/News Ltd)

In Australia, beer brands tend to mark local, not national, identities. The quintessential Queenslandness of XXXX was essential to *Praise*, even though, in the end, the film had to be shot in New South Wales. For much of the twentieth century, the brand of beer one drank was a strong indicator of where one came from. In retro shops today one might find a set of six plastic mugs in an anodised caddy, as sold in the early 1960s, with each mug adorned with the label of each state's major beer brand. Not until the late twentieth century, with the effects of globalisation, transnational ownership and market segmentation along age and gender lines, did the beer borders begin to soften. In fact, the beer wars between the state breweries could be seen as a dress rehearsal for future problems of globalisation. They were also the continuation of a longer historical process during which what had once been, by physical necessity in the late eighteenth century, a quintessentially local product became, via the industrial revolution, mass produced and widely consumed. The considerable costs associated with mechanisation and refrigeration led to the consolidation of breweries along colonial and state lines and to the demise of smaller town-based breweries.

In more recent times, boutique beers and market segmentation have brought profitable market share to smaller companies. The marketing of beers to consumer segments, paralleling the segmentation of audiences in the mainstream media along age and income lines, has also contributed to a softening of regional identities. But the increased sophistication in this part of the beer-drinking population has been easily exploited by local and international conglomerates: these days Australia's new global citizens drink Beck's, Steinlager, Peroni, Kirin and Stella Artois. However, the larger share of the market is still in local beers, which are promoted along familiar lines of masculinity, sport and patriotism, although inflected along state lines.

To understand how beer became Australia's preeminent alcoholic beverage, and why masculinity and local identity became so important, we must return to Hogarth's prints, *Beer Street* and *Gin Lane*.

★   ★   ★

Given the prominence of beer drinking to Australia's ocker stereotype, it may be difficult to appreciate that beer was once at the forefront of public efforts to civilise an inebriated population. The colony's early problems with spirits — a combination of an inherited navy tradition and economic opportunism — led to a protracted local spirits craze, which continued long after Britain had returned to the comparative virtues of Beer Street. The tyranny of distance and problems of climate prevented a Beer Street policy from taking hold early on in colonial Australia, but not from want of trying. Beer drinking was actively encouraged to curb excessive spirits drinking in New South Wales. Along with licensing, it had limited impact. Both strategies connoted a level of acceptance of the constant alcohol supply in the colony and a desire to reduce consumption to 'amiable' and 'useful' levels.

As in Britain, the sale of alcoholic beverages was restricted to those holding a licence. Governors differed greatly in their approach. Governor Hunter's liquor licences in 1796 had little effect on the spirits trade. By 1810, the number of licences had risen to 101, of which seventy-five vendors were in Sydney. Although Governor Macquarie was considerably stricter, he too seemed to favour Beer Street by severely limiting licences except for alehouses. Governor Darling, however, believed in issuing licences to whoever requested them, with the exception of those considered to be of 'unworthy character'.[11] This included both male and female applicants.

Being a licensee provided a few women with a significant opportunity for financial independence and social influence. In Britain, only widowed women held licences; in New South Wales, single women were eligible. Single women had already been employed by NSW Corps officers to retail their general goods. Sarah Bird, a 27-year-old unmarried ex-convict, became the first woman licensee in 1797. She operated the Three Jolly Settlers.[12] By 1815, twelve of the ninety-six public houses in Sydney were in female hands.[13] Some thought the presence of female licensees curbed some of the excesses of male behaviour, at least at the pub, and this was advantageous for publicans and investors. However, it did not seem to have an effect on public drunkenness, which continued to concern many observers, especially visitors from overseas.

In the earliest days of New South Wales, being a publican, although potentially lucrative, had its own challenges. Plenty of liquor trading continued outside of the licensed pubs. Merchant ships stocked with rum regularly landed in the colony and some of the officers conducted a black market of surplus rum, selling it to the convicts on the sly. Some convicts bought extra rum direct from the ships when they were given permission to visit the vessels to buy their essential supplies. Others set up distilleries, even though Hunter had banned distilling. These were mostly Irish convicts, continuing their tradition of home distilling.[14] If the illegal flow of drink (sly-grogging and distilling) could have been contained, then licensing would have been extremely successful, but both activities often ran in parallel.

Another factor affecting the success of licensing, often debated among historians, is the possibility that the early colonists were, in fact, more sober than we have come to believe. When it comes to alcoholic drinking as a social problem, visibility is an important factor. Public drunkenness, a problem then, as now, is just that — public — and so more noticeable and therefore observable than the abstemious lives of the majority. Writing in 1827, Peter Cunningham, a surgeon and pastoral settler in what we now call Queensland, remarked that in his area the native-born 'did not drink so heavily' and had an undeserved reputation from 'a few roguishly prolific families'.[15] A reliable estimate is that average spirit consumption for New South Wales between 1790 and 1820 was not much more than that of Britain.[16] The shiploads of rum reached their peak during Hunter's governorship, who allowed 7 gallons per annum for each white inhabitant of the Botany Bay settlement. This would have amounted to a little over a pint a week, and considering the vast majority of the colony's population consisted of adult males, is, perhaps, not a significant amount. When King succeeded as governor, he cut the arriving cargo of rum to 3 gallons per head, which would mean an even more moderate drinking culture than that of Britain and Ireland.[17] The colony may at times have been awash in a sea of spirits, but a good deal of it was being stored and traded rather than consumed. After adjusting for the predominantly male–female ratio of 3:1 in the colony (compared to 1:1 in the UK) Australia's per capita yearly consumption of alcohol was unexceptional. New South Wales's consumption per capita of litres of absolute alcohol (taking into account the different strengths of drinks) were between 1800–04 and 1811–15, 13.1 litres and 12.6 litres between 1816–20; in the United Kingdom per capita consumption was 14.3 litres in 1800 and 11 litres in 1816.[18] The main era of heavy drinking appears to have been during the 1830s when wine and imported beers added to the figures. Although this put the Australian colonists ahead of the United Kingdom, they still consumed less than their United States counterparts, who at the time drank the same amount as the Scots and the French, but less than the Swedes.[19] Hence Australians may not be as unique as we often think, at least in regard to levels of alcohol consumption.

With the amount of concern about public drunkenness so commonly expressed, it is likely that much of this consumption was in the form of sustained, heavy drinking. This was probably truest of those convicts who had been granted their own land, as they would not have feared the 100 lashes that was the penalty in the convict settlement for drunkenness. Anecdotal accounts certainly refer to heavy rum drinking among the farmers on the Hawkesbury, where many of the first emancipists set up. British visitors were astounded by the habit of public houses of serving rum in a full wine glass. Perhaps this is evidence of a high level of physical tolerance — a sign of frequent, heavy drinking — among some inhabitants; but more likely the refined visitors did not observe that the precious grog was routinely watered down.

The idea that the harsh circumstances of the early settlers contributed to excessive drinking by some is supported by the fact that the other emerging colonies did not share the levels of consumption of New South Wales. Port Phillip residents, for example, drank half as much spirits as their northern counterparts in the 1830s.[20] To obtain a licence, a prospective southern publican had to get a certificate from a magistrate testifying to his or her good character and pay a fee of £25. Both fee and certificate had to reach the Sydney treasury within fourteen days of signing. This proved an impossible task for those who settled in Port Phillip in 1835: ships could take more than fourteen days to reach Sydney from there. John Pascoe Fawkner decided to cut through the red tape and set up his own public house. Technically, this was a sly-grog business, but a blind eye was turned as it was agreed that he was performing a necessary service. Fawkner was alleged to have taken full advantage of his monopoly of this essential service by insisting that his clients be compliant. Customers could eat only what he decided to serve, with no rights of request, and many meals were accompanied by a tirade of his opinions on the affairs of the day. Any criticism or refusal of his meals, or disagreement with his opinions, would be met with a demand that drinkers shut up or leave. Fortunately for Port Phillip pub-goers, the law was soon changed to allow a licence to be issued in the settlement. Fawkner's monopoly was rapidly undercut and public houses sprang up all over Melbourne.[21]

Liquor could also be bought for consumption off the premises. In the first half of the century, however, it could only be bought in bulk, in quantities of 5 gallons or more. It was only after 1864 that licensed

'Diggers' breakfast'. Coffee and soup at the front and sly grog out the back. Victorian goldfields, 1852. (State Library of Victoria)

stores, including grocers, could sell by the bottle. A royal commission in Victoria in 1867 into the effects of these changes found a decline in sly-grog selling. Sly-grog venues weren't just shanties frequented by the poor and criminal classes, or responses to prohibition such as that declared on the goldfields: much sly-grog selling was a side venture by practitioners of other trades, in particular butchers, bakers, greengrocers and those who provided common essentials. Interestingly, their customers were typically those who switched to buying from the grocer once the single-bottle licence was introduced. Such people thought themselves too respectable to be seen entering a public house.[22]

In those days, alcohol served a necessary function other than intoxication and social lubrication. The available water was often foul tasting and unhygienic; it needed to be mixed with alcohol to kill the taste and to disinfect it. In 1768, as the *Endeavour* was being prepared for its voyage, Nathaniel Hulme wrote to Joseph Banks advising that he take 'a quantity of Molasses and Turpentine, in order to brew Beer with, for your daily drink, when your Water becomes bad'. In his experience, he claimed, 'The smell of stinking water will be entirely destroyed by the process of fermentation.'[23]

Journalist Edmund Finn, writing under the name of 'Garryowen', described the River Yarra's water as unfit for man or beast: 'The people of Melbourne had to swallow it, though often rectified with large dashes of execrable rum or brandy.'[24] He described how rural labourers visiting Melbourne to spend their pay cheque would typically order spirits, their favourite drink being a cocktail of brandy and ginger beer known as a 'spider'.[25] A decline in spirits drinking had been reversed by the gold rushes, but the preferred drop turned from rum to brandy. By the mid-nineteenth century, brandy had surpassed rum as the most popular alcoholic drink in Australia. Despite the large number of Irish and Scottish immigrants, whisky did not become a common drink in Australia until the late nineteenth century.

Whether or not Captain James Cook accepted the virtues of Beer Street, he believed beer had health-giving properties. One gallon per man was the daily ration; he took 4 tonnes of it on board the *Endeavour*. Within a month, it was all consumed save for two casks, which he wanted 'to keep for some time longer'. Instead he served wine to the ship's company, though he kept some in reserve for the officers.[26] The lack of keeping qualities and its bulk severely limited beer's usefulness to a naval expedition, but it was carried nonetheless because several leading medical figures of the time, including Nathaniel Hulme, believed it was suitable for treating scurvy, a disease caused by dietary deficiency of vitamin C. Scurvy was a common problem on long sea voyages; its symptoms were swollen, bleeding gums, amnesia, bruising and pain in the joints. Other advocates of beer for preventing scurvy included Gilbert Blane, physician to the West Indies fleet in the early 1780s; John Clephane, physician to the New York fleet in the 1750s; and Dr David Macbride, an Irish physician who believed that scurvy was caused by putrefaction. Decaying animal and vegetable matter was accompanied by the release of 'fixed air'. Believing that healthy living tissue trapped this fixed air, he thought the effects of putrefaction could be countered by ingesting the fixed air trapped in fresh vegetables and in fermented drinks.[27]

The *Endeavour* carried not only beer, but also sweet wort (an infusion of malt) and malt extract to make experimental batches of beer, as well as spruce beer, a concoction made from leaves and wood shavings of spruce fir and molasses. Cook reported favourably on his experiments in his first two voyages, having succeeded in preventing scurvy among his crew. These experiments, however, were not conducted with scientific rigour. Cook had used such a wide variety of methods — not only the beer, wort and malt, but also the juice of lemons and oranges — to treat scurvy that he could not reliably pinpoint the source of his success. The assumption that beer would be good for treating scurvy was based on the long-standing observation that the rapid deterioration of the sailors on long voyages often coincided with the depletion of beer supplies. Given our present understanding of the cause of the disease, we know that 'the depletion of the sea stock of beer would coincide with the depletions of bodily reserves of ascorbic acid in the absences of a dietary source'.[28] If Cook had not administered his treatments simultaneously, he would have observed that lemon juice and spruce beer were the more successful. The latter, in particular, was a better source of vitamin C than traditional beers and had long been used in North America and northern Europe to prevent scurvy. The HMS *Pandora*, for example, dispatched in 1790 to capture the mutineers of the HMS *Bounty* in Tahiti, carried 340 pots of spruce essence for making spruce beer. (The *Pandora* was shipwrecked on the Great Barrier Reef in August 1791 and 150 of the intact spruce jars are now held in the Townsville Museum.) Nevertheless, Macbride's misguided putrefaction theory continued to hold sway, representing a triumph of theory over practice. Even Governor Arthur Phillip came under its thrall, complaining that provisions to counter scurvy had not been supplied for the convicts and marines for the voyage to New South Wales. He was eventually given supplies of essence of malt, but they had little effect. Lemon juice was officially adopted for use against scurvy in 1795, and the Admiralty discontinued the use of essence of malt to treat scurvy in 1798.[29]

The local climate in New South Wales compounded the problems of establishing Beer Street in the Great South Land by brewing it there. Average temperatures were neither conducive to successful floor-mashing techniques nor to the growing of raw ingredients. The First Fleet arrived in a land where no hops or barley grew. John Boston, a surgeon and apothecary who arrived in Botany Bay in 1794, became Australia's first brewer. He used maize instead of barley and, in the absence of hops, the leaves and stalks of a plant that he referred to as Cape gooseberry but which later historians believed was tomato. The home-brewing ventures of this period also sought native plants as substitutes for the hops of Britain. In 1804, when Governor King established a government-controlled brewery at Parramatta — eager to produce native beer in the hope that a ready supply would wean the convicts off rum — the favoured hops substitute was the bitter Tasmanian columba root.

James Squire, a convicted highwayman, is accredited with producing Australia's first commercial beer. He began his brewing career with hops and brewing equipment purchased from visiting store ships. From his brewery, built at government expense at Kissing Point on the shores of the Parramatta River, he produced a familiar British-type beer, rather than John Boston's colonial adaptation.

Squire sold his product at the Malting Shovel Tavern, strategically located halfway between Sydney Town and Parramatta.

Soon, settlers began cultivating barley. They would take their crop to the government brewery at Parramatta and receive 32 gallons of the brewed product in return.[30] In 1806, this brewery passed into private hands. By the end of the first decade of the nineteenth century, several breweries had emerged in Sydney, both government owned and privately owned. None lasted for long. High licensing fees played a part, but New South Wales simply didn't have the right climate for growing hops. Although James Squire produced Australia's first hop plants in 1805 from 200 poles planted for his brewing operations, the industry in New South Wales soon expired and hops were again imported. Some breweries used their own barley, but again the conditions were detrimental to the quality, so barley was also often imported. The grain would be transported to New South Wales after the floor malting process, which involved shovelling grain on the ground and depended on cool temperatures.

Even with the appropriate raw ingredients, brewing was precarious in a warm climate. Harmful bacteria thrived in the high temperatures of an Australian summer, and the beer could become contaminated to the point of being undrinkable.[31] As late as 1834, there were complaints in Sydney that the various substitutes for hops in the local beers created a brew that 'produces the heaviest sleep, pain in the head and irregularity of the bowels'.[32] Adapting brewing techniques to Australian conditions was a matter of trial and error. Not until 1876 would Louis Pasteur's studies on beer reveal the microbiology involved in both pure and contaminated beer. (Indeed, such breakthroughs formed the basis of Pasteur's germ theory and would revolutionise not only the food industry but also medicine and surgery.) In 1883, Emil Christian Hansen, a scientist at the Carlsberg brewery in Copenhagen, developed the pure strains of yeast that changed the beer industry forever. And in 1871, Carl von Linde, a

German engineer, developed a refrigeration machine that helped control the temperature-sensitive yeasts and allowed beer to be produced throughout the year. With the help of several European breweries, the machine was commercialised and patented in 1873.

Owing to the low temperatures required for floor malting, the main beer drinking countries of Europe were in the north — Germany and Scandinavia. On the other side of the world, it seemed logical that beer production should be more successful in the south. Even so, the brewing industry started relatively late in Tasmania. Although some individuals had brewed on a small scale since the earliest days, in 1806 Governor Collins forbade brewing in order to preserve the grain supply for making bread. It wasn't until 1821 that the first proper breweries were established (unsuccessfully) — one by emancipist George Gatehouse, one by the unscrupulous merchant Roland Walpole Loane, and one by John Henry Cawthorne. More dedicated hands were destined to succeed. The relatively cool Tasmanian climate was best suited to growing the raw materials necessary for British-style beer — hops and barley. The Methodist William Shoobridge, who came from a long line of hop growers in Kent, successfully established hops in the Derwent Valley in 1822, and it became the main hops-growing area of Australia. Its barley was also of better quality than on the mainland. Most importantly, the climate was ideal for brewing, and for this reason the Tasmanian breweries had more staying power than their northern counterparts. By 1850, Tasmania had forty-eight breweries. Cascade, founded in 1824 by Peter Degraves, is still running and claims to be 'Australia's oldest continuously operating brewery'.[33] Boag's Brewery in Launceston is currently located on a site — on the Esplanade beside the Esk River — where the Cornwall Brewery was established by John Fawns in 1829.[34]

Despite the difficulties, brewing in the Australian sun was possible. Even Queensland had a few breweries in its early years; however, they had to import their raw ingredients from other colonies, especially

Tasmania. The barley had to be imported after it had been malted; and in Victoria and South Australia, the malting had to be performed in the winter months. [35]

In New South Wales, of the numerous breweries that had emerged during the first half of the nineteenth century, only Tooth's was still standing in 1860. In 1835, John Tooth, of Kent in England, along with Charles Newnham, an experienced brewer also from Kent, had opened a brewery at Blackwattle Creek, now the Broadway in the Glebe area of inner Sydney. Eight years later it passed to Tooth's nephews, Robert and Edwin Tooth. The Tooth family typified the emerging players in the brewing industry, having a range of business interests, rural and urban — as merchants, pastoralists, cheese-makers and bankers.[36] Two brothers, John Thomas Toohey and James Matthew Toohey, from another family of prosperous graziers, bought the Darling Brewery in Sydney in 1872, after John had acquired his brewing licence in 1869. By the late nineteenth century, surviving in the brewing industry required large outlays of capital. Later, in the twentieth century, cartels and conglomerates would further dominate the industry.

When each colony in Australia was founded, a brewery soon emerged. In 1837, John Stokes founded the first Emu brewery in Perth. Victoria's first brewery was established by Thomas Capel that same year, and within another two years there were a total of five Victorian breweries. Some brewers, such as Henry Condell, set up in more than one colony — Condell ran a brewery in Hobart in 1830, and established another in Melbourne in 1839, but it burned down in 1845.

From the 1860s, breweries started to multiply and Tooth's lost their monopoly in Sydney, although they remained one of the largest. Beer's relatively poor keeping qualities meant only small distribution ranges were possible and so breweries spread not only throughout the large cities but also in country towns. In New South Wales, there were about eighty breweries by the 1880s, with eight out of every ten located in non-metropolitan areas. They thrived during the prosperous 1880s but many did not survive the economic depression and declining consumption of beer in the 1890s. By 1932, the number of country breweries in New South Wales would be reduced to two, as the Sydney-centred railway network opened the rural market up to the larger metropolitan breweries. Many of the struggling country breweries, with their increasingly out-of-date equipment, were taken over by city breweries.[37]

Despite the growth of the Australian brewing industry, many still preferred to drink imported beer from Europe and the US, denouncing the colonial beers as somewhat inferior and watery. Most of the imports were in draught form, as bottling techniques were not sufficiently developed until the mid-nineteenth century to suit long sea voyages. The beer produced in Tasmania's British-type climate was the most popular among British Australians, and Tasmania was an early exporter of beer to other colonies. Victoria was the next colony for good beer. From the 1860s, Victorian local brew was more widely

Before the era of refrigeration, brewing beer in many parts of Australia was a risky business, as demonstrated by the fate of Charleville's only brewery established in Queensland in the 1890s. It failed owing to unsuitable water. (State Library of Queensland)

drunk in that colony than imported beers. This was particularly so when small towns acquired their own breweries. Indeed, Victoria had the heaviest consumption of beer of all the colonies in the nineteenth century — higher even than Tasmania.

The climatic determinants of brewing in the pre-Pasteur era were reflected in the consumption rates of wine, beer and spirits for the various colonies. The figures for the 1880s, just before modern brewing techniques were introduced (and the earliest period for which we have comprehensive drinking statistics), show marked differences between the northern and southern colonies. The inhabitants of Tasmania, Victoria and South Australia drank more than seventeen times the volume of beer as compared to spirits, whereas residents of Queensland and New South Wales only consumed nine times as much.[38]

Throughout the nineteenth century, Australians drank considerably less beer than the British. Even the residents of Victoria, the biggest beer drinkers, only drank half as much as the British at the end of the century.[39]

In the northern colonies, bringing beer to the hinterland away from the large towns proved a major problem. Before the age of railways and refrigeration, beer was unlikely to stay fresh during a horse-drawn journey. For that reason, it remained the drink of the large towns — particularly those with their own breweries. As Richard Twopenny in his famous account of Australian town life noted, urban dwellers may have drunk beer regularly with their midday meal, but in the small rural towns durable spirits was the drink of choice and necessity.[40]

One type of beer that kept better than the others, in all temperatures, was the lager beer of Bavaria. Lager — from the German *Lagerbier*, or 'beer for keeping' — was made with bottom-fermenting yeast (which falls to the bottom of the liquid after fermentation) as opposed to the top-fermenting strain, which releases carbon dioxide and rises to the surface forming a 'head'. Despite the popularity of lager in Germany, it wasn't produced in Australia for the first 100 years of brewing, even though it would have suited our climate. Lager also became popular in the US in the mid-nineteenth century, but Australian brewers stuck rigidly to British-style beers. It was only in 1882 that lager first became available in Australia, when the Cohn brothers of Bendigo began producing it. In 1886, the fortunes of lager kicked on when William Foster arrived in Melbourne from New York and set up a brewery in Collingwood. Foster's brewing team had both German and American experience. They began brewing in November 1888 and sold their mainly bottled product to the public in February 1889. The labels proudly declared that the contents were 'warranted to keep in any climate'.[41] Foster's American-style enterprise and government protection combined to stop him being undercut by German and American-produced imports. He also revolutionised the serving of fresh beer by supplying hotels with free ice during the summer months, thereby providing both cold beer and an early example of supplying promotional 'freebies' to licensed premises.[42]

The 1880s saw a number of important new technologies and changes in beer production. A mechanised malting process was introduced, which involved placing the grains in revolving drums. This new 'pneumatic' malting replaced the old floor malting, which made the process much less labour-intensive and it could be carried out all year around, rather than just in the winter months. Auguste de Bavay came to Melbourne from Belgium in 1884 and immediately followed the method of Emil Christian Hansen, the Dane who several years earlier had revolutionised brewing in Europe by developing yeast strains from one cell, thus developing a pure form of yeast. De Bavay developed 'Australian No. 2', which was 'the first pure top-fermentation yeast used commercially in Australia and possibly the world'.[43] De Bavay joined Foster's in 1894.

Those factors which had worked against beer in the early years — too hot a climate for brewing and poor keeping qualities —

'Specifically suitable for tropical climates'. The beer, perhaps, but surely not the costume. Modern brewing, handling and refrigeration brought cold beer to a thirsty population. Advertisement for Bulimba Beer Gold Top, 1900. (State Library of Queensland)

soon turned in its favour. With successful modern brewing, handling and refrigeration, Australians had a refreshing, cold brew on tap to slake a thirst when the weather was hot. But the capital outlays required to take advantage of the new techniques also led to the demise of the local, independent breweries and ushered in an era of takeovers and conglomeration that continues today. Two conglomerates, Foster's Group and Lion Nathan, dominate brewing in 21st-century Australia.

One by-product of the new brewing techniques was to become an Australian icon. Initially, Carlton and United Brewery produced an extract from the spent yeast called Cubex, but it was short-lived. Fred Walker & Company then contracted to buy the spent yeast. Their young chemist, C. P. Callister, developed a version of the English product Marmite, calling it Vegemite. At first, sales were poor, but in

1935 the company increased its marketing of the new product by diverting proceeds from the successful sale of its processed cheese. Coupons for free Vegemite were given away with every purchase of a Fred Walker food product. Belying its humble origins as a brewery waste product, Vegemite was promoted as a health food; indeed, it was the 'World's Wonder Food', capable of producing 'Happy Little Vegemites'.[44] There was heavy irony in the promotion of Vegemite as a health product: a 1959 study found that most children already had sufficient amounts of the vitamins that Vegemite claimed to add to a child's diet. As Michael Symons observed, 'Alcoholics, rather than children, would have been more likely to gain from the advertising of this brewery waste product.'[45]

Young chemist C. P. Callister created Vegemite, using spent yeast supplied by Carlton and United Brewery. Despite initially poor sales, it was later successfully promoted as a health food for children. (Advertisement from the 1920s)

★　★　★

Despite the level of national and international conglomeration, beer sales today still rely heavily on local appeal: the majority of Australians mainly want to drink 'their beer', and that means their state's beer. One would expect the steady process of brewery amalgamation to have led to the emergence of a dominant national beer brand, particularly when one considers that, despite respective labelling as ales and bitters, lagers have been Australians' preferred beer for the last 100 years. But even Foster's, Australia's most internationally recognised beer brand, is not a national bestseller. In Australia, the localism of traditional British-style ales' production was refigured to state levels by the economics of efficient manufacture, marketing and transport costs. The pre-Federation colonial traditions also played their part. The six colonies already celebrated their separateness in many areas of life: post offices, stamps, lighthouses, railways, immigration programs, clocks, armed forces and customs duties.[46] Until Federation in 1901, when free trade between the states was enshrined in the Constitution, 'a Wodonga hotel-keeper who wished to import beer from the other side of the Murray River paid an import duty of twopence a bottle, the same duty he paid on a bottle from Germany'.[47] Although a local brand dominated in each state, each major brewing conglomerate also maintained a local market share, a situation that provoked occasional beer wars.

The cost of the new lager technology contributed to the decline of the smaller breweries. Both New South Wales and Victoria had fewer than forty breweries by the 1890s and Tasmania had only eleven. General economic conditions worsened in the 1890s, leading to a further decline in small brewers. In Melbourne in 1903, Carlton, Foster's, Victoria, Shamrock, Castlemaine and McCracken breweries formed the Society of Melbourne Brewers. This decreased competition in the market and higher prices followed, but the breweries survived. In 1907, they formed into a company, Carlton & United Breweries

(CUB), which went public in 1913. The centre of gravity of innovative brewing had shifted from Tasmania to Melbourne.

In the 1850s, two Irish brothers, Nicholas and Edward Fitzgerald, established a successful brewery in the gold-mining township of Castlemaine in Victoria. They expanded their operations to Melbourne, and in 1877, in partnership with local merchants Quinlan and Gray, purchased a distillery in the Brisbane suburb of Milton, which had fallen on hard times following some failed sugar crops. The Fitzgeralds converted it into a brewery and within a year began selling their Castlemaine brand XXX 'sparkling ale'. With their presence in two states, Castlemaine 'could lay claim to being Australia's first national brand'.[48] The *Brisbane Courier* described the beer as 'delicious ale of the brightest amber, pleasant to taste, with a peculiarity of flavour not easily described and aroma of an appetising nature by itself'.[49] Not content to simply look at and sniff it, the locals drank it in prodigious quantities. Castlemaine's most famous brand, however, originated in 1924 when they began selling XXXX Bitter, although it was in fact a lager. The brand XXXX has come to epitomise the rabid regionalism of popular beer drinking and the 'promotion by parish' marketing strategies of the beer conglomerates.[50] The company made itself the centre of attention from the beginning, with an image of the brewery featuring on the label. It stands 'high on Milton Hill, like a great church complete with crosses',[51] at least since the 1950s when it was emblazoned with a large XXXX sign. Also helping the image of the company was a dapper little chap, Mr Fourex. With his straw boater, wink and a beer raised in one hand, his image was the face of XXXX beer from 1924 to 1967, when he went into semi-retirement from advertising campaigns. In 2005 he returned to the company's outside billboard advertising. Mr Fourex had been 'declared by the National Trust of Queensland to be the state's second-most recognised heritage icon behind the mango tree'.[52]

Castlemaine took over the rival Perkins Brewery in 1928 to become Castlemaine Perkins Brewery. In 1982, Castlemaine Perkins

An ad from the bodyline era of cricket featuring Mr Fourex. The Queensland National Trust has declared Mr Fourex to be a heritage icon in the Sunshine State. (State Library of Queensland)

merged with the New South Wales brewer Tooheys, and the new entity was bought out by Bond Corporation in 1985. This amalgamation with Tooheys didn't seem to greatly affect the XXXX base in Queensland; after all, both states played the same dominant brand of football — rugby league — and each brew kept to its own state. But the purchase of Castlemaine Tooheys by developer-turned-entrepreneur Alan Bond provoked xenophobic reactions. Bond's image as a brewer wasn't helped by his product Swan Light, an ultra-light alcohol beer (cashing in on harsher penalties for drink driving) considered by Queenslanders unfortunate enough to have to drink it as a literally 'piss-weak' product threatening to one's manhood. Despite being a national sporting hero for helping fund the syndicate that won the America's Cup yacht race in 1983, Bond seriously misread the importance of regionalism to beer sales. He replaced the XXXX on the Milton brewery with a Bond Corporation logo. 'To make matters worse, the beer labels underwent a similar facelift and even included a reference to Western Australia.'[53] When Bond Corporation put local hoteliers on seven-day rather than thirty-day accounts, one of them, Bernie Power, correctly reading a building groundswell of popular discontent, established his own brewery.

Localism rules when it comes to beer. 'New' Queenslander, future Australian cricket captain Alan Border, pitching for XXXX in the early 1980s.
Originally from New South Wales, he is surrounded by Queensland images — tropical palms, beaches, bikinis and a relaxed attitude. Even Border's Alvey fishing reel is a distinctly Queensland creation.

Within two years, Power Brewing Company had gained 10 per cent of market share, and outmanoeuvred Bond Corporation by gaining the sponsorship of the new Brisbane rugby league team, the Brisbane Broncos. As one of the first Queensland teams to enter the Sydney-based New South Wales rugby league competition in 1988 (the other was the Gold Coast–Tweed Heads Giants), the Broncos were able to draw on the support base that had been built up by the Queensland rugby league's State of Origin team. XXXX and Lang Park (now called Suncorp Stadium), the home of Queensland rugby league, are virtual neighbours in Milton. XXXX's sponsorship of the Queensland team, the Maroons, had allowed them to maintain significant regional support; however, the rapid inroad by Power's was worrying. Certainly, Power's gained market share, but it wasn't all at the expense of XXXX. To sustain its 80 per cent market share XXXX had always to contend with local products from the Carlton & United Breweries' stable. More worrying this time was Power's attack on the creditability of XXXX's regional identity.

Swan itself was a strong regional brand. It was first brewed in Perth in 1857, taking its brand name from Western Australia's state emblem, the black swan. But the Bond Corporation wasn't primarily in the brewery business, it was in the money business. For Bond, breweries were cash cows to finance the massive levels of debt required to conduct corporate takeovers. He had paid over $1200 million for Castlemaine Tooheys Ltd; his own company was only worth a quarter of that. In the heady 1980s, the word 'entrepreneur' was being so overworked that it came to signify a mixture of pretentiousness and shark-like menace. Norman Gunston, the satirical creation of actor Garry McDonald, gave the word such a mock exaggerated Frenchiness that it conjured an image of a sleazy lounge lizard rather than a businessman.

While trying to hold its ground in Queensland, Bond Corporation was fighting opposition on another front. In New South

Wales, it wanted to divest itself of its pubs in exchange for a quick injection of cash. This required letting current leases expire without offering to renew them, but also not offering to pay the former lessees any goodwill; that is, the value of the favour or prestige that a business accrues beyond the value of what it sells. Tooheys had previously credited this surplus value to the talents and efforts of the lessee. Many of the lessees did not want to forgo their leases, nor did they want to buy the pubs, so they refused to be evicted. After a bitter battle, the courts granted them compensation. After Bond Corporation's takeover, sales of Tooheys had fallen by 20 per cent from 1985 to 1989. In 1990, New Zealand brewer Lion Nathan put them out of their misery, buying out Bond and becoming, at the time, Australasia's largest beverage producer.

By 2008, two corporations dominated brewing in Australia — Lion Nathan and the Foster's Group. Lion Nathan's brands include Tooheys, Castlemaine Perkins, Hahn, Swan, West End and James Squire. In 1983, CUB was acquired by Elders IXL, a conglomerate with interests not only in food but also in pastoral production and finance. Elders IXL was under the helm of John Elliott, a former president of the Liberal Party and a long-serving president of the Carlton Football Club. The Elders brewing group expanded overseas and in 1990 changed its name to Foster's Group. It includes a range of former CUB brands, including Foster's, Crown Lager, Carlton Draught, Victoria Bitter and Cascade.

In Australia, smaller brewery operations have emerged from time to time, seeking that part of the market that is indifferent to regionalism and responsive to taste differentiation. Hahn Brewery in Camperdown in Sydney, for example, began trading in 1988, producing a premium (high-strength) beer with a bitter finish. Power Brewing in Queensland had also ensured that their product tasted different from XXXX. For a short while, Eumundi Brewing in the

Sunshine Coast hinterland offered an alternative to drinkers disaffected by the over-corporatised world that brewing appeared to have become, but in fact had always been. Most often these smaller brewers were fated to be reabsorbed into the major corporations. Both Power's and Eumundi eventually became part of Queensland Brewing, and not only their products, but also southern beer brands, were manufactured at the Yatala site which had been created by Power's to take on the might of XXXX. The site currently produces a range of CUB brands, including Foster's, Victoria Bitter and Cascade Light, supplying them to the New South Wales market after CUB closed down the Tooth's Kent Brewery. (Up until the CUB takeover, workers at Tooth's had been entitled to one schooner of beer at morning tea, lunch, afternoon tea and at the end of their working day from one of three bars in the brewery. Later, drinking on the job was replaced by a system of tokens, allowing workers to take home one carton of beer per week.)

Hahn Brewery was acquired by Lion Nathan in 1993. Dr Chuck Hahn remained chief brewer until 1998, when he returned to his small Camperdown brewery, The Malt Shovel Brewery, to brew a unique range of handcrafted beers named after James Squire, Australia's first commercial brewer.[54] One brewery that remained for a long time outside the fold of the two major groups was the northern Tasmanian brewery J. Boag & Son. In the 1990s 'a vigorous capital expenditure policy'[55] saw Boag's purchase more than twenty small local and boutique breweries, including for a while Hahn Brewing's Camperdown brewery and the Redback Brewery in South Australia, and boutique breweries such as Kelly's Brewery in South Brisbane. Many of these smaller breweries had flourished in the bull markets that underpinned the corporate takeovers, but were vulnerable to economic downturns. Boag's success was built on its Premium Lager and Premium Light beers. In 2000, J. Boag & Son was acquired by San Miguel Corporation, the largest food and beverage company in Asia, headquartered in the Philippines. In 2007, Boag's was sold to Lion Nathan for $325 million.

Distaste for big business also provided a fillip to South Australian brewer Coopers, privately owned by the Cooper family. Coopers was established in 1862 by Thomas Cooper, a stonemason by trade, in Norwood in Adelaide. In 1881, the brewery relocated to a bigger site at Leabrook. Although freely available on tap in South Australia, Coopers' distance from the major corporations is seen as part of its current appeal. It also produces a range of beers, including its Sparkling Ale and Pale Ale, which have the distinction of being produced by secondary fermentation techniques — some yeast is left in the bottle, producing cloudy sediment, to the delight of trendies and connoisseurs alike. In 2005, Coopers was the subject of a takeover bid by Lion Nathan. This was prevented by the company's constitution, which makes it difficult for non-family members to acquire a large number of shares.

The prospect of a genuinely national beer emerging has been boosted in recent years by the relative success of Victoria Bitter, or VB as it is more widely known. VB is the most popular beer sold in Australia. Part of this success may be a peculiar kind of taste differentiation: VB is an unambiguously full-strength beer. In response to increasing community concerns over drink-driving, the dominant state brands entered the low-alcohol beer market with some trepidation in the late 1970s and early 1980s. Initially treated as a niche market, the segment took a boost from excise concessions for lower-strength beers. Initially, brewers distinguished low-strength beers from their major brands, but then entered energetically into the mid-strength market by making those beers look as much as possible like their major brands. XXXX Gold and Carlton Mid-Strength picked up sales by drawing on existing brand loyalty. Hahn Light and Cascade Premium Light used taste differentiation. So successful has

XXXX Gold become that full-strength XXXX has abandoned its traditional yellow livery to the newcomer and is now sold in a predominantly black can. In 2007, confirming the seismic shift, a mid-strength VB entered the market, also in golden colours. Until that time, there had been no room for a light VB beer.

Moreover, while the other brands were being marketed through association with fun and leisure, VB has maintained its image of being a working man's beer — a 'big cold beer' for 'a hard-earned thirst' as the ad's voice-over puts it. Overseas, Foster's sells well by appealing to images of Australianness, which don't work as well at home, where regional rivalries are more influential. VB's appeal to strength, maleness — and a discounted slab price — have given it national penetration. However, it is probably fair to say that in states other

Foster's identity as Australia's favourite beer is primarily for overseas consumption. The misconception that all Australians drink Foster's can be partly attributed to the influence of Barry Humphries' comic creation, Barry 'Bazza' MacKenzie, brought to life on screen in the 1970s by Barry Crocker. Bazza was originally created for the pages of the UK satirical magazine *Private Eye*. (Tony Feder/Fairfaxphotos)

than Victoria, drinkers see themselves as drinking a 'VB' rather than a 'Victoria Bitter'.

Sales of VB benefited from Lion Nathan's unsuccessful attempt to establish its Tooheys New brand in the Melbourne beer market. In what became known as the Melbourne beer wars, Lion Nathan made a conscious grab for an increased market share in the south by purchasing pubs and other venues for about $50–60 million. Local patrons proved resistant. They also secured naming rights for the iconic Melbourne Cup from 1999 to 2009, but relinquished them to the international airline Emirates in 2004.

One essential part of the strategy for selling regionally identified beers beyond their borders was the selling of slabs — a package of four six-packs of stubbies or cans — for discounted prices interstate. It appears that VB has been the major beneficiary of this strategy; by 2006 it had about a third of the packaged beer market in Australia. The 2007 move to add a VB mid-strength lager to the range is an indication of the current thirst for mid-strength beers, especially in the Western Australian and Queensland markets. The need to appeal to traditional mythic images remains, however. The company's website observes: 'No, Aussies are not going soft. Blokes are still blokes — sports mad, willing to have a go and still dead keen on a beer with mates and the occasional late night lamb sandwich. But drinking habits are changing.'[56]

The normative equation of masculinity and mateship with drinking alcohol has had a long history in Australia. Barry Humphries' great vaudeville character Sir Leslie Colin Patterson, the dribbling, dipsomaniacal, Australian Ambassador to the Court of St James, Chairman of the Australian Cheese Board and 'cultural attaché for the arts', sings *Never Trust a Man Who Doesn't Drink*, as told to young Les Patterson by his father — who died 'trustworthy' in his sleep, halfway between the public bar and the dunny:

Never trust a man who doesn't drink.
Though he may not throw up in your kitchen sink.
I'd rather be half-hearted,
Than be a blue-nosed wowser bastard.
So *never* trust a man who doesn't drink.[57]

Even now, many men and women in Australia don't trust a person who doesn't drink alcohol. Recently at a party Ross Fitzgerald overheard a bloke saying to a friend, 'Watch her, she doesn't drink.' The sentiment, attributed also to American comedian W. C. Fields, actor John Wayne and Admiral William Halsey, as well as a great many male Australians sums up the attitude that there is something wrong with a person who doesn't drink. It is a suspicion that can affect the behaviour of even our top leaders. According to politician John Anderson as he sculled a beer on the *Stateline* televison program in 2001: 'You can't cut the mustard in the Australian bush if you can't put a beer down.'[58] At the time, he was leader of the National Party and deputy prime minister.

There is little differentiation from state to state in the core advertising images used to sell beer. As Jonathan Dawson points out, 'Moving cases of beer in Queensland seems set to forever inscribe and reassert the primacy of those old mythic structures, mateship, sun and the bush.'[59] Yet these images are not uniquely Australian. In the 1980s, images promoting tourism in Durban, South Africa, contained 'identical clusters of shots promoting a mythic, sun-drenched arcadia using the same proportion of shots of dawnlit bikini girls, swooping chopper runs and fast beach runs intercut with outback work images as in … the Brisbane Bitter launch in the late seventies and the latest Our Beer [XXXX] series'.[60] Dawson refers to such images, when used in a marketing context, as 'transnational archetypes'.[61] Whether one considers them archetypical or merely stereotypical, these amalgamations of images of horses at gallop, shearers, landscapes at dawn and dusk, and good sports ogling good sorts, all project ideas of 'masculinity'. The pastoral aspects of these advertising campaigns echo much of what Russel Ward called 'the Australian Legend' — a literary construction from the 1890s, in which the Australian nation defined itself by the values and attitudes of the upcountry bushman.[62] This self-image was 'the often romanticised and exaggerated stereotype in men's minds of what the *typical*, not the *average*, Australian likes (or in some cases *dis*likes) to believe he is like'.[63] Part of that image was of 'a practical man, rough and ready in his manners' who 'drinks deeply on occasion,' and was based on outback employees — the 'semi-nomadic drovers, shepherds, shearers, bullock-drivers, stockmen, boundary-riders, station-hands and others of the pastoral industry'.[64] It was a population in which men vastly outnumbered women, and where the bush tradition of 'work and bust' led to widespread binge drinking.

Similar patterns of behaviour have been associated with heavy drinking in other parts of the world. Jack Blocker, for example, identified three factors determining an individual's drink consumption in the US: gender, marital status and distance from family.[65] Attributing Australia's heavy drinking in the early days to its lopsidedly male population would suggest that gender was the key factor, and indeed the historian A. E. Dingle attributes the declining rate of alcohol consumption throughout the nineteenth century to the higher number of women and families in the colony. Australians were growing up and settling down.[66] But was gender really the determining factor in rates of alcohol consumption? One way to examine the relative influences of gender, marital status and distance from family on drinking patterns in Australia is to compare regional differences in consumption. This can be done most successfully in the period after 1880, when the best records of drinking rates in the various colonies were kept. It was only in this decade that New South Wales included its locally produced beer figures and that the colony of Western Australia produced drinking figures.

Looking at Western Australia, it may seem that Blocker's three factors apply. In 1889, this colony consumed more than twice as much proof alcohol as any other colony, and 10 per cent more than the United Kingdom. In 1896, while other colonies' consumption had declined, Western Australia's had risen by nearly 50 per cent and was higher than most European countries. Western Australia happened to be the colony with the greatest number of men in comparison with women. In 1891, there were 66 women per 100 men. This went down to 50 women in 1896 and back up to 64 in 1901. The gender gap widened in different age groups. The greatest imbalance was in the 35–40 age group where there were only two-thirds as many women as men.[67] If you look at the statistic for marital status, it seems that Western Australia fitted Blocker's model: according to the 1901 census, there were about three married men to five never married men aged fourteen years and upwards. Of those men who were married, a substantial number were living away from their wives on census night, presumably having left them at home while going off to seek gold. The highest proportion was in the north and north-western district where there was also the highest gender imbalance.[68] Thus, Western Australia appears to confirm the theory that being male, a bachelor or removed from family determined heavy drinking.

Queensland, however, had an even higher proportion of males in 1889, and in the 25–30 age group there were just over half as many women as men.[69] It also had the highest immigrant population, including European and Irish immigrants (in 1881, only 40 per cent of Queenslanders were Australian born).[70] Although Queensland resembled Australia's early days in terms of its predominantly young, single male population this did not produce similar drinking rates. In 1889, Queensland had much lower alcohol consumption than Western Australia. Indeed, in 1885 it was only very slightly higher than South Australia and considerably lower than Victoria — the two

Gender differences observed at a Mackay ball in the 1890s. Wallflowers on
the left, and propping up the bar and falling down drunk on the right.
(State Library of Queensland, no. 00078)

most gender-balanced colonies. Queenslanders' drinking patterns
were like those of early Australia in one respect — they drank more
spirits than Victorians and South Australians. As noted previously,
spirits were more durable in the warm climate. Yet they didn't drink
spirits in anywhere near the same quantities — about half as much as
New South Wales in the 1830s.[71]

Why the huge discrepancy between Queensland and Western
Australia, given that both were male-dominated? Part of the reason
becomes clear if we compare alcohol consumption with consumption
of other luxury foods. In 1896, T. A. Coghlan, the government
statistician for New South Wales, gathered data on the consumption
rates per head for various foods in all seven colonies of Australasia.
Western Australia stood out dramatically, with high figures not only for
alcohol but also for tea, coffee, wheat, rice, butter, cheese and mutton.
Clearly, Western Australians spent more on food and beverages of all
types.[72] The colony with the lowest alcohol consumption per head was
Tasmania. Oddly, considering it was the main beer producer, this
included the lowest beer consumption. Were more Tasmanians
brewing their own? Perhaps, but a more likely explanation can be

found when we examine figures for other foods. Tasmania was also the colony with the lowest consumption of tobacco (despite the fact it didn't have the lowest percentage of males), tea and coffee, sugar, salt and beef. The Tasmanians weren't high purchasers of non-essential groceries in general, including alcohol, which isn't surprising if we consider that Tasmania was the poorest of the colonies. Its inhabitants were high consumers of potatoes — the traditional food of the less well-to-do and much cheaper per bulk than meat.[73]

Coghlan's figures would have excluded not only home-brew but also the sly-grog market. Nevertheless, if we assume that these factors were constant across colonies and between decades (and we have no reason to assume otherwise), it seems that periods and regions of increasing wealth were similarly those of increased drinking. If these colonial differences are a guide, it seems that an important factor that distinguished the heavy drinkers from the more sober was wealth. More money for luxuries such as tea, sugar and tobacco also meant more expenditure on alcohol. In fact, the substance whose popularity correlated with the proportion of males in a colony was not alcohol but tobacco. Western Australia had the highest tobacco use per inhabitant, followed by Queensland, with Victoria down below New South Wales.[74]

If we contrast the drinking rates between the 1880s and the 1890s, the correlation between alcohol consumption rates and the economy stands out even more. This was most pronounced in spirits: every colony saw a pronounced decline in consumption during the 1890s.[75] Beer also declined. Wine was the exception, with Victoria and South Australia showing significant increases. The 1890s happened to be a period of economic depression. In 1896, however, Western Australia's consumption rate rose by a third. (Admittedly, this was the first time there were reliable statistics for that colony.) Its male–female discrepancy had widened further, but something else was clearly a factor: Western Australia in the 1890s was the scene of an amazing economic boom; in particular, a mining boom. In this sense it was very similar to Victoria in the 1850s.

Queensland, with its high percentage of single males, showed one drinking pattern that was different from the more family-dominated colonies. The drinking rates there didn't go down in the depressed 1890s, as they did in the other colonies, but there was a switch from spirits to beer — perhaps due to the increased use of iceboxes. Yet in Queensland between 1889 and 1896, the use of tobacco, the other popular stimulant, decreased considerably. Interestingly, Queensland was the only colony that saw a decline in tea drinking (from 8.7 to 7.8 pounds a year) in those difficult years. In other colonies, tea was clearly treated as an essential, an item to be fitted into the budget through good times and bad; whereas alcohol was a disposable luxury. In Queensland, the reverse appears to have been true.

We know that the rich colonies like Victoria drank more than poor colonies such as Tasmania, but what do these alcohol consumption figures tell us about the rate of drunkenness in a particular colony? Was the annual drink quantity for the colony spread evenly amongst the inhabitants? Or were there a substantial number of non-drinkers compensated for by another group of big drinkers?

When it comes to patterns of excessive alcohol consumption it might seem natural to look at the figures for arrests for drunkenness. Such figures are available for each of the colonies and show differences between the two sexes, different age groups, the various religions and denominations as well as the different colonies. From these figures, we might conclude that the average drunk was male, in his twenties or thirties, Catholic, and living in New South Wales. New South Wales had by far the highest rate of arrests for drunkenness in the 1880s (27 per 1000) compared to 15.8 in Queensland and 13.9 in Tasmania (the lowest), even though it had the second lowest drinking rate (though second highest of spirits).[76] T. A. Coghlan, however, the colonial statistician, dismissed figures for drunken arrests as unrepresentative of anything but the presence and stringency of police.[77] In his 1891 comparison of arrest rates for drunkenness, he deduced that the colonies with the highest rates (New South Wales, Victoria and Queensland) were those with the most favourable ratio of police per head of population.[78]

These days, the sportsman has replaced the shearer and drover as the primary image of a masculine ideal. Leisure time, rather than work time, is the locus of a more relaxed maleness, one in which the democracy of skill and the sympathy of drink often submerges distinctions of class. The frosty beer is an easily achievable reward for the exertions of sport. Moreover, while hotels and bars are open all hours to one and all, Australia's sporting fields remain heavily segregated along gender lines even in the age of anti-discrimination laws.

In the early decades of the Australian colonies, there was a strong connection between the public house and recreational sport. This wasn't surprising considering that the public house was the community's central meeting place and the focus not just of drinking but of leisure. The public house, as an all-purpose recreation centre, would provide facilities for playing billiards, quoits or skittles — the types of games that involved small spaces and equipment. Some hoteliers provided for more expansive outdoor sports. Indeed, amateur sport often depended on the local hotel for essential supplies; for instance, cricketers might hire their bats and balls from there. Most importantly, the hotel was a meeting place for sporting clubs, and many such sporting clubs became associated closely with the hotels. Sydney's first cricket clubs, for example, were associated with their local hotel, which would be the venue for meetings and club dinners.[79]

Other publicans opened sporting facilities around their establishments, and were often central to the foundation of Australia's first sports. One such example was Thomas Shaw, the licensee of the

Woolpack Inn, who founded the Petersham racecourse behind his hotel. This became the second most important racecourse in Sydney, and its annual carnival attracted visitors from many miles around. Shaw also founded one of the first bowling greens in Australia in 1845.[80] Hotels were particularly important to racing events. The Sportsman Inn in Sydney was used as the venue for entering horses in races. Sometimes one hotel was the place from where trotting races would start and another was the site of the finishing line. Horse racing's close association with hotels was also connected with gambling, and hotels and gambling had always had a close relationship in both Britain and Australia.

Another sport that had close associations with the public house in the early days was wrestling. The Cornish immigrants to South Australia had been instrumental in promoting wrestling in the colonies, and in 1851, Adelaide held the Cornish Wrestling Championships: a three-day event, organised by a hotel, held adjacent to that hotel and attended by 2000 people.[81] The generally masculine nature of such sports linked them naturally with alcohol and the public house. Wrestling and boxing were also sports that excluded women, even as spectators, due to their brutal nature and the lack of clothing worn by competitors. When the American writer Jack London, on a reporting assignment for the Sydney *Star* and the *New York Herald*, took his wife to the Burns–Johnston prize fight in Sydney in 1908, her presence was something new and shocking.[82]

Breweries as well as public houses were significant in the sporting world. Often they provided alcoholic refreshments for sporting clubs not tied to hotels. For example, the Richmond Brewery provided beer for the Mercantile Rowing Club of Melbourne.[83] The Gippsland Hop Bitters Brewery provided the silver trophies that in 1886 were presented to the winners of the Mercantile Club's eights race.[84] One reason for the strong association of sport with alcohol was the belief that alcohol increased size and strength — and alcohol is a known source of calories.

In the later years of the nineteenth century, a decline in drinking and the rise of teetotalism and the temperance movement had an effect on sport. For twenty years, from 1903–23, Victoria Park, home of the Collingwood football team, was a dry venue. This was the decision of the Collingwood City Council, which had taken over Victoria Park's management a few years previously. Up until then, liquor booths had been present in the park on match days — between the outer and the reserve. The prohibition of the liquor booth didn't stop drinking; it just meant that the half-time break had to be extended so spectators had time to frequent nearby hotels. Entertainment had to be provided for those who stayed in the park, such as the Aboriginal boomerang thrower Mulga Fred, or other sporting activities such as running races.[85] The ban on drinks in the park was a boon for the local hotels. Many displayed the Collingwood scores so their patrons had no urgency to return to the game. In 1923, however, liquor booths were once again allowed to operate in Victoria Park.

By 1940, Collingwood not only had liquor at its games, it had received a club liquor licence before other Victorian football clubs. As a result of its privileged status as a licenced club, in the 1940s Collingwood became the wealthiest Victorian football club.

The temperance movement affected other sports besides football. Even a sport as tough and masculine as boxing was sometimes transformed. The boxer and manager Jimmy Sharman, who professionalised boxing, insisted that all boxers in his employment must sign a contract promising to refrain from alcohol and other drugs. He himself was a very light drinker and would not permit intoxicated men in his boxing ring.[86]

Cricketers were notorious for their alcohol consumption in earlier years, but the game underwent something of a clean-up in the 1890s. British cricket had certainly been boosted by the efforts of the Yorkshireman Lord (Martin Bladen) Hawke, the English cricket administrator who had transformed the game with winter pay and

Bulimba beer, XXXX's local competitor, linked its Gold Top beer to
Australia's spin bowling attack. 'Other bowling theories' refers to the
infamous bodyline pace attack of the touring English cricket team in
1932–1933. (State Library of Queensland)

travel allowances. He also aimed to alter the cricketing culture by instilling sobriety in players and administrators alike.[87] In 1906, *The Australasian Star* asked a number of sportsmen — including a footballer, a bowler, a boxer, a cricketer and an 'aquatic enthusiast' — whether it was true, as advertisements claimed, that alcohol was good for athletes. They all said that they never drank. A 'prominent batsman' replied that cricketers these days 'are noted for their temperance'.[88] Certainly there were noted teetotal cricketers in the twentieth-century era, such as the great batsman Victor Trumper, and Sir Donald Bradman, until he stopped playing. However, there were famous cricketers who clearly imbibed, such as Warwick Armstrong, who carried a bottle of whisky in his cricket bag, and Reggie Duff, his test teammate in 1901, 1902 and 1905, who died of alcohol poisoning at the age of thirty-three.[89]

Many sporting figures had been moderate drinkers or teetotallers even in the earlier decades. For example, the Aboriginal cricketer Jumgumjenanuke (Dick-a-Dick), who had played in Australia's first official touring squad to England in 1868 (an all-Aboriginal team), was described as having a 'horror' of drunkenness and was praised in *The Australasian* for his abstemious tendencies. The Aboriginal cricketers faced particular dangers from alcohol, having come from a culture that traditionally had little or no alcohol, and some of Jumgumjenanuke's teammates died of alcoholism.[90]

The degree of female drinking in Australia's history, and the female presence in pubs, has been a subject of controversy and disagreement. The historian Marilyn Lake insisted that the Australian pastime of heavy drinking was an essentially male affair and that to women alcohol was most often a source of anguish.[91] Husbands spent their wages at the pub, and the women were financially deprived or even victims of drink-related violence. Referring to Janet McCalman's study of Richmond, *Struggletown*, and to studies of domestic violence in Queensland, Lake insisted that drinking was a masculine privilege and that women could actually be punished for drinking. She claimed that the temperance movement was to some extent a sex war. Chris McConville, on the other hand, drawing on the testimonies of temperance and police reports, spoke of young working-class men and women drinking together at the Rose of Melbourne at Fitzroy, and saw the public house as a heterosocial space. He claimed that class, not gender, was the main dividing line between pub-goers and temperance reformers.[92] Reports from the time, however, suggest that in the middle of the nineteenth century women were avoiding the public houses, although some women bought grog from public houses in jugs to drink at home. Byrne O'Reilly, sergeant of police, spoke of drunken women he encountered in their homes when he was collecting rates, which he attributed to the growing number of pubs in their neighbourhoods and the fact that beer was so cheap. Robert Barnfield, a Melbourne publican, told an 1867 royal commission into alcohol sales that no respectable woman would be seen in a public house. As O'Reilly expressed it: 'Men can go and drink anywhere, but women, if they are not quite devoid of feminine delicacy, will only send for it and drink in the house.'[93]

Many women preferred not to be seen buying takeaway grog from a public house; instead, they were catered for by tradesmen who slipped liquor to their respectable customers. The 1867 royal commission showed particular concern about licensed grocers providing alcohol to women. Interestingly, public house customers drank mainly beer, whereas the licensed grocers' customers mostly drank brandy. The commission heard of women who kept their drinking habits from their husbands by having alcohol included on the grocer's bill under the heading of groceries. Many women used alcohol as a medicine or painkiller to soothe their ailments. Indeed, doctors often sent female patients to sly grog tradesmen and grocers to obtain their 'medicine' without a loss of face. According to temperance advocates, many women developed alcoholism from constantly imbibing medically prescribed spirits.

The commission also heard of working-class wives who liked to drink at the end of a hard week's work, as did some well-to-do women. Women's drinking, however, tended to have a different social pattern and function. Indeed, Byrne O'Reilly told the commission that men drink 'in company and to pass away the time, but the women drink to get drunk'.[94] Whether they drank to get drunk or to ease the pain of their ailments, women's drinking, being largely confined to the home, was probably more solitary.

Some writers tend to assume that most female drunkenness occurred mostly among working-class women.[95] However, the existence of Emily Harcourt's home in Cheltenham for women inebriates 'of the better class' suggests otherwise.[96]

Among the middle or upper classes there were more opportunities for women to drink alcohol socially at private functions, as witnessed by W. M. James Mercer's famous Ballarat-based temperance novel *Emily Graham*, in which boarding school girls used alcohol as a coming-of-age ritual.[97] It is possible that it was in homes with a good disposable income that many female drinkers were to be found.

If drinking alcohol at home was compatible with female respectability, drunkenness was not. Visiting Women's Christian Temperance Union missionary Mary Leavitt found that a hurdle to getting women to temperance meetings was the association of the temperance movement with ex-drunks. Ladies did not want to associate with alcoholic women, or even ex-alcoholics.[98] Respectability proved no guarantee against alcoholism. The 1867 commission heard of husbands who were being ruined financially by their wives' drinking. Drunkenness could afflict women of any class.

How, in the light of the statements to the 1867 royal commission, do we explain McConville's findings of young men and women cavorting together at the Rose of Melbourne hotel? And this was not a sole case: many concerned observers at the turn of the century referred to young women in pubs. Donald Lucas, the Canadian temperance reformer, was surprised on his 1887 visit to Melbourne to see women in a public house. Other temperance reports referred to public houses frequented by women. The Wesley Central Mission magazine described the clientele of the pubs that were violating Sunday closing: they were young people under twenty-one, including many girls. Judith Allen has poured scorn on McConville's picture of a free and equal camaraderie between the sexes at the pub, suggesting that these girls were most likely prostitutes.[99]

Two important differences stand out between the female patrons of the Rose of Melbourne and the women referred to in the commission: their respective time periods and their ages. There is reason to believe that the late nineteenth century saw the emergence of different gendered drinking patterns. The 1890s was a period in which women took up other previously unfeminine behaviours, such as smoking, and, in the middle classes, earning a living and riding a bicycle. The working-class pub-going woman could be seen as a further manifestation of that phenomenon. Another important distinction was the women's youth — they were 'girls' and presumably unmarried. They most likely earned their own wages and weren't subject to the same round of domestic responsibilities as married women. American accounts show that the recreational life of working-class youth became more heterosocial in the late nineteenth century, with both sexes frequenting public amusements unchaperoned, the young men often 'treating' the 'girls' whose low wages precluded them from paying for their own leisure.[100]

Women certainly came to frequent the public house more often as the twentieth century got underway. Clare Wright has shown how, by the 1920s, housewives often frequented the ladies' lounge of the local in the afternoons, bringing their vegetables, which they would sit and chop up, preparing for the evening meal. While fewer men were drinking in the public house than half a century before, women were moving back there. In those states with six o'clock closing, most men had to squeeze in their pub drinking between leaving work at five and closing time at six. Women's more flexible hours of housework, however, allowed for pub time.

In the twenty-first century, beer marketers claim to have moved away from stereotypical associations of beer drinking with maleness and sport. Certainly, both Carlton & United Breweries' so-called 'Big Ad' and a Tooheys New commercial featuring an army of people working together to induce the heavens to rain beer feature none of the sun-drenched images that were typical of Australian beer ads in the 1970s and 1980s. But these newer commercials differ from past efforts not because of some nascent feminism in beer marketing but because they were produced to take advantage of new marketing possibilities via the internet. Both ads were part of so-called 'viral marketing' campaigns, which involved pre-releasing them to thousands of staff and customers, who were emailed a web address that allowed them to view the ad and pass it on. As few would be interested in circulating a 'normal' beer ad, the content had to be sufficiently different to motivate the initial recipient to forward the email to friends. The new ads also blurred the usual regional focus because they were aimed at increasing national market share in the annual $5.3 billion full-strength beer market. Thus, Tooheys $1 million ad for the best-selling beer in New South Wales was filmed in Melbourne.

With the concentration of most Australian beer sales in the hands of two large players — the Foster's Group and Lion Nathan — the task of increasing national market share could be likened to trench warfare, with many attempted forays into enemy territory for modest gains. In 2004–05, overall domestic beer sales (by litres) were down by 1.2 per cent. Full-strength sales were down by 1.9 per cent and light beer sales by a whopping 9.8 per cent. Mid-strength sales were up by 3.1 per cent and premium beers, mostly full-strength but a smaller market, were up by 8.4 per cent.[101] Lion Nathan had 60 per cent of the overall beer market in Queensland, while Foster's had only 40 per cent. Mid-strength beers accounted for 48.6 per cent of the Queensland market and were worth $451 million. XXXX Gold was the national number one in the mid-strength category. Foster's saw this area as a strategic means of increasing sales. With the largest investment in a single brand in the state in seventy-five years, they launched an advertising campaign directly aimed at the connection between masculinity, sport, regionalism and beer. The Male Intelligence Division (MID) ads depicted leading Queensland sporting heroes — Wally Lewis, Gordon Tallis, Michael Voss, Trevor Gillmeister and Matthew Hayden — enjoying mid-strength beers in a male-only environment while robotic lookalikes took their place in the real world, undertaking unpleasant domestic chores that included interacting with their significant others.

Selling more beer has effectively meant entering the global market. Lion Nathan was already the product of a cross-Tasman merger, and by 2006 was 46 per cent owned by Japan's biggest beverage maker, Kirin.[102] Both Foster's and Lion Nathan tried in the 1990s to cash in on the lucrative Asian market, with ventures in Vietnam, India and China. This 'China fever' was compared to a gold rush in reverse, but instead of thousands of Chinese prospectors pouring into Australia, Australian companies were pouring money into China, hoping to get a share of the world's fastest-growing economy.[103] In 1993 alone, Australian beer companies poured $1 billion into China. Foster's bought breweries in Guangdong, Tianjin and Shanghai. They planned to 'Fosterise' China, and then the world, but may have done better if they'd concentrated on producing local beers. By 2003, China had overtaken the US as the largest beer market in the world, but Lion Nathan pulled out of its three Chinese breweries in 2004 and Foster's eventually pulled out after less than six years' involvement. By mid-2006, Foster's had vacated China, Vietnam and India, effectively exiting the Asian market. Having sold the Foster's brand in Europe to the company Scottish & Newcastle, they showed a profit for that year, but from sales of breweries and brands rather than sales of beer.

Producing foreign beers locally, under licence, has been a far more successful outcome of globalisation for local brewers than their forays into overseas markets. However, to the surprise of brewers, local consumers of overseas beers complained that the local products were inferior to the original.[104] According to Lion Nathan's chief brewer at the time, Bill Taylor, enthusiasts for foreign beers were being confused by the freshness of the locally produced beer; their acquired taste for the overseas product being partly determined by the three-month shipping time it often took to arrive in Australia. Beck's beer, for example, is locally produced by Lion Nathan to the German Purity Law of 1516 using carbon-filtered local water, imported malt and hops and the original 100-year-old cultivated Beck's yeast strain. Why does it taste different? Because Beck's is fresher, drinkers 'may be noticing more flavour characters'.[105] It is somewhat ironic that a select minority of beer drinkers today may be equating a lack of freshness with a superior taste, when their forebears from yesteryear longed for fresh beer.

CHAPTER 3

Glass Distinctions

In the summer of 1867, Prince Alfred, Queen Victoria's son, undertook the first royal tour of Australia. A local Melbourne business leader, Mr L. L. Smith, hosted a free banquet for the prince and the city's poor on the banks of the Yarra River. Donations of food and drink were arranged and volunteers marshalled. The ladies' auxiliary set up by the governor's wife estimated that they would be able to serve up to 4000 people at a time. The Reverend Dr J. I. Bleasdale — a Roman Catholic priest and trained viticulturalist — selected 1000 gallons of local wine to toast the prince's health. Bleasdale had made many contributions to the Medical Society of Victoria on the usefulness of wine in treating the sick, arguing that it was a 'natural antidote to spirit drinking, and all its baleful effects' in Victoria's hot and dry climate.[1] The *Argus* editorialised that the free banquet for the prince was turning into a free guzzle. The day of the picnic turned out to be hot and dry. High in the trees, huge wine barrels fed wine fountains. A crowd of 40,000 (three times the number predicted) gathered early. When they were finally let in, there was a rush for the inadequate supplies of water. Members of the ladies' auxiliary and attending clergy pleaded for patience, but by early afternoon the crowd was famished, thirsty and restless. Melbourne's police chief rode to Government House to warn that the prince's safety could not be assured, and his visit was called off. When the organisers announced that the prince wasn't coming, the crowd stampeded for the food and drink. It was a scene described by the *Argus* as 'a bacchanalian picture of unbelievable horror', while *The Age* called it a 'disgusting debauch'.[2] Crowds grabbed food, cases of champagne and attempted to fill any available containers with wine. The patron, Mr Smith, denounced the police chief's meddlesome interference, indignantly claiming that 'if members of the Ladies Committee were brave enough to attend, the Prince ought not have been deterred'.[3]

This ambitious event, supposedly offering the prince and the poor alike their place in the sun, not only severely tested antipodean egalitarianism, but also challenged some prevailing myths about the naturally civilising effects of certain select beverages. The provision of wine, an amiable and useful tool of celebration, was intended to be both a civilising influence and a gesture towards moderation. As it turned out, whatever form it came in, alcohol was often not a civilising influence in Australia. Nevertheless, the ability to handle alcoholic drink without becoming drunk was widely regarded as an important marker of one's character. To be amiable while remaining useful was laudable. In Britain, table wines were never the drink of the hoi polloi; consuming them marked off a person from the common mass. The Reverend Bleasdale's belief in the socially elevating effects of drinking wine was profoundly misplaced. Wine was more a reflector of social distinctions than a creator of them. Who drinks alcohol and what they drink are significant caste marks. Those secure in their class or cultural identity usually drink happily from their traditional founts, but for those in the grip of status anxiety — the middle classes, but also those negotiating the boundaries between

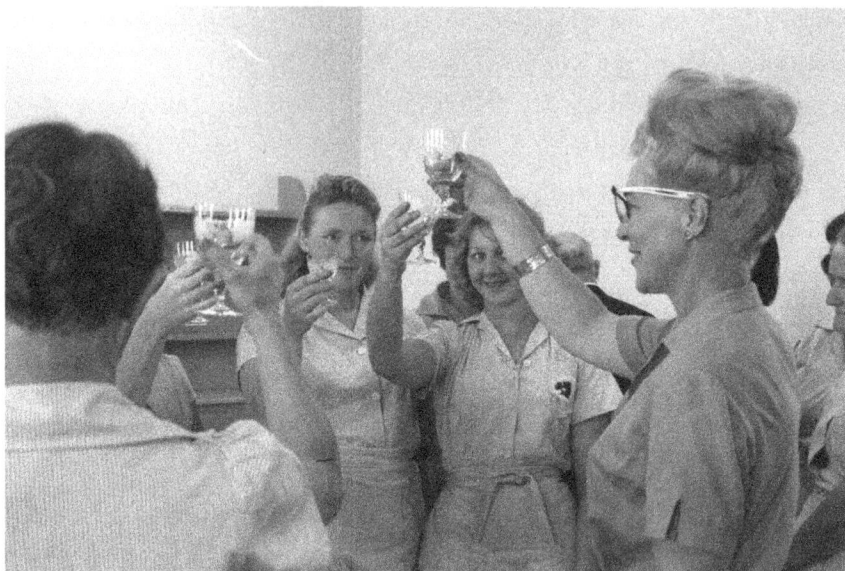

Wine has long been regarded as a civilising influence. In this photo a group of women from the State Reformatory, Long Bay, Sydney, in the 1960s are being taught the finer points of drinking wine. (National Library of Australia)

cultures — knowing what form of alcohol to drink can provoke a profound un-ease, if not dis-ease.

When the First Fleet arrived at Botany Bay, wine wasn't as popular in Britain as beer and spirits. The climatic influences favouring beer and spirit production weren't conducive to vineyards. Wine, predominantly the drink of the Mediterranean countries, was imported and, therefore, more costly, so wine drinking began to reflect class differences. Although the Scottish highlanders, for example, were renowned as whisky drinkers, the drink of the Scottish lowland middle classes was imported claret.[4] Religious differences also played a part. Dr John Dunmore Lang (1799–1878), Australia's first Presbyterian clergyman, who feared that the colony would be swamped by Roman Catholic Irishmen, 'believed people should be taken off whisky and shown the pleasures of light wine'.[5] The wine Captain James Cook was forced to serve when the beer ran out on his voyage of discovery had been intended for medicinal purposes and the enjoyment of the officers. That was why he held some in reserve. For those who belonged to the middle class, wine embodied the virtues of amiability and usefulness, and so it's not surprising that, as with beer, it came to be seen as an alternative to the socially disadvantageous consumption of spirits. Wine also had an advantage over beer in being more readily transportable, particularly in its fortified forms, and this was to prove some disincentive towards efforts to produce a local product.

Captain Arthur Phillip observed that 'in a climate so favourable, the cultivation of the vine may doubtless be carried to any degree of perfection, and ... the wines of New South Wales may perhaps hereafter be sought with civility and become an indispensable part of the luxury of European table' — a statement that conveyed accurately the contemporary belief in wine's civilising effects but overstated the case for the prospects of early success for its local production. Vine cuttings brought with the First Fleet — acquired from the Cape of Good Hope and described as 'claret', probably of cabernet sauvignon variety[6] — were planted in the area that would later become the Sydney Botanic Gardens. They produced some fruit but it was neglected and left to decay on the vine. Grapes from the next crop were eagerly consumed, and the prospects for grape growing looked promising. Cuttings planted at Parramatta were to yield further modest amounts of table grapes. Based on his success in his own garden with growing strawberries, the colony's first chaplain, the Reverend Richard Johnson, promised a friend in England that he would soon toast his health 'in a Bumper of New Holland wine'.[7] Ultimately, however, those initial vines did not take hold in the new southern land.

The first successful vines for making wine were planted in the antipodes in 1791 by Philip Schaffer, a German whose father owned a vineyard by the Rhine, and whose inability to speak English fluently had been no impediment to him coming to Botany Bay as a superintendent of convicts, particularly as he had some farming experience. Schaffer was granted 56 hectares of land at Parramatta, which he called The Vineyard, and within a few months had 5 hectares under mixed cultivation, mostly maize and some wheat, tobacco and grapes. In 1795 he produced 10 litres of the first documented wine grown in Australia. Captain William Paterson, who acted as the colony's administrator between the departure of Major Francis Grose and the arrival of Governor John Hunter, observed that in a couple more years the administration might be able to purchase wine and brandy from him. Schaffer did not last long as a vigneron, however, selling his property two years later. According to the Reverend Dr John Dunmore Lang, he died a drunkard. Eventually the land would be bought by the Roman Catholic Church for a convent, which produced altar wines until the 1960s.[8]

In truth, the climate around Sydney was hot enough but too humid to consistently produce successful table wines. The stills Governor Bligh had seized from John Macarthur had been intended to produce a fortified wine from peaches as well as rum. During Macarthur's period of de facto exile, he became interested in producing wine from grapes. In 1815 and 1816 he travelled to Europe with his then teenage sons, William and James, as William later recollected, 'for the express purpose of collecting vines and of obtaining information respecting their culture'. The Macarthurs left what in their estimation were 'about thirty of the best varieties of vine (from six to twelve cuttings of plants of each)' with a nurseryman near London. In April 1817, this collection — or, as William later put it, 'what was said to be this collection' — went with them back to Australia.[9] In 1820, William and his brother James planted and then carefully cultivated over many years a large vineyard containing what turned out to be very ordinary grape varieties, half of which had been already introduced to the colony.[10] Had the Macarthurs been stiffed by the nurseryman? William claimed so, and certainly it was not a common Macarthur trait to admit one's failings. Although this venture was a failure, twenty years later, after much further study and endeavour, William did manage to produce a thriving vineyard on the family's property at Camden. In 1840, they exhibited wines and brandies in London under the label 'Australian Wine, Camden Park, James & William Macarthur'. There was no information on the precise type of wine, but it had the reputation 'of enormous richness'.[11]

Other vignerons were also setting up in New South Wales at the time the Macarthur brothers returned from France. One was Gregory Blaxland, the explorer of the Blue Mountains, who planted vines at Brush Farm near Parramatta. He sent his first pipe of fortified wine to England in 1822, and he was awarded a silver medal by the Royal Society of Arts in 1823 and a gold medal in 1827.[12] The Royal Society medals were a kind of encouragement award to stimulate the

The wines and brandies of John Macarthur's sons, James and William, were some of the first produced in Australia and were exhibited in London before 1840. Their label provides no clue as to the type of wine.

production of wine in New South Wales. The judges pronounced the first wine to be 'light but sound' and observed that it smelled and tasted like 'ordinary claret'. Taking into account the 'inexpertness' of its maker and the 'youth' of the wine, it afforded 'a reasonable ground of expectation that by care and time it may become a valuable article of export'.[13] The 1827 wine they found 'decidedly better'.

Another successful promoter of early Australian wines was James Busby, who had studied viticulture in France and who, in 1825, wrote *A Treatise on the Culture of the Vine and the Art of Making Wine*. He was one of the first vintners of the Hunter Valley, which from the 1820s became a notable vine-growing region. Busby himself never made a drop of wine; he bought the land, but his brother-in-law, William Kelman, became the winemaker. Busby believed the distinctiveness of wine created a morally uplifting effect and promoted temperance against 'ardent spirits'. (Temperance at that time meant the temperate use of wine and beer as opposed to drinking spirits.) His writing was intended to show 'the respectable portion of the community' how to produce wine, an activity suitable to 'increase the comforts, and promote the morality of the power classes of the Colony, and more especially of native-born youth'.[14] Busby had collected 543 vine varieties in France and Spain, of which 362 reached Sydney. They were not only planted in his Hunter vineyards but also formed the basis of a collection in the Sydney Botanic Gardens, from where cuttings made their way to Camden Park and to Melbourne and South Australia.

As Busby saw it, the main problems confronting wine growing in Australia were cultural not meteorological. He noted that Australia, while possessing the perfect climate, suffered because its inhabitants were from non-wine-growing cultures. Vineyards would be plentiful if only the country had French, Swiss and Germans to pass on their knowledge and skills. Subsequently, he and other keen vignerons starting employing skilled immigrants to develop the fledgling wine industry. Sir John Jamison, physician, landowner and constitutional reformer, employed the Rhenish vigneron F. A. Meyer at Regentville on the Nepean River. By the 1830s, winemaking was becoming a hobby of the moneyed classes and Meyer and local nurseryman Thomas Shephard were kept busy tending the vineyards of the wealthy. William Macarthur also successfully lobbied the government to allow the importing of skilled European labour, obtaining permission for six German families to come to Camden Park in 1837.[15]

Swiss immigrants were to be especially influential in developing Australia's wine culture in Victoria, where they became the earliest viticulturists and winemakers. In 1850, Paul de Castella and Adolphe de Meuron (both Swiss) bought Yering Station vineyard — Victoria's first large vineyard, established in the Yarra Valley in 1838 — from William Ryrie. De Meuron was a nephew of Madame Sophie La Trobe, wife of Governor Charles La Trobe. The La Trobe family connection made Melbourne conducive for many Swiss immigrants. Deschamps of Kyneton, another Swiss vigneron, was also connected to the La Trobes. Geelong was another great vine-growing area in the 1840s. One of the earliest vineyards was John Belperroud's Berramongo property on the banks of the Barwon River. German vintners also contributed to Victoria's industry, mostly further north along the Murray River.

While growers struggled hard to prove that the Australian climate was conducive to growing grapes and producing wine, writers like the Melbourne journalist John Stanley James, who wrote under the nom de plume The Vagabond, continued to assert that it was certainly ideal for wine drinking. After visiting the Victorian Yering Valley wineries he stated: 'In such a climate as this, the constant use of malt and spirituous liquors is a mistake, and wine is the only natural drink.'[16] By the 1830s, Australians had already been consuming considerably more wine than the British. Mostly it was imported from overseas, particularly Britain or France. Excavations from the early days of Port Phillip have revealed bottles of sauternes and champagne, and these two styles of wine continued to be the most popular for some time. Champagne, particularly, appears to have been Australia's favourite wine, and its popularity was remarked upon by the South Australian journalist Richard Twopenny and other observers of Australian customs. It was the drink of celebrations: the upper classes imbibed it at their clubs or the races, yet it was drunk by stockmen too. According to Twopenny's observations in 1883, wine in Australia was drunk by all classes, but he confirmed that the working classes had a preference for sweet fortified wines such as port and sherry.[17] Preference for dry wines rather than sweet would remain one indicator of social distinction and refined taste into the 1980s, during the white wine boom.

In South Australia, the first commercial vines were planted in 1837 on land bought by the South Australian Company, a joint stock company set up by George Fife Angas, a prominent Baptist and businessman, and a group of merchants to promote agrarian settlement. Within months of the foundation of the settlement in Adelaide, vines had been planted at Underdale by H. H. Davis, using a large quantity of cuttings from James Busby's collection of vines in Sydney. Despite the colony's reputation for German vintners, it was actually Englishman John Barton Hack who planted the first private vineyard at Echunga Springs and produced South Australia's first wine, in 1843.[18]

Throughout the 1840s, Prussian immigrants, many of them Lutherans, arrived in the Barossa, encouraged by the god-fearing promoter of dissenters and non-conformists George Angas. They brought with them their native vine-growing and winemaking methods. The Bavarian Johann Gramp arrived in the Barossa in 1847; he had already been in the colony for ten years working as a labourer and a baker. He brought with him the vine variety Rhine riesling, ordered from Germany, and planted the cutting at Jacob's Creek. The first vintage in 1850 produced 64 litres of white hock-style wine, later known as Carte Blanche.[19]

Not all the Barossa settlers were German. Englishman Dr Christopher Rawson Penfold arrived in 1844 at his estate at Magill (first called Makgill), bought sight unseen, which he called The Grange. Basing his medical practice there, he planted vine cuttings which he had brought with him from the south of France. Initially the sweet produce from those grenache vines 'was only for private medical prescription, never for public consumption',[20] and Penfold prescribed it for anaemia, believing it to be strong in iron.

Samuel Smith, a Dorset brewer, came to work as a gardener for George Angas. In 1849, he bought a 12-hectare block of land which he named Yalumba (an Aboriginal word meaning 'all the country around') and worked it in his spare time. He struggled in the early years, but after a successful four-month trip to the Victorian goldfields in 1852, he returned with enough money to invest in modest farm equipment and extra land, which he rented out. He also produced his first wine that year and planted extensive amounts of shiraz. He gave out cuttings to neighbours and bought their grapes to make into wine, quickly establishing a reputation for quality.[21]

South Australia now has the reputation for being the wine-producing state, and it is certainly true that the German migrants brought their wine culture to a largely British beer- and spirits-dominated environment. Nevertheless, Victoria remained the wine capital of Australia in the latter half of the nineteenth century. It not only had the largest wine-producing industry but Melbourne was the largest market for wines in Australia at the time. It had not always been so. Thomas Hutchins Bear's wine-selling business was not a success in the late 1850s, and in 1860 Victoria had only half the acreage of vines that New South Wales did. However, the 1862 Land Act, which offered land leases for agriculture, including 'novel industries' such as viticulture, gave a great boost to the Victorian wine industry. By the late 1860s Australian wines had become popular, and within the next few years they received greater publicity and became more fashionable. In 1868, the Victorian government issued special licences — the Colonial wine licence — for vendors of local wines. At the 1873 International Exhibition in Vienna, several Victorian wines from the vineyards of J. S. Johnston of Sunbury and Carl Pohl of Strathfieldsaye near Bendigo received medals. [22]

In Western Australia, the first winemaker was Thomas Waters, who had arrived as a passenger on HMS *Parmelia* in 1829. Waters was a botanist, with practical experience of viticulture and winemaking in South Africa. He was granted 20 hectares of land on the Swan River, and dug the first wine cellar in the colony at Olive Farm.[23] Western Australia is perhaps better known as the home of Houghton's wines, named after Lieutenant Colonel Richmond Houghton, an officer of the Indian army who purchased land at Middle Swan in 1836. The first commercial vintage of 25 gallons was produced in 1859. According to John Beeston, Houghton was 'the most famous absentee vigneron in Perth's history, as he is reported never to have set eyes on his property'.[24]

During the gold rushes, those who sought gold took their chances, while almost all those who sold food and drink did very well. In Victoria, Joseph and Henry Best invested in cattle yards and a slaughterhouse at Great Western, to supply the nearby goldfields at Ararat and Stawell. By 1863, when French couple Jean and Ann Marie Trouette, and Ann Marie's brother Emile Blampied, purchased land at Great Western and planted vines, the gold was declining. Jean had winemaking experience in France and produced good-quality wines which won some awards. Joseph Best bought his Great Western property in 1865. He obtained cuttings from the Trouette vineyard and also from the Yarra Valley. In the following year, his brother Henry, a religious man who never worked on Sundays except to record the weather in his diary, bought a separate property, Concongella. Both brothers had little knowledge of viticulture, but Joseph Best had a cellar, which the *Ararat Advertiser* observed consisted of 'two lofty stories sunk beneath the surface where the temperature cannot be but cool',[25] and which would later prove crucial to the production of champagne. Australian champagne had already been made in Albury in the 1880s with the help of imported French technicians,[26] and when Hans Irvine, a Ballarat businessman and politician, bought Joseph Best's property, he hired Charles Pierot, a winemaker from the House of Pommery in France, to develop a champagne-style wine at Great Western. When Irvine retired in 1918, he sold the property to the eccentric wine pioneer Benno Seppelt. Legend has it that Seppelt, who designed his own clothes, seldom went anywhere without an umbrella and a violin, though the latter was sometimes left behind when he rode the across the region on a white stallion.[27]

If, as Claude Lévi-Strauss maintained, culture is about transforming the raw into the cooked, and there are hierarchies of cooking methods,[28] then traditional champagne techniques are the apotheosis

UNDERGROUND TUNNELS. 12,000 DOZEN CHAMPAGNE IN SIGHT. 35 FEET BELOW SURFACE.

The underground tunnels at Great Western provided ideal conditions for making and storing champagne-style wines. The time and effort put into making these styles of wine usually means a higher price, but it has been Australia's favourite big occasion celebration beverage since the time of the gold rushes. (State Library of Victoria) of beverage civilisation. Few who relish sparkling wines in times of celebration and festivity appreciate the time and trouble involved in producing them by traditional champagne methods. Fully ripe grapes are crushed and then fermented until there is no residual sugar. The wine is pumped off the lees, filtered and stored in wood. If required, it is blended with other wines, fined (clarified) and pumped into vats where *liqueur de tirage* (made from invert cane sugar, which is less prone to crystallisation than sugar) is added to feed the special yeast responsible for a second fermentation. It is bottled, temporarily corked, and stored in special racks that allow the lees to gather slowly in the neck of the bottle. The bottle is then dipped in brine, the plug of lees is removed — with some loss of wine, which is replaced — and the bottle is topped off with *liqueur d'expedition* (sugared brandy) in varying amounts, thus determining the wine's final degree of sweetness. The bottle is then corked and wired with a *muselet*. It is a complex process, which requires constant attention to maintaining cool temperatures to prevent excessive build-up of gas in the bottles.[29] This complexity may enhance the sense of appreciation for the connoisseur, but it also means a high price for quality product.

Other less expensive methods have evolved to produce sparkling wines, viewed by wine snobs as more technical but less civilised — such as carrying out the process in vats rather than bottles (the *charmat* process, which originated in Italy in 1895) or simply directly injecting carbon dioxide into wine. Differences in taste arise from the method by which the gas in sparkling wine is produced; not because of the gas itself, which is odourless and tasteless, but because of the imperfections and unpredictability of the traditional method, which give these wines their distinctive character. The impact of regional differences on grape production also dictates that sparkling wine produced in the Champagne region of France will taste differently from wines produced by the same methods in Australia. The French industry has fought hard for the term 'champagne' to be applied only to wines from the Champagne region. In the latter twentieth century, Australian laws also protected the rights of those using traditional methods here. The description Méthode Champenoise was only to be applied if the second fermentation took place in the bottle, and was allowed by law to cover the possible final transfer of contents to another bottle. Many makers, however, still proudly claim on the label that the content 'has been fermented and aged on its lees in *this* bottle'.

The Great Western region was fortuitous in being spared the scourge of *Phylloxera vastatrix*, a parasitic disease of the vine which caused enormous damage to the Victorian and New South Wales wine industries at the turn of the twentieth century. This root louse, a kind of aphid, was an inheritance of those early European vine cuttings (*Vinus vinifera*). The industry was saved by grafting onto American rootstock (*Vinus labrusca*), which is resistant to the louse, and confining the outbreak to the eastern vineyards. The surprising effect of this was that many unaffected vineyards in South Australia were planted on original European rootstocks that no longer exist in most of the classical wine-growing areas of Europe.[30]

By the early 1900s, winemaking had been established in all the colonies, but it was a small industry in need of wider market. When Samuel Smith, the founder of Yalumba, died in 1889, his son Sidney took over, and two of Sidney's sons, Percival and Walter, became involved in the business. Walter took on responsibility for sales and marketing, and his sales tours were often to countries where he could indulge his passion for big-game hunting. His marketing style 'stressed the excitement of wine' with often bizarre messages. One poster depicted 'the Indian North West Frontier War with gruesome detail of severed arms, pools of blood and the battle cry "Yalumba Wines to the Front!"'. Others recalled what today would be regarded as shameful memories of our past, such as the murder of Aborigines, with the caption 'Yalumba Wines are pure and wholesome'.[31]

Walter Smith from Yalumba, South Australia, extensively promoted his family's wines in overseas countries known for their big game hunting. He is pictured here, in 1919, with tiger skins and deer heads from India. Smith's promotional ideas were vivid and outrageous by today's standards, with posters depicting a massacre in the Indian North West Frontier and the shooting of Aborigines. (Searcy Collection, State Library of South Australia)

Despite his methods, Walter Smith was right to pursue selling wine to other parts of the empire. By the end of the 1800s, experimentation with growing vines near Australian capital cities had been abandoned and hundreds of thousands of gallons of red and white table wines were being successfully produced in a range of micro-environments in New South Wales, Victoria and Adelaide. Although these wines were predominantly for local consumption, they often bore familiar British and European names such as claret, burgundy, chablis and hock. Arguably, these names 'were simply an attempt by people in a new and hostile environment to remind themselves of familiar things from the other side of the world',[32] but according to Osmar White's *A Guide and Dictionary to Australian Wine*, such nostalgia was unfortunate on two counts. It often misrepresented what was in the bottle, 'provoking rather than inviting a critical comparison between the "genuine" article and the "imitation"'; and it obscured 'the undeniable fact that the "imitation" could often turn out to be more satisfying'.[33] In truth, the industry needed these generic names because it relied on exports for its continuing existence. In 1936 and 1937, 18 million litres of wine were exported and only 16 million litres were drunk domestically.[34] The future did not look bright for the expansion of domestic wine consumption.

There was some hope that Australians' love of champagne might hold the key, but creating the wine using traditional methods was time-consuming and expensive. Carbonated wines were much cheaper to produce, and the direct infusion of carbon dioxide could also produce sparkling wines held at differing pressures. The high-pressure wines were sold in champagne-style bottles, while the lesser pressures produced 'pearl' wine (from the German *Perlwein*, a pearl or bead being the term used to describe the bubbles in beer and wines), which could be sold in normal wine bottles with a screw-top. Contributing to the Orlando company's reputation for innovation was their introduction of controlled fermentation in 1953, and the launch of Barossa Pearl in 1956 to coincide with the Melbourne Olympics. Indeed, Barossa Pearl helped change the drinking habits of the nation and revolutionised the Australian wine industry. Certainly, in Australia, sparkling wines played a significant role in making wine accessible to the broader public, breaking down barriers of mystique and price. In the 1970s, White observed that Australian sparkling wines were 'decorative, refreshing and occasionally subtle' and that they played 'a persuasive part in teaching Australians that beverage wines can be enjoyed without the drinker serving a painful apprenticeship in appreciation'.[35]

At the beginning of the 1960s, Australian wine sales fell, and in areas like the Hunter Valley smaller wineries went bust. By the mid-1960s, however, something had clicked with the Australian public, because sales of table wines began to increase relative to the still dominant fortified wines. Long-serving Liberal Prime Minister Robert Gordon Menzies played his part by regularly drinking Australian table wines in public. Even more significantly, Australian wines were being written about in the press. In 1962, Len Evans's 'Cellarmaster' column started in *The Bulletin* magazine and Evans's relatively youthful outlook (he was then in his thirties) blew some of the cobwebs off a dust-laden subject. In 1965, Evans was appointed inaugural director of the Australian Wine Bureau, the first domestic promotional body for the wine industry, financially assisted by the Wine and Brandy Producers Association.[36] Despite an apparent conflict of interest, Evans continued to write about wine when he became a vineyard owner, forming the Rothbury Estate syndicate in the Hunter Valley in 1968.

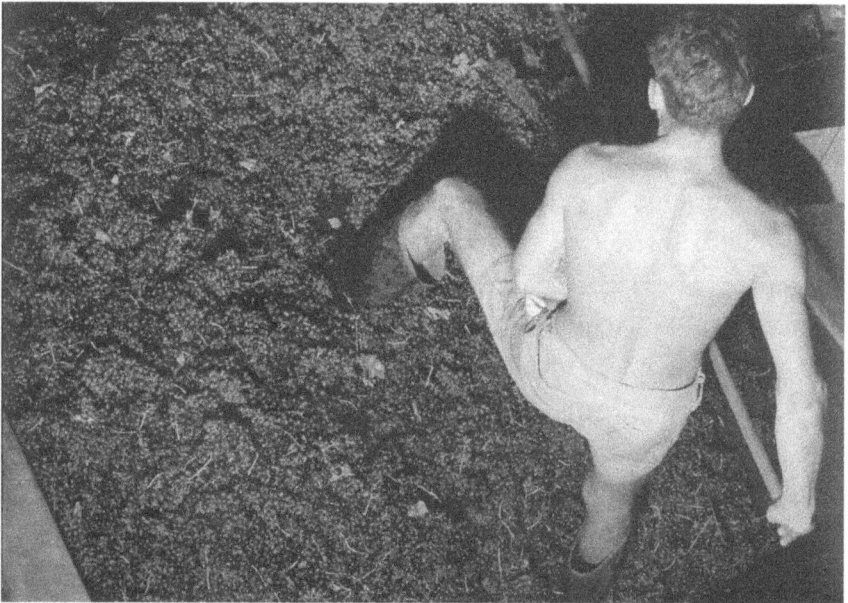

There is a lot of hard work involved in creating pleasure for others, as shown in this study of a worker at Mt Pleasant vineyard in the Hunter Valley, NSW. It was taken by one of Australia's leading photographers, Max Dupain, in 1950. (National Library of Australia/Max Dupain)

Certainly throughout the 1960s, the emergence of a wine press was a fillip to the level of public wine appreciation, and it helped contribute to a boom in red wine sales, which had hitherto somewhat intimidated the average drinker. The expanding post-war migrant culture also played a part, as did Australia's emerging youth culture, many of whom travelled the world and encountered 'the civilised use of table wine as an everyday beverage, a practice with which their parents were as a rule totally unfamiliar'.[37] Cashing in on this boom was difficult for many in the wine industry, however, as it meant not only meeting the increased demand for grapes to fulfil the increased demand for table wines, but coping with a concomitant reduction in the demand for fortified wines. The economics of producing fine red table wines were not suitable to meeting the increased wider demand and producing lesser quality table wines in bulk would eventually put downward pressure on prices at all levels of production. Bigger players such as Seppelts saw an opportunity to establish new vineyards in the Padthaway–Keppoch area near Coonawarra in South Australia. The boom also increased pressures on independent winemakers to adapt to the demands of managing larger enterprises.

By the middle of the 1960s, many of the smaller struggling wineries had been taken over by an enthusiastic breed of new owner, often from the professions of medicine and law. Wine historian John Beeston, a lawyer at the time, was one of them; he joined with Tony Albert and James Halliday to create Brokenwood, one example of the rush to replant the Hunter that proceeded apace during this time. By then, as Beeston pointed out, the big battalions were forming, though on what rational basis it is difficult to see even in hindsight. Tax minimisation, future capital gain, perhaps even lifestyle are the only reasons that can be advanced.[38] Productive capacity of the land and rational economics seemingly played little part.

The smaller wineries in New South Wales opened their doors to direct sales and set up mailing lists. Wine enthusiasts made weekend visits from Sydney to sample and buy new vintages for their home cellars. The mid–1960s also saw the first Hunter winery acquired by a multinational, when Reed Paper bought out Tulloch's at Pokolbin. Both the family and the company benefited from the injection of capital. Many operators, large and small, planned to cash in on booming red wine sales, but they would be disappointed by the fickleness of public taste. However, one company, Rosemount, planted 50 hectares from 1969–74 with a variety of grapes, including what were at the time experimental varieties — chardonnay and pinot noir. Its first whites were well marketed and critically acclaimed.[39]

Ultimately, the increased interest in red wine, prompted by a newly informed minority, would be overtaken by a white wine boom in the 1970s that finally delivered the hoi polloi to the industry. Initially, this explosion in white wine sales was an Australian phenomenon: 'From a sales base of 17.5 million litres in 1970 (including sparkling wines), sales of white table wine soared past red in 1975 to reach almost 160 million in litres in mid-1980.'[40] There was some truth in the contention that this was a revolt against poor red wine, 'for many a poor red was hastily cobbled together from the callow vineyards of the early 1970s'.[41] But at a time when more beer than ever was being consumed, the 'drink now' styles of white wine were more attractive to those who had no interest in cellaring a wine until it was drinkable. White wine became the beer alternative and reds stayed at the food table where they belonged.[42]

Just as technology had helped bring beer, in the form of lager, to the masses, new technology would also help deliver wine to the wider Australian population. Despite the fact that there were many immediately drinkable reds on the market, red wine's indelible association with wine 'appreciation' was a drawback to more widespread, if not mass, marketing. New technologies not only extracted more wine from the lees, but also increased consistency and prevented oxidation, so that makers of white wine were producing 'the attractive nectar whose aromaticity and fruit flavours made it an extremely pleasant drink at almost any time of day'.[43] This newfound consistency was advantageous to producers of white wines in the middle and upper market, who needed to provide quality product in quantity to domestic and export markets, yet the real boon from the new technologies would be at the lower end of the market. Over time, technology simply helped to increase the drinkability of cheaper wines.

Technology was also helping to deliver these cheaper wines in new ways. In 1965, Angove's at Renmark in South Australia's Riverland area was the first company to introduce the 'bag in a box' or the wine cask. The idea originated in America, where it was used for packaging milk, but Australian winemakers and drinkers made it their own. In the wine industry's view, the technology required to make and fill the casks was surprisingly sophisticated. The Japanese five-layered inner bag, with a metallised coating on one layer, was 'claimed to give a "shelf life" of 12 months, but this was not always the case'.[44] Initially, inherent problems with the technology forced the withdrawal of the cask in 1971. Air entered through the seal and minute pores in the plastic lining giving the cask a relatively short shelf life. It was a case of drink now or never, and several Australian states required winemakers to stamp a 'use by' date on their products. Nevertheless, the great virtue of the cask was that it was a very convenient form of packaging, particularly suited to the Australian outdoors lifestyle. By the mid-1980s almost half of Australia's wine was sold in casks.[45] It was also an early example of what today would be called 'supersizing', and the increased capacity of the wine cask compared to bottles and flagons may also have played a part in the white wine boom. A standard 4-litre cask — a convenient, stable and unbreakable package — contained the equivalent of two flagons, or just over five standard bottles of wine.

At the time, the industry informed the public that, 'as a sweeping generalisation, flagon wines are usually better in quality than cask wines'.[46] For a while, a hierarchy developed: bottled wine was considered superior to flagon wines, which in turn were considered superior to cask wines. But ultimately casks proved themselves more suited to bulk white wine sales. For growers, the type of wines sold in casks also had the advantage of being blended with grapes such as sultana and muscat gordo blanco, supplied from the large vineyards in the heavily irrigated areas. By the late 1980s, wine drinkers, though by now wedded to the convenience of casks, were becoming wary of an overly cheap product and more self-conscious about its underprivileged status in the hierarchy of taste. One part of the industry was keen to keep supplying the boom market, while those relying on the quality table market were hoping for a flow-on effect. Large winemakers hedged their bets by introducing higher-quality varietal wines in one-litre casks.

As this marketing of wines to the masses was occurring, winemakers were taking advantage of new production techniques. Appellation control — government certification that a product bearing the name of a region (for example, Bordeaux, Burgundy or Champagne) originates from that region — meant that exporting generically labelled wines to European markets was no longer possible. And the industry had matured enough to realise there was no need to compete with overseas traditions. Perhaps reflecting a new confidence in most things Australian, there was a positive commitment to the production of quality varietal and blended wines not only with their own distinctive attributes but also, with the aid of technology, produced with consistency and in quantities that would be economical to market across the globe.

One variety that took off in the 1980s was chardonnay. It had hardly been heard of in the 1970s, but had been among James Busby's imported cuttings. The first to realise the commercial implication of the variety in Australia was Murray Tyrrell in the Hunter Valley.[47] In 1967, so the story goes, Tyrrell jumped a barbed-wire fence to 'liberate' chardonnay cuttings from an experimental vineyard owned by Penfolds. He grafted them onto his own vine rootstock.[48] In 1971, he produced his first chardonnay — Vat 47. After two years of experimentation, he produced it using new French oak. It was a white wine blessed with many of the nuances that had appealed to the red wine appreciator — at least in theory. Tyrrell had certainly produced a cellarable white wine. Initially, only a small few appreciated his efforts, and didn't include those in wine-judging circles who at the time were more used to the 'elegance' of Rhine rieslings. Perhaps one factor in its favour for those early discerning consumers was that chardonnay had never been associated with the wine cask or flagon. Also in its favour was the fact that there were enough ways of dealing with it (aging it in wooded or unwooded casks, for example) that the combined output of this single variety could appeal to a phenomenally wide range of tastes.

A notable exception to the trend towards producing white wine and selling lots of it cheap to the lower end of the market was Wolf Blass, who successfully created blended red wines for the middle and upper segments of the market. Blass had been a viticulture apprentice in the lower Rhine area and later studied champagne making in France. He came to Australia in 1961 on behalf of Kaiser Stuhl (the Barossa Valley Cooperative) to share his knowledge of sparkling wine production using the *charmat* method of tank fermentation. From 1966 onwards, Blass began producing his own red wines by artfully blending carefully sourced materials; initially, often using the equipment of his wine consultancy clients. He firmly believed that 'man as well as nature makes wine', and he experimented with many combinations of grape sources, blends and techniques, never releasing wines onto the market unless they met high standards. As he put it: 'I learned very forcefully at the time that there were no prizes for coming second.'[49]

Blass also broke with the tradition of selling red wines to customers to 'lay down' in cellars. Aside from the dubious assumption that the customer would have reliable cellaring facilities, this marketing attitude required that the customer rely on his or her own judgment, or, failing that, the judgment of a wine writer, to determine what would be a suitable purchase. In effect, customers were being asked to pay premium prices to take home an undrinkable product in the hope that it would one day become drinkable. Previously, most buyers of premium wines had assumed that dry reds had to be cellared for a couple of years or more after their release before they were really enjoyable. Wolf Blass showed 'it was possible to make a wine which was balanced, smooth, soft, fruity with depth of palate, which was drinkable from the moment it was put on sale while still having fifteen more years of life ahead'.[50]

Although big firms continued to make quality wines, the middle and upper market was now being driven by winemaker-proprietors rather than wine growers. The market appeared to be divided between boutiques wines for the upper market and bag-in-a-box wines for the lower end. Many boutique wineries, however, had relied heavily on red grape varieties and few anticipated that the white wine dominance would lead to the emergence of the chardonnay variety as the wine appreciator's alternative. The grape was still in relative short supply in the early 1980s.

The wine appreciator's preference for boutiques wines was also fuelled by an emerging distrust of big business. As in the beer industry, the 1970s and 1980s were times of corporate takeovers in the wine industry. The Penfold family sold to the brewers Tooth & Company in 1976, who later sold to Adsteam. During these decades, Penfold took over Kaiser Stuhl, Wynns, Seaview, Tollana and Lindemans. Mildara took over, in turn, Hamilton, Yellowglen, Balgowie, Krondorf, and then merged with Wolf Blass Wines, who had taken over Tim Knappstein Wines and Quelltaler. Seppelt eventually sold to South Australian Brewing, who also gained Adsteam in 1990 and so acquired 45 per cent of the local industry.[51] The company was subsequently incorporated into the diverse industrial group Southcorp.

The stakes were high. Per capita consumption of wine in Australia had increased from 17.3 litres in 1980 to 21.3 litres in 1987. The 1988 total sales of 370 million litres (local and export) included 204 million litres of white wine sold compared to only 44.5 million litres of red. Consumers were turning away from sweet wines, with dry white wines accounting for two-thirds of sales. Wine casks accounted for over 67 per cent of sales. The sweetness gap was taken up by wine coolers: refrigerated carbonated blends of white wine and fruit juices with lower levels of alcohol, marketed mainly to young women.

The late 1980s saw an increased interest in building export markets and the introduction of a Labelling Integrity Program to ensure quality and honesty at all levels, from growing to sales. Records would be kept at various sites of the year of vintage, location of vineyard, grape variety, tonnage, and name of the grower. Winemakers had to identify the volume of wine, details of blending, and the release dates of the finished wines. For retailed wines, records had to show the total production of vintage, variety of regional wine, how much was in stock and how much had been sold. This universal recording system could validate all claims as to vintage and region of origin. It certainly communicated seriousness to export markets, which by 2005 accounted for 60 per cent of Australian wine sales.[52]

In Australia, alcohol is by far the most commonly used drug of choice. The acceptability of alcohol in Australian social life is largely due to the long cultural history of its use and its legal status, which makes it readily available and which even now carries with it minimal social stigma. Of the wide range of drugs available for consumption in 1998, 89 per cent of Australians aged fourteen or over had ever used alcohol and roughly 83 per cent had used it in the past twelve months. This compares to 67 per cent of the population that had ever used tobacco and only 27 per cent who had smoked in the past twelve months. As for illegal drugs, 40 per cent of the population had used cannabis and 18 per cent used it in the last twelve months, and at the extreme end of the spectrum, about 2 per cent of Australians had ever used heroin and 1 per cent had used it in the last twelve months.[53] Of the people who drank alcohol, almost half (49 per cent) were self-described as regular drinkers (males, 59 per cent; females, 38 per cent).[54]

Surprisingly, in the late 1990s, Australians with higher levels of education and employment qualifications were more likely to be regular drinkers (meaning those who drink alcohol at least once a week) than those with lower educational levels and employment qualifications. In 1998, 59.8 per cent of Australians with tertiary education were regular drinkers, contrasted with 40.3 per cent of those with no formal qualifications. White-collar workers made up 60.4 per cent of regular drinkers, contrasted with 41.2 per cent of blue-collar workers. However, a lower percentage of tertiary-qualified people were ex-drinkers (7 per cent) as compared to those with no formal qualifications (13.6 per cent), and a lower percentage of white-collar workers (7.7 per cent) were abstainers as compared to blue-collar workers (12.8 per cent).[55] As many ex-drinkers tend to have been problem drinkers, or in some cases dependent drinkers or alcoholics, these figures could indicate either that those in the lower socio-economic brackets drink at more problematic rates, or that perhaps those in higher socio-economic brackets are more able to continue with or hide their problematic drinking. It could also reflect the fact that being a regular drinker is costly.

In terms of geography, the rates of alcohol use across urban and rural Australia in the late 1990s were similar. In urban Australia, 49.4 per cent of the population drank alcohol regularly and 10.7 per cent never drank. In rural and remote Australia, 46.7 per cent of the population drank regularly and 6 per cent of the population never drank.[56] However, the difference between Aboriginal and non-Aboriginal drinking rates was marked, with only 33 per cent of the Aboriginal population drinking regularly as opposed to almost 50 per cent of the non-Aboriginal population.[57] In terms of country of birth, of the Australian-born population 49.2 per cent were regular drinkers and 8 per cent never drank. Of those born in other English-speaking countries 58.8 per cent were regular drinkers and 3.6 per cent never drank. Of those born in non-English speaking countries 32.5 per cent were regular drinkers and 24.5 per cent never drank.[58] A considerably higher number of people who migrated to Australia from English-speaking countries drank regularly compared to Australian-born

The late Slim Dusty's pub with no beer might be an iconic and lonesome place for a lot of Australians but, surprisingly, almost half of us do not drink alcohol regularly and one in ten Australians don't drink it at all. (National Library of Australia/Bruce Howard)

citizens, and a considerably lower number of people who migrated from non-English speaking countries drank regularly compared to the Australian-born. The lower prevalence of alcohol drinkers in people from non-English speaking countries is clearly influenced by the number of Muslim migrants who generally abstain from alcohol, and migrants from Asia where, until recent industrialisation and westernisation, regular and especially heavy drinking was not generally widespread or acceptable.

Challenging the myth of hard-drinking Australians are studies that show that Australia also has its fair share of total abstainers. Again, figures taken in 1998 looking at the population from the age of fourteen upwards showed there were various populations that had a very high percentage of abstainers: people from non-English-speaking backgrounds, (25 per cent); widowed persons, (23 per cent); and, surprisingly, students, (22 per cent).[59] Another group with a high number of abstainers was the Aboriginal population: 15 per cent of Aboriginal people never used alcohol, which was similar to the non-Aboriginal rate of 13 per cent. However, ex-drinkers made up 22 per cent of the Aboriginal population, as opposed to 9 per cent of non-Aboriginal ex-drinkers.[60] As with rates of drinking across socio-economic strata discussed above, this high number of ex-drinkers is almost certainly the result of the high rate of problem drinking in Aboriginal communities, as well as the more immediate deleterious impact that problem drinking has on Aboriginal people, as opposed to non-Aboriginal people, because of socio-economic and cultural factors.

One area of Australian life where alcohol plays an important role, either by its presence or its absence, is that of religion. Before the medical interest in alcohol in the nineteenth century, religious and moral disapproval were means for the social control of alcohol abuse. But this was somewhat complicated by the central role of wine in religious symbolism. Wine (or a substance representing wine) is used for symbolic purposes in both Jewish and Christian religious ceremonies. It has been shown that when a drug is used under strict cultural demarcation, such as part of a religious ritual, there is little risk of harm to the person using the drug or of the drug being abused. For instance, in Brazil, many Christian churches use a very powerful hallucinogen, ayahuasca tea, as part of their religious celebration. The tea is drunk by the whole congregation throughout the service, which can last from four to six hours. However, because it is used within a strict cultural boundary, it seems to cause little damage to the general population.[61] In contrast, wine is not imbibed in the Christian and Jewish rituals for its effects; its use is symbolic. In most cases it is sipped; and some Protestant churches use unfermented grape juice rather than wine. Until recent times, in the case of most Catholic ceremonies wine was used but often only drunk by the priest and his assistants. However, because wine is widely used outside of the ritual context in ways markedly different from the way in which it is used in ritual, the ritual has very limited educative effects.[62]

In the case of Islam, there are two schools of thought on alcohol and drugs in general. One school forbids the use of alcohol, and the other forbids intoxication of any sort. For Muslim Australians, therefore, religion is more likely to play a protective role against the abuse of alcohol, although it may not necessarily protect against other forms of substance abuse. In the case of Eastern religions such as Hinduism and Buddhism, intemperance in general is shunned and, therefore, the heavy use of alcohol is not readily accepted. Again, this may have a protective effect on these populations.

However, given that Australia is a secular society in which many Australians either do not follow a religion or do not adhere closely to the observances of their religion, it is more likely that other social aspects of drinking have a stronger influence on who is and isn't a drinker.

Drinking alcohol in most cases is a social event, and solitary drinking is often seen as inappropriate, uncouth or, at worst, a sign of having a drinking problem. In fact, the act of drinking together has often been a way of staving off loneliness, a means of making contact with strangers, or obtaining and sharing news and information. In the nineteenth-century Australian outback, pubs were the equivalent of the modern-day internet.[63] People exchanged news conversationally, and in more elegant pubs the latest Australian and English periodicals were made available for patrons.[64] In contemporary Australia, the country pub continues to be a place where a lonely person or visitor can chat to other people. The drinking of a disinhibiting substance like alcohol, may also have the effect — or more importantly, the perceived effect — of allowing people to be more sociable than they might usually be.[65]

According to one theory, the practice of 'shouting', or the 'grand custom' as it was originally known in colonial times, was a technique used for overcoming loneliness by itinerant workers, such as shepherds and drovers on the nineteenth-century bush frontier. Many of these workers spent long periods of time alone or in small groups and were keen for company on coming to town. As the pubs were often crowded and rowdy, a lone drinker would have to grab someone's attention literally by shouting out to them and offering to pay for their drink.[66] Another theory is that the man ordering the drinks had to shout over the ruckus so the barman or barmaid could understand what he was saying.[67]

In *Booze Built Australia*, Wayne Kelly argues that to be part of a shout means to agree in advance to drink the same number of drinks as there are people in the group, regardless of personal limits or of how the drinker feels as the drinking session progresses.[68] In a positive light, shouting is seen as an act that allows people to socialise on an equal level with equal levels of obligation and consumption, and where the wishes of the group are put before the wishes of the individual. In this view, shouting is an act of egalitarian communalism. Seen in a negative light, shouting is an act that promotes alcoholic excess through social pressure at the expense of personal needs and limits and to the obvious financial advantage of publicans everywhere.

In the 1966 movie *They're a Weird Mob*, shouting is encountered for the first time by an Italian immigrant newly arrived in Sydney. The main character, Nino Culotta, goes to have a drink at the Marble Bar, one of the more elegant pubs in Sydney at the time. He is shouted a beer by a drinker sitting next to him at the bar. After they both finish their beers, the Australian drinker explains to Nino that it's now his turn to shout. Nino is baffled by the idea that he needs to shout (literally) to obtain a drink. Once his drinking companion explains to him the meaning of the shout, he is even more baffled. He asks whether it would be insulting for him to buy only his companion a second beer, saying that he himself doesn't feel like having another one. He is told that it would be a huge insult, and so Nino is initiated into the world of Australian pub-drinking culture by shouting, and reluctantly drinking, a second, unwanted beer.[69] The scene in the movie shows the extent to which, even in the latter half of the twentieth century, the practice of shouting was still well-entrenched and the extent to which it was seen by many as quintessentially Australian.

In the twenty-first century, rural and outback pubs continue to be places where lonely people or outsiders will congregate with locals. As in the frontier era, many people who move to rural areas or the outback today do so to make a significant change or sometimes to get away from their old life. A study of drinking in Alice Springs carried out in 1991 claimed that, 'Only missionaries, mercenaries and misfits come to the Territory, so the cliché goes.' Historically, the Northern Territory (and Alice Springs) was considered the end of the line, a place as far away as possible from all that was familiar in suburban life without actually leaving Australia. The study aptly continued: 'Alcohol, of course, is frequently the balm of the disaffected.'[70]

133

This study also showed that hard drinking was portrayed as normal and even 'traditional' by both the Aboriginal and non-Aboriginal population in Alice Springs: 'For Aborigines, it is the traditional system of kin-based sharing that helps to sustain excessive consumption. Among "Europeans", it is the "shout system" and an almost belligerent … "ocker" cultural pride in drinking.'[71] Social drinking in this context works as a quasi-ritual to give members of certain populations a sense of togetherness, despite the damage it may also be causing. Yet drinking in this manner may also work to reinforce social divisions, depending on how the various styles of drinking are perceived by each group. The ritual not only makes the group by creating and sustaining internal bonds, it also marks the group to outsiders. An Alice Springs police officer made a telling remark about how he perceived the difference between Aboriginal and non-Aboriginal drinking in the town: 'Aboriginals certainly have a problem with alcohol. As for Europeans in Alice Springs I don't know if you'd call it a problem. They just drink like Australians.'[72] Social drinking can, therefore, be used as a marker of social identity for the drinker, or as a vehicle for the stereotyping of drinkers belonging to other groups. Like most stereotypes they are usually the result of what the new science of heuristics would call accidental anchoring to selective observable phenomena and do not reflect the wider realities.[73] Significantly, the number of non-drinkers is higher in the Aboriginal population, so the social bonding effects may be confined to the drinking group themselves rather than the culture as a whole.

The same applies to the perceived link between heavy drinking and Australian national identity. Even today, some Australians are quite proud of the idea of belonging to one of the biggest-drinking nations in the world, but the reality falls short of the myth. Compared to other nations, Australia is certainly among the top thirty countries for alcohol consumption, but not as close to the top of the list as many might expect. In 2001, international comparisons of per capita consumption of total pure alcohol for the year had Australia ranked a mere twentieth (at 7.5 litres) out of the top fifty alcohol-consuming countries in the world. Luxembourg ranked first (11.8 litres). Even in terms of litres of beer consumed per capita, Australia ranked only ninth (95.4 litres); the Czech Republic was first (160 litres). When it came to litres of wine consumed per capita, Australia ranked seventeenth (18.2 litres) and Portugal was first (60.6 litres). With spirits, Australia ranked a miserly thirtieth (1.4 litres), with Russia first (5.3 litres).[74] These figures confirmed Australia as a predominantly beer-drinking nation, with wine second, and spirits — which were hugely popular in the eighteenth and nineteenth centuries — now much less popular. Thankfully, none of these figures makes us heroes of drinking. The reputation of Australians as world leaders in boozing remains quite literally legendary.

How much one drinks is only one mark of distinction; what one drinks is another. The relative popularity of various types of alcoholic beverages in Australia has been an indicator of social change over time, as have been the various social meanings given to each type of drink. Throughout the twentieth century, beer and wine consumption increased markedly, whereas spirits consumption slightly decreased. In 1911, the per capita volume of beer consumed by Australians was 56.4 litres. In 1931, beer consumption dropped dramatically to 36.8 litres, presumably due to the effects of the Great Depression. By 1941, consumption was at 61.8 litres and then steadily increased until it peaked at 129.3 litres in 1981. By the late 1990s, beer consumption had dropped to roughly 95 litres per capita, but was still almost double the amount being drunk in 1911.[75]

The consumption of wine has steadily increased. In 1961, only 1.4 litres per capita was consumed. Like beer, consumption increased, and there was a considerable peak in 1981 when 14.5 litres per capita were being consumed. By 1990, the figure was 16.2 litres, and stayed around this level then increased to 17.3 in 1997.[76]

American serviceman living it up in a wet canteen in Brisbane during World War II. Although beer was rationed during the war, alcohol sales did not decline as they had done in World War I. It was often alleged that US soldiers, who were better paid than their Australian counterparts, had no trouble getting supplies. (State Library of Queensland)

As for spirits, in 1911 Australians were drinking 2.2 litres per capita. By 1921, this amount had fallen to 0.9 litres, and by 1931 there had been a large drop to 0.5 litres. From 1941 to 1981 consumption increased only slightly, and in the 1970s and 1980s it increased to around 1.1 litres. Throughout the 1990s, it averaged only 1.3 litres per capita, higher than it was during most of the twentieth century, but still lower than the 1911 figure of 2.2 litres.[77] In 2005, Australians were again drinking on average 2.12 litres of spirits a year, an increase no doubt fuelled by increasing sales of ready-to-drink spirit mixes.[78]

Of all the changes that have occurred in consumption levels and attitudes towards the drinking of beer, wine and spirits, the two biggest shifts have been the move away from spirits consumption (predominantly rum) in the nineteenth century to beer, and the huge increase in the acceptability and popularity of wine drinking in the twentieth century. These changes are gender inflected. In Australia today, the male drinking population's first choice of drink is regular beer, as opposed to light beer (54.3 per cent), followed by bottled wine (40.6 per cent) and bottled spirits (39.4 per cent). The female drinking population prefers bottled wine (57.4 per cent), followed by bottled spirits (38.2 per cent) and cask wine (23.8 per cent). For the whole population combined, the preference is for bottled wine first (48.7 per cent), then bottled spirits (38.9 per cent), and, thirdly, regular beer (36.8 per cent).[79] Beer and wine, therefore, have considerable gender significance, with beer continuing to be a more predominantly masculine choice and wine a predominantly feminine choice, with spirits being drunk by an almost equivalent percentage of men and women, but higher on the list of favourites for women. Significantly, there is a noticeable increase in alcoholic drinking — particularly of spirits and so-called 'mixed drinks' — among teenage girls.[80]

According to the 1977 *Report of the Senate Standing Committee on Social Welfare*, 'Few changes in social behaviour have been quite as dramatic as Australians' changing attitude to wine.'[81] In the 1970s, the wine bar began to develop in competition with the pub. It was seen as an alternative, more sophisticated venue, where young men and women could socialise together in an atmosphere more accepting of and respectful to women.[82] To a younger generation, the male exclusivity of the public bar was becoming nonsensical. There was no need for women to chain themselves to a wine bar to demand the right to be served, as Ro Bogner and Merle Thornton had done in an ultimately successful series of protests in male-only public hotel bars in the 1960s.[83] Significantly, the focus on it being a bar that served wine was part of the alternative identity. Yet by the end of the twentieth century, with the proliferation of restaurants and cafés, the wine bar as such had virtually died out, to be replaced by the private bar which often served food on the side.

At the same time as the wine bar came the wine cask, which, as we have seen, helped to establish wine as a casual, everyday drink in competition with beer. More importantly, the cask fitted the casual, outdoor lifestyle Australians were increasingly enjoying. The noisy, smoke-filled, dank interior of the pub was no match for the natural settings in which many Australians could now enjoy a tipple. While public drunkenness was still widely considered to be unacceptable, drinking wine with meals and the appearance of the friendly-looking bag-in-a-box helped break down social taboos against drinking in public places. Wine was becoming the drink of choice not only for the young, alternative set, but also as an alternative to beer for Australians in everyday settings.

Wine drinking boomed in the 1980s and consumption continued to increase into the 1990s. There was also a considerable swing in the 1980s from a preference for red wine to a preference for white. It was so dramatic that various members of the wine industry who had concentrated on producing red wines and were therefore losing a considerable amount of business to the 'white wine boom' commissioned a study to investigate the phenomenon.[84] They wanted to know whether the boom would be a passing phase or whether they needed to increase the quantity of white grape varieties in their vineyards. The study, completed in 1985, found that the newly emerging 'meaning' and social role of white wine, as opposed to red wine or other types of alcoholic drinks, was the main reason for the increase in its popularity. The study confirmed that, at the time, beer was seen as a predominantly masculine beverage. Women felt uncomfortable about beer drinking by other women, but sometimes also by men, because of its heavy masculine and sometimes 'ocker' identity.[85] Men also reported that seeing a woman drink beer was off-putting as it made her appear unfeminine.[86] The study showed that young women and older women enjoyed spirits, and it was seen as acceptable for women to drink spirits in company, although young

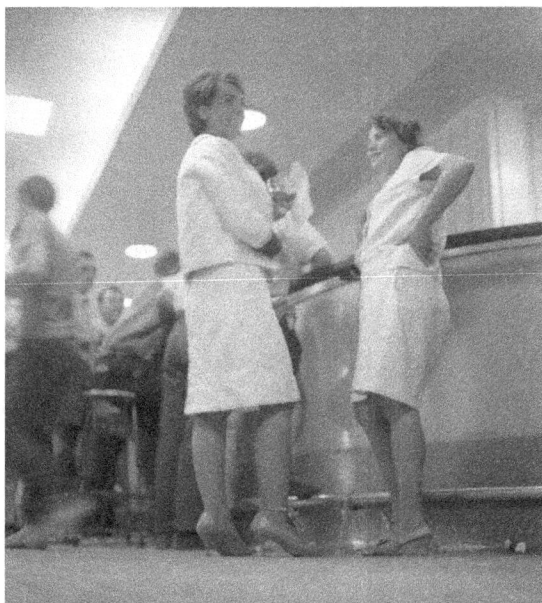

Chained to the foot rail in the public bar of the Regatta Hotel in Brisbane in 1965, Ro Bogner and Merle Thornton relax with a glass of beer bought for them by a hotel patron. They were drawing attention to their campaign to give women the right to drink side-by-side with men in public bars.
(© Newspix/Bruce Postle)

women were more likely to drink spirits mixed with soda or soft drink. Young people and people on lower incomes were also seen as spirit drinkers, as well as 'sophisticated' men who drank their spirits unmixed.[87] When it came to wine, the study found that people associated red wine with 'high culture'. Red wine was known to be more variable in quality than white wine and therefore to select a good red wine required expert knowledge.[88] The corollary was that white wine came to be seen by the general public as being much more accessible. There was no need to be a wine connoisseur to choose a drinkable white wine and there was less of a concern that a bad choice might be made.[89]

In one sense, the study was a blow to any theory about an increasing sophistication in the Australian market. If beer, red wine and, to a lesser extent, spirits already had strong social connotations, white wine by contrast was seen as a 'neutral' drink. According to the study, the influence of post-World War II migration was negligible in this trend, as the shift towards white wine consumption was uniquely

Australian and not seen in the Mediterranean countries of origin of the majority of post-World War II migrants.[90] Additionally, the figures about consumption of wine did not take into account the homemade wine that was often drunk by migrants from Mediterranean countries. Nevertheless, it is likely that everyday social exchanges between the migrant and non-migrant population may well have had an influence on overall wine consumption in Australia, along with the commercial production of wine by migrants from traditional winemaking countries. Generally, as the acceptability of men and women drinking together in company and in public increased, and as Australian society became less differentiated, with men and women of various ages and backgrounds mixing socially, white wine became the most appropriate drink to serve in mixed company.[91] The fact

In the 1960s, wine bars and other non-pub settings became increasingly popular as venues for drinking in mixed company. This photograph shows patrons at the Stage Coach Inn, Melbourne. (State Library of Victoria)

that it was seen as gender, age and class neutral made it a drink that could be used to bring together people from various backgrounds. Its increasing popularity seemed assured.[92]

It is clear from the study of the social meanings attached to drinking white wine that the various types of alcoholic beverages carry with them particular social and cultural connotations. Alcohol can be used by a drinker to actively assert an identity, even in destructive ways. In Australia today, the increasing acceptability of hard drinking among young women has been part of a continuing desire to be able to behave in a manner not constrained by sexual stereotypes. This trend has been exploited by advertising agencies, which produce alcohol advertisements in which young women are depicted as just as rowdy or tough as young men, or sometimes impress the men by being even tougher. In 2004, a female marketing executive was quoted as saying, 'The girls are able to misbehave as much as the boys. The girls are keeping up.'[93] The trend for hard drinking in youth in general is also a sign of self-assertiveness, although often a destructive one. Teenagers in contemporary Australia have shown a preference for consuming high-alcohol drinks and rejecting low-alcohol drinks — 63 per cent of teenagers (14–19 years of age) drink high-alcohol drinks, decreasing in higher age groups.[94] As for low-alcohol beer, only 9 per cent of teenagers (14–19 years) drink it, though consumption increases in higher age groups.[95]

Alcohol as a signifier of a range of identities in twentieth-century Australia was well illustrated in the 1976 film *Don's Party*, based on the play by David Williamson. The film is set in Sydney on the day of the 1969 federal election, in which John Gorton, the incumbent Liberal prime minister and Gough Whitlam, the Labor opposition leader at the time, are contesting the position of prime minister and government. The Liberal Party has been in power for twenty years, the Vietnam War is in progress, and Don, a middle-class, left-wing,

Anglo-Celtic Australian male, is holding a party to watch the election results on television, in the hope that the Liberal Party will finally be toppled in a Labor victory. In preparation, large quantities of beer are bought and it is questionable as to whether the focus of the party will be the election or the alcohol.

> Don's wife: 'I can't see the point of coming to a party
> with the sole intention of drinking yourself into a
> stupor.'
> Don: 'Well, that's not the intention. We're celebrating
> the end of twenty years of conservative rule.'
> Don's wife: 'It's just an excuse for a booze up.'[96]

In the next scene, Don is shown filling the laundry tubs to brimming with beer bottles and ice. He says to his wife: 'You may not be, but most of the people here are going to be very concerned about what happens tonight — very concerned indeed.'[97]

What happens that night is the government doesn't change and the copious amounts of alcohol consumed, along with frictions between the party-goers, leave everyone more than a little worse for wear. During the course of the party, the alcohol-consumption patterns of the guests provide an insight into their political and other affiliations. They are all middle-class, Anglo-Celtic Australians, like Don, and so the main division depicted is between the men and the women. The women drink mixed spirits and to a lesser extent flagon wine, whereas the men mainly drink beer. However, one of the characters, who describes himself as politically neutral but is seen by the others as a conservative, is very knowledgeable about red wine. This character so impresses the crowd with his knowledge of various reds and his recent trip to the Barossa to shop for wine (again, mainly reds) that one of the other male characters comments with reserved admiration: 'Our conservative friend knows a good drop when he sees one.'[98] Other class differences are highlighted when this character, presumably of a higher socio-economic background or affiliation, storms off in disgust at the drunken behaviour of the other men, all drinking beer, commenting that he 'never knew that university-educated people could be so uncouth'.[99]

Don's Party provided an entertaining snapshot of the confused and often contradictory social meanings attributed to drinking habits of one segment of Australian society in the late 1960s.

CHAPTER 4

A Pub With No Beer

In 1895, when the Federal Council was preparing a constitution for the soon to be federated Australia, another convention was being held in Hobart at which members of so-called temperance organisations met to discuss solutions to the widespread problem of alcohol abuse in the colonies. The Hobart convention resolved to petition the Federal Council to insert a clause in the new Australian Constitution that would prohibit the manufacture, sale and import of alcohol for all but strictly medical purposes, providing that the Australian citizens approved such a measure in a referendum.[1]

Unlike the United States, Australia has never had alcohol prohibition; however, a significant number of Australians had hoped to see it introduced. The Hobart convention delegates were representatives of a number of temperance organisations, some international and some local. The Independent Order of Rechabites, Sons of Temperance, Good Templars and Woman's Christian Temperance Union were all American organisations which had spread throughout the world in the mid-nineteenth century. By the

1890s, these bodies had 70,000 members in Australia.[2] In addition, individual towns and cities had their own temperance societies, such as the Sydney Total Abstinence Society. Popular support for the idea of prohibition can most accurately be measured by the results of referenda held thirty years later in various Australian states — almost one in three Australian voters expressed their support for prohibition of alcohol in their state. In Queensland, the temperance movement, led by the church-backed Prohibition League, was so strong that in the state referendum of October 1923 almost 40 per cent of Queenslanders voted in favour of prohibition.[3]

The referenda were the climax of the temperance movement's 100-year battle to create an alcohol-free society. The temperance campaign was twofold. On the one hand, it aimed to educate the public towards total abstinence from alcohol; on the other, it agitated for laws to restrict the availability of alcohol and undermine the liquor industry. The campaigns could claim a degree of success. From

An anti-prohibition rally in Brisbane's Albert Square in 1923. At a referendum that year, 58 per cent of voters favoured a continuation for the liquor laws (8 o'clock closing in Queensland) and 37 per cent voted for prohibition. Another 4 per cent favoured state management of the liquor trade. (*Sunday-Mail*, 1923)

being a country of tipplers in the early days, by the end of the nineteenth century Australians were drinking less than the British.[4] On the legal front, the temperance campaign achieved six o'clock closing in four states, the closing down of some hotels and the introduction of dry suburbs.

Until the nineteenth century, total abstinence from alcohol was not a common demand. A few of the Puritans of the seventeenth century, such as the New England preacher Cotton Mather, preached against drunken excess, but mostly they did not regard moderate drinking as a sin. Cotton Mather's father, Increase Mather, had called alcohol 'God's good gift'.[5] John Wesley, founder of the Methodists in the late eighteenth century, denounced the drinking of spirits, and thus began an anti-spirits crusade within the wave of evangelicalism that swept the United States and Britain during this era, although these early evangelicals accepted wine, beer and cider within moderate limits, as had Wesley. In the 1830s, however, societies emerged which were against alcohol in all its forms. Why single out spirits when wine and beer also caused intoxication and subsequent social problems? They also saw a certain class bias in singling out spirits, as these were the drink of the poor. Why should the upper classes hang on to their drink of choice? As Lilian Lewis Shiman has noted, anti-spirits societies, mostly concentrated in the south of England, were middle class in membership, while the total abstinence societies, which emerged in the industrial north, were more working class.[6]

Throughout the 1830s a number of temperance societies emerged in Australia. Some were strictly anti-spirits, such as the one that visiting Quakers James Backhouse and George Washington Walker formed in Hobart in 1832; others were committed to total abstinence. Melbourne and Sydney each formed their own total abstinence societies and other Australian cities soon followed. Initially, the total abstinence societies were considered to be somewhat eccentric, but by the late 1840s the movement had grown and the word 'temperance' in Australia had generally come to denote total abstinence from alcohol, as it did in Britain and the US.

These anti-alcohol societies began largely as educational endeavours. They published leaflets, journal articles and works of fiction on the personal dangers as well as the dire social costs of alcoholism, and presented the principle of total abstinence as the best manner of avoidance. They ran libraries and book rooms and held public lectures. Indeed, the first public lecture ever to be held in Melbourne was about temperance.[7] In the major cities, the societies erected temperance halls, where lectures and other public functions would take place. In the temperance hall in North Melbourne, the Total Abstinence Society held regular Tuesday night concerts whose purpose was to provide an alternative entertainment to the public house and to attract the public to a forum promoting the temperance message. Temperance societies also favoured elaborate public processions at which huge crowds and brass bands filled the city streets.[8] In 1847, the Independent Order of Rechabites entered Australia. This was a friendly society as well as a temperance group. Rechabite tents (as the local branches were known) demanded abstinence from alcohol as a condition of membership and eligibility for benefits, and also waged an aggressive recruitment campaign for the temperance cause. Rechabite tents took on most particularly in Victoria and South Australia. The Sons of Temperance, another international friendly society with total abstinence principles, launched branches throughout Australia in 1864.

Throughout the nineteenth century, temperance societies ebbed and flowed. The Victorian gold rush, for example, caused a draining of temperance societies despite the banning of alcohol sales on the goldfields themselves. At other times, temperance societies surged in popularity, mainly due to the efforts of some notable overseas temperance advocates who toured throughout Australia, inspiring

Creative public activism was important to temperance societies. A 'suitcase parade' of women opposed to changes to 6 o'clock closing in South Australia in 1938. (Mortlock Pictorial Collection, State Library of South Australia)

public support for the total abstinence ethos. These were often evangelical preachers, for whom total abstinence was a keystone of their Christian message. Their favoured tactic, in addition to fiery sermons, was to invite members of their audience to 'take the pledge', which involved signing a document promising to permanently renounce alcohol. Matthew Burnett from Britain, who travelled around Australia in the 1860s, conducted what he termed 'love feasts', and his visits inspired the launch of numerous local temperance societies and pledges. In the Victorian town of Cobden, the Cricketers Arms Hotel went out of business following Burnett's visit, as the local cricketers took the pledge and joined the Rechabites.[9] Richard T. Booth and Thomas Glover arrived in Australia from the United States in 1882 to conduct Blue Ribbon missions. The Blue Ribbon movement, also known as gospel temperance, was launched originally in the United States by Francis Murphy, an alcoholic and former rum-seller who had spent time in gaol but had recovered after taking the pledge. Murphy devoted the rest of his life to spreading the principle of total abstinence — not just for personal health and wellbeing but as part and parcel of a born-again religious conversion.[10] Those who took the pledge were given a blue ribbon to wear on the lapel, allowing pledge-takers to recognise each other as fellow travellers.

The 1880s was a golden era of temperance pledges. In the six years leading up to 1888, the NSW Alliance procured 24,000 pledges, as many as in the previous twenty-five years. This was mostly due to the evangelical efforts of the Blue Ribboners and the Woman's Christian Temperance Union (WCTU). The WCTU began in the United States in 1873, following an incident known as the 'women's crusade', during which the women of various towns in the north-east and western states staged mass protests outside their local saloons, demanding that the proprietors cease selling liquor to their husbands and sons. The women decided to form their own national organisation and meet every year to discuss ways in which they could stop alcoholic drinking within their communities. By 1883, as a result of the indefatigable efforts of its new president, Frances Willard, the WCTU had become the largest women's organisation in the US with over 150,000 members who belonged to local branches in every state.[11] At this time, the WCTU was becoming an international body, mostly through the efforts of Mary Leavitt, a former Boston schoolteacher who became the WCTU's round-the-world missionary and sailed to Europe, Asia, Africa and Australia. In 1885, she set up WCTU branches in Queensland, New South Wales, Tasmania, South Australia and Victoria.

In Australia, the women of the WCTU vigorously asserted their presence by conducting public meetings and also house-to-house door knocking and hotel and factory visiting, at which they would ask members of the public to sign the pledge. WCTU members wore a white ribbon on their lapel as a sign of their taking the pledge.

The evangelical temperance missionaries brought many church members into the temperance movement and, in the case of the Blue Ribbon Movement, made total abstinence an essential principle of some churches. In the early days of the temperance movement, only a few churches were predominantly teetotal. The Quakers were numerous among the early temperance leaders in both Australia (Backhouse and Walker in Hobart were examples) and Britain. The Primitive Methodists were also prominent — some Australian towns, such as Camden in New South Wales, had their first temperance society introduced by the Primitive Methodists[12] — yet many Wesleyan Methodists were still drinkers in the early 1880s. The

Women's Christian Temperance Union members were asked to wear a white ribbon on their lapel to indicate that they had signed a pledge to abstain from alcohol. (Mitchell Library)

Victorian Methodist magazine, *Spectator*, even carried advertisements for the Chateau Tahbilk winery in the Goulburn Valley.[13] The Blue Ribbon missions, however, converted some Protestant churches to a more stridently anti-alcohol stance, and many Methodist and Presbyterian parishes formed temperance committees. By the end of the decade, many of these churches were serving unfermented wine for communion, and the annual Wesleyan conference advised all ministers to do so. Elizabeth Nicholls, the first president of the Australasian WCTU, claimed that she had been a social drinker, despite being a strict Methodist, until she took the pledge following a Blue Ribbon mission.[14] The women of the WCTU were predominantly the wives of professionals, tradesmen or clergy — what were referred to as the 'middling' classes.[15] Their most distinctive common feature was religion; they were mostly

The Presbyterian minister Reverend George Mackie (1823–1871) was dedicated to the temperance cause in Victoria. He was commemorated in a postcard that reflected one of the main themes of temperance advocates — the impact of drunkenness on the lives of children. (State Library of Victoria)

Methodists, Baptists, Congregationalists and Quakers. Indeed, the Protestant churches were the main conduit for recruitment. It was advised that the WCTU branch vice-presidents be the wives of clergymen, as a means of inducing the women of the parish to join.

Baptist and Congregationalist churches were also overwhelmingly serving unfermented communion wine. Even the Roman Catholic Church, although sticking to fermented communion wine, had its own total abstinence societies, including the League of the Cross and the Catholic Total Abstinence Society.[16] The Jewish community included staunch temperance advocates also; Rabbi Joseph Abrahams, for example, served unfermented wine at his Melbourne synagogue.[17] The Church of England had its own temperance society but not all of its members believed in total abstinence. Some interpreted 'temperance' according to its original literal sense of the moderate use of ale and beer. When the WCTU's Mary Leavitt arrived in Australia she was amazed at how many Church of England women drank wine.[18]

Abstinence from alcohol, both in church and outside, was coming to be strongly identified with the dissenting Protestant churches, although the Salvation Army was the only church that demanded total abstinence as a condition of membership.[19] There were still some secular temperance groups, such as the Melbourne Total Abstinence Society, which shocked the Methodist church by holding raffles (thus sanctioning gambling) and frivolous theatrical entertainments rather than sermons.[20] There were also some notable 'freethinkers' among the Australian temperance movement: Charles Edwin Jones, the Melbourne politician and journalist; Bessie Smyth, the women's suffragist and birth control campaigner; and Louisa Lawson, the feminist journalist, publisher and mother of Henry Lawson. However, the main temperance organisations were dominated by dissenting Protestants. Some, such as the Good Templars and WCTU, insisted on Christian commitment as a condition of membership.

Many advocates of total abstinence realised that drinking was not dangerous for everyone. There were, however, those who could not drink moderately and for whom abstinence was the only means of avoiding alcoholism. In order to persuade them to abstain, everyone must set an example. Moderate drinkers were persuaded to take the pledge 'on behalf of our weaker brethren', as they were often termed. Helen Lyall of the South Australian WCTU explained the concept to a ladies' drawing room meeting: 'Granted that you can enjoy a glass of light wine without being disturbed by it, will you not give it up so that you can help weaker sisters and brothers who are in danger of inebriety?'[21] One Australian pledge card of this era, received by those who signed, read: 'We bind ourselves that others may be free.'[22]

Total abstinence was presented as a Christian duty, part of one's love for one's fellow man. Even though there was no specific injunction against alcohol in the Bible, temperance advocates sometimes explained away the references to alcohol by insisting that the Bible referred to two types of wine. The good wine that St Paul recommended to Timothy was unfermented, and the bad wine that Solomon declared a 'mocker' was fermented.[23] At other times, they insisted that alcohol was against the spirit of the Scriptures, if not the letter. Christ could not promote drink or anything else which 'would cause a brother to stumble'.[24] To the Blue Ribboners, White Ribboners and other religious temperance groups, total abstinence was necessary to Christian living as well as for health and personal and social wellbeing. Similarly, they believed that Christian commitment was necessary to total abstinence. It was commonly said that a religious conversion was necessary if an alcoholic was to keep the pledge.

Alcoholics who kept the pledge were the exception rather than the rule. Temperance advocates noted that those most likely to keep the pledge were children who had not yet begun drinking. For this reason, much temperance preaching targeted children. The Band of

Whether humble tent or hotel, the temperance movement aimed to provide alternatives to the dominant drinking culture. (Mortlock Pictorial Collection, State Library of South Australia)

Hope, a children's temperance organisation, began in Britain in the 1850s and by the 1880s had branches all over Australia.[25] Most of these branches were run by the Sunday school of a Protestant parish church. They hosted activities, songs and games, as well as lessons on the dangers of alcohol. The major temperance organisations such as the Rechabites, WCTU and Good Templars had associated children's societies with similar aims. The temperance advocates also agitated for state schools to teach lessons on the dangers of alcohol in the hope of creating a future generation of total abstainers. In the 1880s, Australian state school students were reading temperance textbooks by Dr T. Broadribb that stressed the deleterious impact of alcohol on the organs of the body,[26] were presented with wall graphs illustrating the physiological effects of alcohol, and were taught that the best way to avoid such disease was by avoiding alcohol at all times.

★   ★   ★

In 1851, the American state of Maine passed a law prohibiting the manufacture and sale of alcohol within its borders. Since the 1830s, individual US counties had gone dry, but now a whole state was alcohol-free. Temperance groups in both the United States and Britain looked to the 'Maine law' as a wonderful groundbreaking experiment and began to dream of the day when a similar prohibition law would be passed in their own part of the world. Some seventy years later, the entire US nation had outlawed the manufacture and sale of alcohol, but the British temperance movement knew that this would be impossible in the immediate future in their country, as drinking was such an integral part of British culture. Public opinion was well disposed towards alcohol, in moderation at least. So in 1853, the British temperance movement, under an umbrella group called the United Kingdom Alliance, devised a policy known as 'local option' or 'local veto', which was similar to the Maine law but on a much more local level. It would allow all the ratepayers of a municipality or shire to eradicate licensed premises from their district by means of a majority vote. The United Kingdom Alliance devoted much of its energy throughout the nineteenth century to agitating for laws that would allow local option.

The temperance movements of Australia followed the British model. In 1859, the New South Wales Alliance for the Suppression of Alcohol (formed in 1857) campaigned to introduce a local option policy in the colony that would allow ratepayers to banish hotels from their locality. In Victoria, Richard Heales, an MP and president of the Melbourne Total Abstinence Society, brought the individual temperance societies under a colonial umbrella called the Temperance League, a lobbying body for local option laws. The local option campaign injected renewed energy into the temperance movement and by the 1870s the agitation for local option laws had become its main legislative objective.

Liberal Party MP for Carlisle, Wilfred Lawson, first proposed a local option measure, known as the Permissive Bill, to the British House of Commons in 1864. His attempt was initially unsuccessful, but it inspired temperance societies elsewhere, including Australia. Temperance societies sent a deluge of petitions to their colonial parliaments demanding a Permissive Bill. They had important allies within the governments. Victoria's local option champions were George Higginbotham and James Casey. Henry Parkes and Francis Abigail worked to introduce such laws in the New South Wales parliament, while Peter McLean, the member for Logan, south of Brisbane, introduced a Permissive Bill to the Queensland parliament in 1874.[27]

The agitation for local option in Australia received a great boost in the 1880s. This was partly the outcome of an intercolonial temperance convention, held in 1881, at which each of the temperance groups decided to unite to form an alliance within their respective colonies and exert more of a force on their respective colonial governments. The Victorian Alliance emerged at this time and also the South Australian Alliance. Yet not all members of the alliances were total abstainers. The Honourable James Casey, for example, who introduced the first local option bill (the Permissive Bill) into Victorian parliament, was himself a drinker.[28] The Victorian Alliance, of which Casey was a vice-president, did not demand that its members be total abstainers. There were some members who believed in local option purely on grounds of residents' rights to determine the quality of their neighbourhood. Nevertheless, the majority of alliance members were total abstainers from alcohol and committed to creating a nation of total abstainers. Indeed, most of the organisations that joined the alliance insisted that all members pledge to give up all alcoholic drinks and actively persuade others to do the same.

Local option received huge popular support in the 1880s due to the efforts of the Blue Ribbon movement and other evangelical pledge-signing crusades. The temperance movement had come to be dominated by specific religions — Methodist, Congregationalist, Baptist and Quaker — and these churches expressed their commitment to local option at their annual conventions. Also, a large number of individual parishes petitioned their colonial parliaments to pass local option laws. Some churches, however, did not support the measure. When a poll held at Kyneton in 1888 resulted in a vote for no reduction, the Victorian Alliance blamed the Roman Catholic Church. At Warrnambool that same year, the local Roman Catholic and the Church of England clergy were blamed for the no-reduction vote.[29] Nevertheless, the temperance organisations continued their agitation, hoping to see in every colony laws that would allow inhabitants of a municipality the power to veto all licences — including special licences for grocers, wine shops or private clubs — and thus create a completely dry neighbourhood. Moreover, they wanted local option voting rights for all adult residents, whether ratepayers or not.

Significantly, many of the early members of the United Kingdom Alliance had also been members of Chartist organisations, agitating for universal adult male suffrage. This explains why they were drawn to voters' polls as a means of eradicating public houses.[30] They promoted expansion of democracy by campaigning to give the public an extra vote in addition to the right to elect representatives in parliament — a vote that would directly determine the existence or absence of hotels in their neighbourhood.[31] That the democratic principle was important to the Australian temperance organisations and that they saw local option as an important part of democracy in action is strongly evident in the language they used to describe the local option cause. The Victorian Alliance claimed its goal was to: 'Give to the people of each district power to protect themselves from these terrible evils by effective local option.'[32] The South Australian Alliance described local option as giving to 'the people' the power which was currently in the hands of the licensing bench.[33]

Australia was more successful than Britain in the battle for local option. By the 1890s, every Australian colony except for Western Australia had introduced local option or some modified form of it. In 1881, the New South Wales government gave ratepayers the right to veto any new licences in their district for the next three years. The polls were to be held concurrently with colonial government elections. South Australia and Tasmania had introduced measures which similarly gave ratepayers the right to veto all new licences. The Victorian Licensing Act of 1885 gave residents the right to reduce the number of hotels in a suburb to one for every five hundred inhabitants. Queensland, however, had the best measures from the temperance viewpoint. The Licensing Act of 1885 allowed the ratepayers of a municipality or division thereof to hold a poll at which they could elect to veto all future licences, reduce the number of current licences or totally eradicate liquor sale from the district. Queensland had started its local option campaign more than a decade after the south-eastern states. The Rechabites, who were the driving force in the campaigns of the south-eastern states, were not in evidence in Queensland in the 1860s. It was only with the arrival of the Good Templars, in 1871, that Queensland temperance advocates started the drive for local option.[34]

While the main temperance bodies were fighting for local option laws and eventually total prohibition, other voices were suggesting alternative solutions to the drink problem. In the 1890s, the Gothenburg system became an increasingly popular proposal among temperance activists.[35] Named after the Swedish town of Gothenburg, where it had first been implemented, this program placed the sale of alcohol exclusively in the hands of the local government, which would use the proceeds for municipal expenditure. While some churches remained largely committed to the idea of local option, others came to favour the idea of municipal control. In Australia, the Presbyterian Church favoured this solution to the 'drink problem'. The Victorian Council of Churches also supported it, antagonising the Victorian Alliance as a result.[36] Gothenburg advocates agreed with local optionists that greed for profit was the reason why drink was peddled so aggressively and irresponsibly, often with little regard for laws demanding regulated hours and minimum age of customers. Take the drink away from private profit and it could be delivered to the public within strict regulations. Like local optionists, they saw themselves as handing over trade regulation to the people, but the people would control the revenue through their local government rather than banish the trade outright. Local optionists countered that governments would merely replace the publicans as the profiteers of the liquid poison. In due time, however, state control was favoured side by side with local option. In Western Australia's first local option polls in 1911, voters were asked if they would permit an increase in the number of licences in their district and also if they wished to place the entire liquor industry in state hands. Citizens voted overwhelmingly in favour of no increase in the number of licences and state management of hotels in their districts.[37]

Municipal control of the liquor trade was also favoured by many trade unions. In 1902, the Victorian Trades Hall Council joined with church representatives at a convention to discuss alcohol control. The convention decided on the Gothenburg system as the best solution, rather than local option.[38] Local option, and the prospect of the liquor and hotel industry shrinking, was not an attractive idea to the employees of the hotels, breweries or distilleries. Handing the industry over to government control would preserve jobs, and state control was perfectly in accordance with labour principles. In New South Wales, and to some extent in Victoria, the Labor party at the turn of the century came to be identified as the party of liquor interests, with the Liberals as the temperance party.[39] Some labour leaders, however, were fervent prohibitionists. When the Brisbane-based William Lane attempted to establish his socialist utopian community in Paraguay he declared that they stood for 'Communism, Home Life and Temperance'. The frictions that led to the community's dissolution frequently involved the flaunting of his ban on alcohol.[40] Perhaps because of Lane's influence, the Queensland labour movement was much more receptive to the idea of prohibition, as well as to state control of hotels and the liquor industry.

Once local option rights had been won for ratepayers, the temperance organisations sought to expand those rights to include all residents, whether ratepayers or not. The Victorian 1885 Licensing Act gave local option rights to all those entitled to vote in parliamentary elections; that is, nearly all adult males. The temperance groups hoped for a similar measure in other colonies. Moreover, at the intercolonial temperance convention held in Melbourne in 1888, after the Reverend David O'Donnell stated that the aim was 'to make the will of the people the law of the country', it was proposed that this should also include women.[41]

In Australia, as in the United States, women had been joining temperance organisations in large numbers since the 1830s. The Sons of Temperance had a corresponding Daughters of Temperance who conducted their own meetings. The Rechabites had female tents with their own officeholders. The strong support among women for local option and measures to suppress the public house can be seen from a Victorian petition of 1885, signed by 44,500 women, requesting that the colonial government pass the Amending Licensing Act which would allow ratepayers to limit the number of hotels in their neighbourhood. The petition was a third of a mile in length and 'came down like the fall of a bale of wool from a dray' when Alfred Deakin presented it to the Victorian parliament.[42] It had been drawn up by the women's committee of the Victorian Alliance and circulated throughout every suburb and town in Victoria in the previous year. The signatories were all women over the age of sixteen. In some towns, according to the Victorian *Alliance Record*, every woman, except for the publicans' wives and daughters, had signed the petition.[43] The enthusiasm with which women greeted local option measures and the prospect of suppressing the public house can be explained in the words of the petition: 'There are numerous women who are exposed to constant ill usage, or who suffer equally cruel neglect, because those from whom they should receive protection are made brutal by intemperance.'[44]

Feminist historian Marilyn Lake has described the temperance campaign as embodying a battle between men and women.[45] In nineteenth-century Australia, heavy drinking was mostly a masculine activity, although judging by the private 'inebriate homes' for women

'Now Boys, Vote Six or the Girls Won't Love You'. Stooping to sexual politics to bring about six o'clock closing in 1912. Oddly, the sign was upside down when the picture was taken. Was it considered inappropriate and recycled? (Brooker Collection, State Library of South Australia)

161

'of the better class',[46] out-of-control drinking appears also to have occurred among more well-to-do women. However, in households where disposable income was scarce, the luxury of alcohol would mainly be reserved for the men. In working-class families especially, men's drinking was often a source of women's anger. If men spent their wages on drink, the wife and children often went without food, clothing and other basic needs. Also, alcoholic drinking quite often led to violence, much of which was directed at wives. Before the days of equal pay, women could not support their children on their own so were totally dependent on their husbands' earning and spending. A husband's alcohol abuse too often meant a wife's desperate suffering in a situation from which she could not escape.

This explains why the campaign to restrict hotels was the first political movement in Australia to involve large numbers of women and, indeed, the first instance of women uniting to effect legal reform and assert their rights. Not only did the temperance societies attract numerous women, they also allowed women to undertake tasks formerly reserved for men. The ladies' committee of the Tasmanian Temperance Alliance edited their own magazine, the *Ladies Bazaar*, as early as 1857.[47] The Good Templars, who established branches in Australia in the early 1870s, was one of the most progressive associations in the world as it allowed women to be officeholders on the same terms as men. Although it was rare for a woman to hold a state or national post, women took leadership positions in local branches throughout Australia.[48]

The temperance movement became the forum for feminist ideas even more emphatically in the 1880s when the Women's Christian Temperance Union emerged. The WCTU was instrumental in breaking down the nineteenth-century stereotype that a woman's place was in the home. It was an organisation run entirely by women, with meetings chaired by women. The members held public meetings, drafted petitions, organised deputations to parliament, and wrote articles for local newspapers. The WCTU soon spread to every colony in Australia and by 1894 its membership had reached 7400. Branches were to be found in the suburbs of big cities and in small rural towns, even in places as remote as Angledool, 75 miles from Lightning Ridge in New South Wales. Each branch was affiliated with the colonial branch of the WCTU, which in turn was part of the Australasian WCTU, which held a convention every three years. The WCTU prided itself on being the first women's organisation to have a central federal organisation.

Before the WCTU emerged in Australia, it was rare to hear a woman address a crowd in a lecture hall, a church or the open air due to a strict taboo on women speaking in public. In the 1850s, a Mrs Dalgarno of Williamstown, Victoria, delivered temperance speeches to crowds and received considerable disapproval and taunts. In the early 1880s, *Spectator*, the magazine of the Wesleyan Methodist Church, quoted St Paul's words forbidding women speaking in churches.[49] However, WCTU women not only addressed their own members but were soon speaking at public meetings. Women started speaking at the male-led temperance conventions too, and in 1891 the Victorian Alliance hired a WCTU member, Bessie Harrison Lee, as its travelling missionary. Lee had been brought up in Daylesford by an alcoholic uncle and aunt. Her early experiences, plus her brief residence in a Victorian mining town, were influential in her antagonism towards alcohol. Like most girls of her day, she was raised to believe that a woman should stay at home and sew and had initially disapproved of women speakers such as Margaret Hampson, a British evangelist who arrived in Australia in 1883 to preach at huge rallies in the main cities.[50] Bessie Lee soon became one of Australia's most prominent and fiery evangelists, delivering speeches in lecture halls and at open-air rallies and sermons in churches. As the Victorian Alliance missionary she was sent to remote towns to win recruits for the cause, and to agitate for the no-drink vote whenever local option polls were in progress. Attitudes to women speakers continued to change and in 1894 Mary George, secretary of the South Australian WCTU, was ordained as the first woman preacher in the Australian Wesleyan Methodist church.[51]

When the women's petition was presented to the Victorian parliament in 1885, women did not have the vote in any Australian colony. Numerous women's suffrage bodies had been actively lobbying throughout Britain and the United States since the 1860s, but Australia was just launching its first suffrage bodies, which were still small and purely local. Within the next few years, due largely to the WCTU, women's suffrage was to be a subject that gained much public attention.

At the first Australasian WCTU convention, in Melbourne in 1891, the WCTU declared its support for votes for women on the same terms as men.[52] The colonial branches had been discussing the matter since their inception several years earlier and were already delivering speeches, writing newspaper and journal articles and in general raising public awareness of the issue. The men's temperance organisations, as can be seen from the intercolonial 1888 convention, offered their support. Three years later, the Victorian Alliance in conjunction with the Victorian WCTU drew up a women's suffrage petition, signed by 30,000 women.

There was also a correlation between temperance and suffrage in the United States. For example, the Prohibition Party, which stood candidates for the 1884 federal elections, included votes for women in its platform.[53] In Australia, the temperance movement was even more significant to women's suffrage, because it was the main forum for the battle. The United States contained a number of women's suffrage organisations, independent of temperance, but in Australia the WCTU was the only women's organisation dedicated to votes for women that covered the whole of the country. The WCTU also brought into the women's suffrage struggle a broader range of women, including those living on small farms far away from the urban-based suffrage groups.

It is not surprising that the temperance movement was such a staunch supporter of votes for women when we consider the immense expression of enthusiasm for the local option on the part of women. However, once local option measures had been won and local option polls were being regularly held, the temperance call for women's votes became even more urgent. The temperance organisations realised that local option polls had a greater chance of procuring a no-licence victory if women had a vote on the matter. This became most evident in the active support women were giving to local option polls. The Victorian WCTU and Blue Ribbon women's auxiliaries' members stood outside polls encouraging electors to vote for reduction. Others visited factories and warehouses, delivering talks and handing out leaflets. Some provided refreshments at the polls. John Vale declared at the Victorian Alliance Convention of 1888 that the women 'had proved themselves to be the best men', while J. W. Gates, a delegate at the convention, stated that he was converted to the idea of women's suffrage by watching the women campaigning so hard for the Ballarat East local option polls.[54] At the Intercolonial Temperance Convention at Hobart in 1895, the resolution for prohibition by referendum was followed by a resolution that a clause for adult women's suffrage be included in the new Australian Constitution.[55]

Yet in fighting the liquor trade, temperance advocates were fighting women as well as men. In Australia hotel keeping was one of the most female-dominated trades; in fact, it was the most prevalent type of woman-owned business. As Diane Kirkby has shown, in 1891 three out five self-employed women in Sydney were public-house owners. In addition, there were other hotels that were family enterprises in which the wife was the manager.[56] This was a characteristic of the business that the temperance movement rarely alluded to; they usually referred to publicans as 'men', and certainly the political publicans' groups, such as the Licensed Victuallers Association, were made up of men. However, when the temperance groups attended hearings of the licensing courts or set up petitions to oppose a new licence in their district, they were aware that such applicants for licences were very often women.

Women who applied for liquor licences sometimes faced discrimination from the Licensing Bench on account of their sex. In 1895, Margaret Rice applied for a wine licence in Melbourne's notorious Lonsdale Street, known for its brothels and opium dens. Judge Hickman Molesworth refused her the licence on the grounds that the area was too 'unsavoury' for a woman.[57] Despite their suffragette impulses, however, temperance groups did not protest discrimination against women in such cases. In fact, women hotel employees were the subject of particular restrictions by the temperance organisations. One of their aims was to ban the employment of barmaids. They saw a public house as a corrupting place for the customers — male and female — but especially so for girls working behind the bar. Drunken men often made indecent advances to barmaids, and sometimes the barmaid would be offered extra money for sexual services. It was not uncommon for a life of prostitution to begin with a job in a bar. When the first WCTU branch opened in Sydney in 1882, one of its first activities involved petitioning for a law prohibiting the employment of barmaids. At each WCTU annual convention throughout the 1890s, a motion would be passed to fight for women's suffrage, with another to ban barmaids. Hence, the WCTU's campaign to protect women from drunken husbands also meant depriving some women of a livelihood. This irony was not lost on the Licensed Victuallers Association whose members mocked the WCTU for wanting women to vote but at the same time depriving them of a means to an honest living. The WCTU responded by asking how the publicans could show such concern for women's jobs when they refused to support the women's vote.[58]

★　★　★

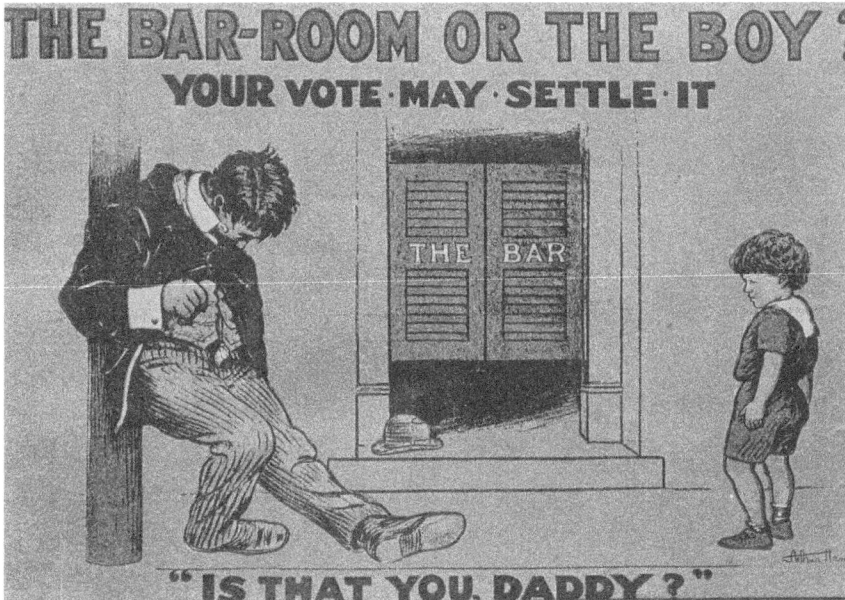

THE BAR-ROOM OR THE BOY?
YOUR VOTE·MAY·SETTLE·IT
THE BAR
"IS THAT YOU, DADDY?"

Pathos was a powerful weapon in the temperance propaganda arsenal, as this poster from the late nineteenth century shows. (Brooker Collection, State Library of South Australia)

Temperance advocates not only believed that alcoholic drink was the primary cause of violence; they believed that hotels and the sale of liquor in general were the cause of public drunkenness. A strong theme in temperance speeches and writings was the idea that the publicans, brewers, distillers and winemakers were responsible for heavy drinking within society and the damage that followed.[59] They perceived drinkers as passive victims: their drunkenness and its consequences were primarily the fault of those who sold them drink. *Australian Temperance World*, the magazine of the New South Wales Good Templars, described drunks as 'robbed of money and character' by the publicans. By seeking to eradicate hotels, temperance advocates saw themselves as 'rescuing' the drunk. They referred to the drink trade as a 'legalised slaughter', while public houses were 'snares' and 'mantraps'.[60] Some suggested that publicans be held liable for drink-related disease or crime — both for what the drinkers themselves suffered and the suffering they inflicted on others. The South Australian WCTU 1893 convention, for example, insisted that 'the publican who takes the cheque and supplies the drink should be responsible for all expenses of the illness'.[61] At the Victorian Alliance 1895 convention, it was suggested that publicans should be liable for injuries and deaths resulting from their clients' drunkenness.[62]

The prohibitionists were totally confident that prohibition of the manufacture and sale of alcohol would solve the drink problem, and considered that this should be obvious to everyone — except for those with vested interests. Bessie Harrison Lee spent six weeks in bed with 'nervous prostration' after visiting a Melbourne women's prison, unable to stop crying as she thought of the women — 'the ruined souls of Victoria's daughters' — whose lives had been blighted by drink. Her husband told her there was nothing she could do, for the women would only drink again once released. She replied, 'Yes, they *would* get drunk again, the poor, poor creatures! Because at every street corner, licensed pitfalls awaited their stumbling feet.' She wondered why the government licensed the sale of a substance that ruined so many lives. She was told by John Singleton, the philanthropist Melbourne doctor, that alcohol was only legal because 'men really held a human soul of less account than customs returns and excise duties'.[63] If the lawmakers refused to pass local veto laws it was because of greed. The very existence of a liquor trade boiled down to avarice and greed — both of the government for revenue and of the drink traders who destroyed others for mercenary profit. As Mary Merson, editor of the WCTU's *Alliance Record*, asked: 'Why should our youth of both sexes be destroyed by strong drink to enrich a few monopolies?'[64]

Alcoholism was often likened to slavery, with the drunks as the slaves and the publicans as slave owners. Like slavery, the drink trade was trafficking in human misery, sanctioned by the law and community, for the material gain of a small section of the community. In fact, many of the early temperance advocates in Britain and the United States were also abolitionists. The moral and political concepts of abolitionism had left their mark on the Protestant churches, of which so many temperance advocates were members. As British temperance historian Brian Harrison has noted, the abolitionist movement had a significant ideological impact on later British social reform movements, not only shaping attitudes to what could be achieved politically and socially through concerted action, but also highlighting the detrimental social impact of the liquor industry.[65] The temperance advocates believed that the law should punish those who were truly responsible for alcoholism — those who sold the drink — and not the victims.

As well as working towards a prohibition measure that would legally suppress all selling of alcoholic drink, temperance advocates sought for legal reform in the treatment of drunks. In 1899, the

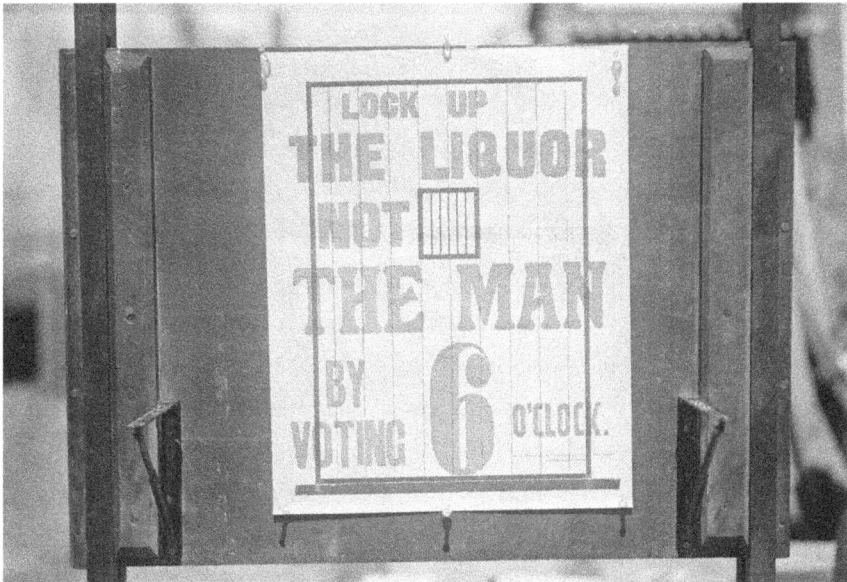

The case for six o'clock closing. Temperance advocates portrayed the heavy drinker as a victim preyed upon by the liquor industry. (Brooker Collection, State Library of South Australia)

Victorian government's report on the treatment of habitual drunkards proposed that, rather than gaol terms, a drunk should be given 'curative influences and discipline suited to his condition'.[66] So, while working to outlaw the drink trade, temperance advocates also tried to decriminalise drunkenness.[67] Some temperance advocates set up institutions for the treatment of drunks as an alternative to gaol. Mrs Swinborn and Mary Christopher of the Victorian WCTU asked the Melbourne courts to send women on drunk-related charges to the Elizabeth Fry Retreat in South Yarra, to spare them the 'injury' of 'the company of old offenders'.[68] The Reverend Courtenay Smith's Cottage Home in Sydney served a similar function. These establishments stressed religious faith, prayer and the strength of the Holy Spirit as essential to curing drunkenness.

During the late nineteenth century, the idea of drunkenness as a disease, with physiological causes and thus solutions, became popular. Vegetarian diets were one favoured method. The Vegetarian Society regularly insisted that eating meat induced the craving for alcohol. The Reverend James Wolfenden set up rehabilitation homes throughout Victoria, in which he administered to alcoholics bi-chloride of gold injections, a method he had learned from an American, Dr Leslie E. Keeley, who opened the first Keeley Institute in Dwight, Illinois, in 1879. By the 1890s every state and nearly every county in the United States had a Keeley Institute, where his 'gold cure' was used to treat the addicted. Keeley claimed an astonishing 72 per cent cure rate for men and 98 per cent for women.[69] By 1900, however, medical opinion had decided that his treatments were only mind cures.

Such cures, dubious though they were, played a part in changing institutional responses to alcoholism. By the first decade of the twentieth century, although drunks in Australia were still forcibly confined in institutions, they were no longer sent to gaol with convicted criminals, but rather to separate institutions for inebriates.

★ ★ ★

By 1911, each state, including Western Australia, had passed Acts that allowed for some type of local option. New South Wales had total local option, by which residents could vote to eradicate all licensed venues from the area or district. In Tasmania only ratepayers were entitled to vote, but in other states the vote was given to all adults.[70] Women were also entitled to participate as they now had the vote in every state.

Despite these successes, temperance advocates realised that nationwide prohibition was a long-term objective and had no chance of working unless the public supported it. The idea of dry neighbourhoods seemed reasonable, and they were confident that the populace, educated in temperance principles, would increasingly vote for no hotels in their area. The number of dry districts would grow and eventually Australia itself would be dry. Nationwide prohibition would enter through the back door. The South Australian *Alliance and Temperance News* predicted that while prohibition would not stop home-brewing, it would mean less than one case of drunkenness for every 100 at present.[71]

However, the introduction of local option did not produce the results that the temperance movement had hoped for. In 1907, New South Wales held its first polls at which all residents included on the state electoral roll could vote to ban all licensed venues (including public houses, wine shops and private clubs) within their electoral district. Thirty-nine per cent voted for a dry district;[72] however, no electorate received the majority vote necessary to institute the measure. It was rare for any suburb in any state to receive the majority vote to go dry. Moreover, legal challenges could render the polls void. For example, in the 1887 local option polls in Melbourne, five districts voted for a reduction of hotel numbers to one for every 500 inhabitants. The publicans challenged the validity of the polls in court, and as a result, four of these districts kept all existing hotels. Only

Geelong went ahead with reduction. The number of hotels in the district decreased, but the number of licensed clubs increased as publicans simply applied for a different type of licence. The other result of local option was the rise in wine shops. Throughout the 1880s in Victoria, these multiplied by a factor of four, as this type of licence was not subject to a local option vote.[73] From a temperance viewpoint, local option polls were most effective in arresting the growth of hotels. When polls were held to determine whether a new licence should be issued in the district, or whether an increase of licences should be permitted, the result was very often against. In Queensland, no new licences were to be issued in a district unless the residents had voted to approve an increase. In 1913, ten districts in the northern state held polls at which five voted against such an increase.

The People's Palace was built in Brisbane by the Salvation Army in 1910–1911. It was a temperance hotel built near the Central Railway Station. The rules were strictly no alcohol or gambling. It existed to provide affordable accommodation for working class people. (State Library of Queensland)

172

Spirits were very important to the early Australian colonists, as beer did not keep well on the long journey from England and local conditions did not suit early brewing techniques. Even when tastes turned towards wine in the nineteenth century, sweet styles of fortified wines were favoured. (State Library of Queensland)

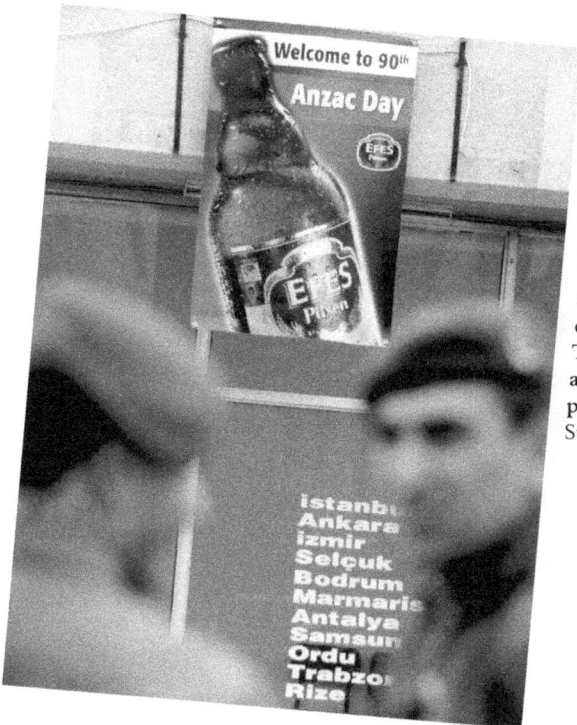

Australians have an international reputation as beer drinkers. This photo shows one of the advertisements for Turkey's bestselling beer that welcomed Australian visitors to the Anzac Day Services at Gallipoli in 2005. That year Efes signed an agreement to brew, market and distribute Foster's Lager in Turkey—a great boon for the annual influx of ANZAC pilgrims. (© Newspix/Innes Stewart)

Beer was considered a healthy alternative to spirits, giving strength for hard-working men, including their Excellencies the Governors-General. (State Library of Victoria)

The tropical beer garden created a relaxed drinking environment for both sexes. Today, the uncrowded atmosphere, generous distance between drinkers, and availability of tables and chairs would be considered useful environmental factors for reducing the incidence of alcohol related harms. (State Library of Queensland)

Today we would call it 'supersizing'. The four-litre 'bag in a box' wine cask provided almost 40 standards drinks of 'imbibe it now or never' product in a convenient, stable and unbreakable package. It may even also have been responsible for tuning Australian palates to predominantly white wines. These look like later, posher versions for those lacking the physical strength to carry, or fridge capacity to store, the equivalent of two wine flagons. (© Newspix/Geoff Ward)

For temperance advocates, war was already a tragedy that did not need to be compounded by the lack of discipline and inefficiency that drunkenness left in its wake. (Mitchell Library)

Temperance subjects were taught in state school as part of health education. This magnificent certificate for passing the temperance physiology examination was awarded to Ken Gooding in 1953 by the Independent Order of Rechabites. The IOR, named after a group of nomadic abstainers in the Old Testament, was founded by Manchester Methodists as a friendly society in 1830. (Courtesy Ken Gooding)

'Beat the Grog.' The negative impact of alcohol in Indigenous communities and the hope of recovery are well summed up in this poster created for the Central Australia Aboriginal Media Association by Michael Callaghan. (National Gallery of Australia/© Michael Callaghan, Redback Graphix, 1986)

For some Indigenous communities, keeping grog out is a matter of survival. Hermannsburg Aboriginal Land Trust boundary notice, 1996. (National Library of Australia/© Robin V. Smith)

GROG KILLS SKILLS

SCORE
DRUNK ☐☐ 0
SOBER ☐ 100

FREDDY'S MESSAGE TO ROOSTERS
ONE BEER AND YOU'RE SACKED

In many ways Indigenous communities have for years been tackling issues only now being taken up in the wider community. (National Gallery of Australia/© Marie McMahon, Licensed by VISCOPY, Australia, 2009)

Back sport page of the *Daily Telegraph* in March 2008. 'One Beer and You're Sacked' was Sydney Roosters NRL coach Brad Fittler's edict to his players to cut out drinking in the week leading up to the game. In 2009, Fittler fined himself $10,000 for drinking excessively. (© Newspix/News Ltd)

Former Prime Minister John Howard and Broncos player Kevin Walters enjoy a beer in the dressing room after Brisbane defeated Canterbury in the 1998 NRL grand final at Sydney Football Stadium. Howard drank a heavy beer and Walters a mid-strength. (© Newspix/News Ltd.)

Then and now. Masking the taste of alcohol is not a new idea. An advertisement for Wimmer's cordial says it can be mixed with whisky, wine, or cordials to form a pleasant liqueur. (State Library Queensland) Forward to the present, where pre-mixed drinks, dubbed 'alcopops', have become the drink of choice for girls between the age of 14 and 19 years. (© Newspix/Justin Lloyd)

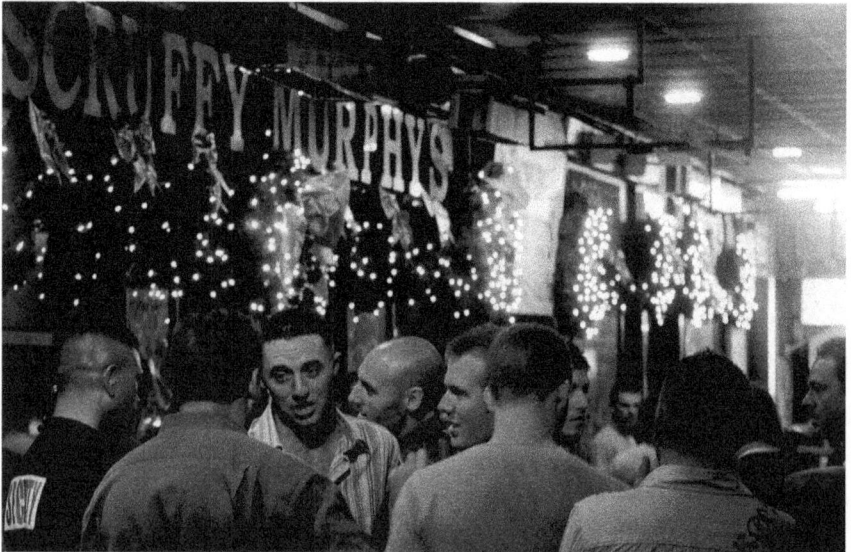

Young men gather outside Scruffy Murphy's in Sydney in December 2008. The pub was one that is required by law to refuse new patrons after 2 am. These measures have been introduced to counteract increased public drunkenness and violent incidents that followed the introduction of 24-hour licences a few years earlier. (Domino Postiglione/Fairfaxphotos)

Released in 2009, this guide to standard drinks attempts to educate drinkers. Many people are still confused when it comes to the idea of a 'standard drink', underestimating quantities and confusing health guidelines with legal limits for driving. Note that the average restaurant serving of wine has 50 per cent more alcohol than a standard drink and there are no low strength ready-to-drink spirits. (© Commonwealth of Australia. Image supplied by Department of Health and Ageing, reproduced by permission.)

NUMBER OF STANDARD DRINKS – BEER

1.1	0.8	0.6	1.6	1.2	0.9	1.4	1	0.8
285ml Full Strength 4.8% Alc Vol	285ml Mid Strength 3.5% Alc Vol	285ml Low Strength 2.7% Alc Vol	425ml Full Strength 4.8% Alc Vol	425ml Mid Strength 3.5% Alc Vol	425ml Low Strength 2.7% Alc Vol	375ml Full Strength 4.8% Alc Vol	375ml Mid Strength 3.5% Alc Vol	375ml Low Strength 2.7% Alc Vol

1.4	1	0.8	34	24	19
375ml Full Strength 4.8% Alc Vol	375ml Mid Strength 3.5% Alc Vol	375ml Low Strength 2.7% Alc Vol	24 x 375ml Full Strength 4.8% Alc Vol	24 x 375ml Mid Strength 3.5% Alc Vol	24 x 375ml Low Strength 2.7% Alc Vol

NUMBER OF STANDARD DRINKS – WINE

1.6	1	0.9	1.4	1	1.4	7.5
150ml Average Restaurant Serving of Red Wine 13.5% Alc Vol	100ml Standard Serve of Red Wine 13.5% Alc Vol	60ml Standard Serve of Port 18% Alc Vol	150ml Average Restaurant Serving of White Wine 11.5% Alc Vol	100ml Standard Serve of White Wine 11.5% Alc Vol	150ml Average Restaurant Serve of Champagne 12% Alc Vol	750ml Bottle of Champagne 12.5% Alc Vol

8	43	21	7.5	39	19.5	28
750ml Bottle of Red Wine 13.5% Alc Vol	4 Litres Cask Red Wine 13.5% Alc Vol	2 Litres Cask Red Wine 13.5% Alc Vol	750ml Bottle of White Wine 12.5% Alc Vol	4 Litres Cask White Wine 12.5% Alc Vol	2 Litres Cask White Wine 12.5% Alc Vol	2 Litres Cask of Port 17.5% Alc Vol

NUMBER OF STANDARD DRINKS – SPIRITS

1	22	1.1	1.2	2.6	1.5	1.8	3.6
30ml High Strength Spirit Nip 40% Alc Vol	700ml High Strength Bottle of Spirits 40% Alc Vol	275ml Full Strength RTD* 5% Alc Vol	330ml Full Strength RTD* 5% Alc Vol	660ml Full Strength RTD* 5% Alc Vol	275ml High Strength RTD* 7% Alc Vol	330ml High Strength RTD* 7% Alc Vol	660ml High Strength RTD* 7% Alc Vol

1	1.2	1.5	1.7	1.4 – 1.9	1.6	2.1	2.4
250ml Full Strength Pre-mix Spirits 5% Alc Vol	300ml Full Strength Pre-mix Spirits 5% Alc Vol	375ml Full Strength Pre-mix Spirits 5% Alc Vol	440ml Full Strength Pre-mix Spirits 5% Alc Vol	250ml High Strength Pre-mix Spirits 7% – 10% Alc Vol	300ml High Strength Pre-mix Spirits 7% Alc Vol	375ml High Strength Pre-mix Spirits 7% Alc Vol	440ml High Strength Pre-mix Spirits 7% Alc Vol

* Ready-to-Drink

Like the early colonists, many Indigenous leaders are concerned that their communities are 'floating on a seas of spirits'. Cape York Indigenous leader Noel Pearson is a strong critic of past alcohol management plans, which have focused on restricting the supply of grog without giving due attention to the demand created by addiction. New measures put in place in Cape York communities are focusing on restricting individuals' rights if they neglect their families as a result of alcohol abuse. (Steven Siewert/Fairfaxphotos)

In Victoria, there were 1337 fewer hotels in 1911 than there had been in 1885, when there was one for every 227 inhabitants. There was now one hotel for 451 persons. Two hundred and seventeen hotels had been closed as a result of local option polls; others had been deprived of their licences by the Licensing Bench due to the conditions of the 1907 Licensing Act. In Sydney, by contrast, there was hardly any reduction in the absolute number of hotels during that period.[74] Temperance advocates realised that the public house performed a crucial service in providing food, accommodation and recreation as well as alcohol, and if they were to attract clients away from the pub they had to provide alternative venues for such needs. For this reason, they set up 'coffee palaces', or hotels that provided every essential hotel service except for alcohol. The grand Windsor Hotel, built in Melbourne in 1888, began as such an establishment.

From the 1880s onwards, there is much anecdotal evidence that the Australian population was becoming more sober. The Reverend F. B. Boyce, chairman of the New South Wales Local Option League, remarked in 1893 that drunkenness was less socially acceptable at upper-class dinner parties than it had been and that the teapot had replaced the beer keg at shearing stations.[75] Many clubs and societies started refusing to meet in pubs; for example, the Victorian Trades Hall Council stopped meeting at the Belvedere Hotel.[76] Boyce grandiosely claimed that as many as three-quarters of all Australians were total abstainers, and James Munro, premier of Victoria, estimated that there were 200,000 total abstainers in the colony.[77] According to the liquor retail figures, drinking rates dropped considerably throughout the 1890s.[78] Some of this may have been due to the economic slump of that decade; however, the trend continued throughout the early part of the twentieth century, suggesting that it was more than finances causing the decline in drinking alcohol. Western Australia was the exception to Australia's growing sobriety: in the first decade of the twentieth century it had a higher rate of spirits consumption than the United Kingdom, and by far the highest beer drinking rate in Australia. The mining boom in the west had the same effect on drinking rates as the gold rush had had in Victoria fifty years before. In all other states, the drinking rate declined dramatically between 1885 and 1908.[79] This was most noticeable in spirits consumption which more than halved over that period. In New South Wales, beer consumption declined from 13.4 gallons per capita in 1886 to 9.8 gallons in 1905. In Victoria, it went from 17.3 gallons in 1886 to 12 gallons in 1909.[80]

In the twentieth century, the most successful victory for the Australian temperance movement was the introduction of six o'clock closing in South Australia, Victoria, New South Wales and Tasmania. The campaign began in the early 1900s when Early Closing Acts in the individual states demanded that shops be closed at six o'clock. Temperance organisations then began agitating for a law that would impose the same requirements on licensed hotels, which were open from five or six o'clock in the morning until eleven or half-past eleven at night.[81] After much petitioning by the temperance groups, referenda were held in the different states. This time, they were successful. In South Australia in 1915, a majority of 56 per cent voted that all hotels be required to close at six o'clock. Victoria, New South Wales and Tasmania followed suit in 1916. (Western Australia reduced opening hours slightly with nine o'clock closing. Queensland did not introduce eight o'clock closing until 1923.)[82] In New South Wales a further referendum was held in 1919, as the original Act was intended as a wartime measure. A majority voted to continue six o'clock closing.

The public mood during and just after World War I seemed promising to the temperance movement, and it was an opportunity to enlist the support of moderate drinkers among the middle classes. Six o'clock closing was not a teetotal proposition; rather, according to the veteran Congregational minister and campaigner for early closing in South Australia, Joseph Coles Kirby, it was a measure 'suited to those foolish people who liked a little liquor in moderation. Those of that persuasion ... could well support it, and prove that their desire was moderation and not excess'.[83]

The effects of six o'clock closing were highly localised and, rather than a booster of the temperance cause, they reflected Australia's already existing culture of moderation. The period after World War I did not see a great change in Australian beer and wine consumption despite the shorter hours available for pub drinking. Spirits drinking continued its decline throughout the 1920s, with Australians consuming about a third of the average per capita of spirits in the 1920s than they had 50 years earlier.[84] Consumption of domestically brewed beer had risen towards the end of the nineteenth century, but the introduction of six o'clock closing resulted in a reduction of the Commonwealth annual per capita consumption of beer by less than a gallon for the years 1916 to 1930 — still roughly half the consumption rate of the British at the time.

The mood in favour of sacrifice and moderation during World War I led the temperance bodies in Australia to raise their ambitions. In 1916, the alliances in the various states united under the Australasian Alliance Prohibition Council. The president was Samuel Mauger, a Victorian Labor MP, and vice-president was Julia Holder, a WCTU president, suffragette, wife of a former premier of South Australia and one of the first women justices of the peace in South Australia. The idea of the council was to work towards a dry Australia. The Volstead Act, passed in the United States in 1920, which banned all manufacture, sale and transport of alcohol nationwide, ignited excitement and there was a wide belief that such a move would be possible for Australia. At its 1921 annual convention, the WCTU declared that the aim should be for Australia-wide prohibition by 1925.[85] Given its relatively lower rates

Temperance advertisements supporting alcohol prohibition used in the 1923 referendum campaign in Queensland. (Courtesy Drug-Arm)

of consumption, Australia might have seemed a more likely candidate for alcohol prohibition than the United States. In 1918, just before the passing of the Volstead Act, the US had nearly three times the per capita consumption rate of spirits in comparison with Australia and a slightly higher beer consumption rate. Even though Australia's wine-drinking volume was nearly twice as high, it still did not equal the amount of total alcohol consumed in the United States.[86]

The strategy of the temperance movement was to extend local option measures to the state level and allow voters to elect not just a dry neighbourhood but a dry state. Throughout the 1920s and 1930s referenda were held in each of the Australian states. Voters were asked whether they wished to see their state prohibit the sale and manufacture of alcohol. The agenda was more modest than the United States' Prohibition law; the import of alcohol purchased in so-called wet states would not be banned. Also, as in the United States, home-brew would be excluded from the ban.

No state in Australia ever went dry; nonetheless, a substantial minority supported statewide prohibition during this era. Victoria received the largest prohibition vote (42 per cent) in March 1930. In other states, around a third of the electorate voted 'yes'. Tasmania, however, showed such a small voter turnout that there was some doubt as to the validity of the poll.[87] Canberra had already been declared an alcohol-free zone when it replaced Melbourne as Australia's capital city. However, a referendum held in 1928 brought an end to Australian temperance advocates' pride in their dry capital city. A majority voted to lift the ban, and Canberra residents were soon legally buying liquor along with the rest of the country.

Australia's alcohol consumption rate took a very obvious dive in the 1930s, most noticeably in spirits and also in beer.[88] The financial year of 1929–30 appears to have been the turning point, suggesting that the Wall Street crash in the US and subsequent economic depression was a major factor. With unemployment at soaring levels how could household budgets accommodate alcohol? Indeed, this

Temperance advocates believed that alcohol weakened the war effort. During World War II they made sure that, where possible, dry canteens were available to servicemen and women as an alternative to wet canteens. *Australian Temperance Advocate*, 1942. (Courtesy Drug-Arm)

177

decade marks the lowest drinking rates in Australia's history. It can be seen as the apex of the early twentieth century's temperance ethos, exacerbated by financial scarcity. In this context of enforced moderation, support for further liquor restrictions and prohibition steadily declined throughout the 1930s. In 1932, Tasmanians voted to extend hotel closing to ten o'clock. In 1937, Victoria held another prohibition referendum; this time, only a third voted 'yes'. No doubt the manifest failure of prohibition and consequent repeal of the Volstead Act in the United States contributed. Perhaps, too, the economic depression had made Victorians reluctant to close down an entire industry and create more job losses, even as they drank less of its products. More likely, the middle-class supporters of moderation no longer saw any pressing need to stand in common cause with prohibitionists.

The golden age of temperance enthusiasm had passed its peak and the movement was to decline steadily throughout the rest of the twentieth century. Since the 1830s, Australian society, like other English-speaking and northern European countries, had been moving towards tougher and more extensive restrictions on liquor supply. From World War II onwards, an opposite trend would be much in evidence as alcohol consumption again steadily increased.

CHAPTER 5

In Harm's Way

Despite the fact that some countries prohibit its use and despite many people's preference for other psychoactive substances, alcohol can reasonably be described as the world's favourite drug. There may be good reasons for this popularity and ... alcohol has many benefits and affords great pleasure to those who drink it ...

Despite its popularity and the benefits it brings to our lives, it should not be forgotten that alcohol is also our most dangerous drug and is responsible for more harm throughout the world than any other psychoactive substance, including illicit drugs and nicotine.

'Pleasures & Pains of Our Favourite Drug', Nick Heather, 2001.[1]

After being seen for many years as either a personal or medical problem, the use and abuse of alcohol has returned to centrestage as a political issue. In 2003, for example, the New South Wales government held a summit on alcohol abuse to discuss issues of alcohol use in the community; Ross Fitzgerald was the keynote speaker. For four days, parliament was dedicated to the discussion of alcohol issues and the development of new strategies for approaching alcohol-related problems. According to the then premier, Bob Carr, the summit was to be 'a way of driving policy change, a way of attempting to build consensus about courses of action'.[2] Apart from a similar New South Wales drug summit held in 1999, it was the first time any Australian parliament had hosted such an event. A wide variety of state politicians and community representatives attended, a range of issues were discussed, and over 300 recommendations were made for consideration by state parliament.

Of the many ideas presented during this summit, one that sharply caught the eye of the media and provoked public debate was Premier Carr's interpretation of the major cause of alcohol abuse in Australian society:

> Is it mateship to let your friend drink himself into
> serious inebriation? Is it mateship to watch your mate
> downing schooner after schooner when you know his
> wife and kids are already afraid of him? Is it funny to
> watch a drunken mate pick a fight with a passer-by?
> What sort of mateship allows a group of girls to go out
> drinking and do nothing when a friend, drunk, gets
> into a car with a stranger who has been drinking? As a
> community are we willing to tolerate this sort of self-
> destructive excess or are we willing to adjust our mores,
> our way of life, to explore better means of managing
> alcohol.[3]

Carr had singled out cultural attitudes towards alcohol as being the main cause of alcohol-related harms, particularly the hallowed Australian concept of 'mateship', or at least a distorted version of it. In arguing that one of Australia's most cherished values was being used to cover up negligent social behaviour and a lack of a sense of

An exchange between health promoters and an avid drinker in the men's urinal of a Sydney RSL Club in 2008 shows how tough the road ahead is for those who put their faith in cultural change as the solution to alcohol abuse. Attitudes are well-entrenched. (Photo courtesy of Ken Gooding)

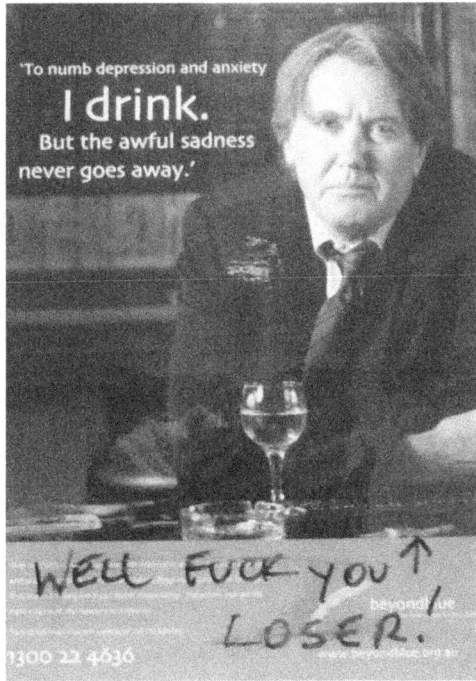

responsibility, he echoed one of the major themes of the summit — the need for cultural change.[4]

Responses to Carr's speech were split. Some commentators agreed that culture was the main culprit in the abuse of alcohol in Australia, while others saw it as an issue peripheral to the major task of government, which was legislative control. As the *Sydney Morning Herald* put it: 'The summit has suggested useful ideas for the Government to refine or tighten existing laws. Its bigger contribution, though, has been to spur the rest of us to question our attitudes to alcohol and to think more deeply about the line between enjoying a drink and abusing it.'[5] At the same time, another observer, John Birmingham, criticised Carr's pronouncement. 'When the Carr Government is serious about dealing with alcohol you'll know. You won't hear a whole lot of waffle about mateship coming from the Premier's office. You'll just hear the screams and howls of the [liquor] industry.'[6]

To put Carr's comments into perspective, by the end of the twentieth century the word 'culture' had become a catch-all for entrenched behaviours and beliefs that could prove resistant to change. Thus, dealing with police corruption meant changing the police culture; public sector reform required addressing the culture of the public sector; and behind every bully was something much bigger and more difficult to deal with — a culture of bullying. The culture ogre had become a ubiquitous contributing factor to an assortment of socially harmful practices and a universal retardant to reform. Some of our most cherished values — even mateship — appeared to be morally dubious; like good soil and gentle rain, they could stimulate growth of weeds as well as flowers. The focus on culture, however, tends to deflect moral responsibility from individual abusers and from the alcohol industry, at the same time reapportioning a considerable amount of blame to us all. It isn't only those who drink to excess or the industry that promotes alcohol's availability that are to blame for alcohol-related abuses, but also those who stand by and allow it to happen. John Birmingham's point was that 'waffle about mateship' — this sharing of the blame — downplays more obvious and palpable political and economic factors. If the ethical framework of a liberal democracy requires a balancing of individual freedoms against possible harm to others, then the issue of defining the precise nature of any harm associated with alcohol consumption has widespread ramifications. The shift in identifying the 'problem' component in so-called problem drinking is itself the outcome of cultural change.

Indeed, this new change-the-culture approach epitomises how far opinions, theories and sentiments about problem drinking and alcohol-related harms have shifted from those current when Europeans first began settling in Australia. Over time, the assessment of the heavy toll of alcohol abuse and the response to it have been influenced by the changing social, political and economic context. In

Australia, one thing that has remained constant is the influence of overseas ideas when it comes to naming the problem, identifying harms, looking for causes and proposing treatments.

That drinking alcohol causes many personal harms and social problems has long been recognised. In ancient Greece, for example, Hippocrates accurately described the physical effects of alcohol consumption, including 'nausea, insomnia, palpitations and delirium', while Aristotle noted alcohol's deleterious effects on sexual function.[7] For most of European history, the social effects of drunkenness were widely perceived as a problem and the individual drinker was seen as the source of that problem. Prior to the nineteenth century, what is most notable about responses to excessive drinking is its perceived connection with licentiousness, sinfulness and crime. English laws against drunkenness enacted in 1552 and in 1606 repressed what was seen at the time as 'the odious and loathsome sin of drunkenness'.[8] Problem drinking and alcohol-related harms hinted at moral defects in individuals, so remedies focused on directly punishing sinful acts or, more indirectly, increasing the wages of sin through taxation and tariffs. For those founding the British colony in New South Wales, who were destined to be the long-term inheritors of European problems and solutions, drunkenness was just one more manifestation of sinful and criminal behaviour to be brought under a regime of regulation and punishment.

From the nineteenth century onwards, however, attention shifted away from the moral shortcomings of the drunk to the powerful influence of alcohol. Increasingly, problem drinkers and society itself came to be seen as victims of a disease induced by a powerful addictive substance. A person was said to 'suffer' from an addiction, with the connotation that such addicts had little control over their personal fates and the consequences of their actions. Interpreting habitual drunkenness as a disease opened up the possibility of treatment rather than punishment and the subsequent possible improvement of both the individual and society. Direct social control of alcohol — even perhaps to the extent of prohibition, a legal form of enforced abstinence — was a kind of medical treatment for the body politic. Such control was a most vivid application of the so-called harm principle: in a liberal democracy, preventing harm to others was the only legitimate reason that the arm of the law could have to reach into the private lives of its citizens. As we have seen, much of the temperance movement's rhetoric was aimed at protecting women and children from the physical and economic consequences of the male breadwinner's drunkenness.

Experiences in the early twentieth century, however, showed that strategies of direct control and prohibition could themselves have unintended social effects; in particular, unworkable prohibition laws could lead to a widespread reduction in respect for law and government. With the subsequent failures of large-scale prohibition in its various manifestations, the focus of dealing with problem drinking retreated from the political and legal domains to the medical domain. From the middle of the twentieth century, direct treatment and health education became the key strategies for dealing with alcohol as a social problem, and the institutions responsible for dealing with the effects of problem drinking became the health department, the clinic, the rehabilitation centre and the asylum. The latter carried a residual burden of a carceral mentality: those found drunk in public places could spend a brief time in the 'drunk tank', while the permanently inebriated might be delivered directly to treatment centres by police. Viewing alcoholism as a disease not only opened increasing avenues for treatment, it also provided a new basis for the moral reform of individuals. The cornerstone of Alcoholics Anonymous, perhaps the world's most enduring and successful self-help group, was the idea that the alcoholic was suffering from an illness which he or she could not control by an individual exercise of the will. The group, co-founded in the United States by a New York stockbroker, Bill Wilson, and an Ohio physician,

Dr Bob Smith in 1935, believed that to solve their problems alcoholics must find and put their trust in a 'Power greater than themselves'.[9] Spiritual sources of power, which previously had been used to cast out the drunkard or to underwrite his or her sinfulness and sense of guilt, were now drawn on as positive resources for the moral or psychological renewal of individual lives in socially supportive group settings.

Medical concerns in the late nineteenth and early twentieth centuries focused mainly on the alcoholic, with the goal of encouraging a restoration of health and the achievement of sobriety. When the latter goal proved to be out of reach, or at least unrealistic, for most if not many, there was a shift in the late twentieth century to other approaches that stressed strategies of prevention and harm minimisation. For the individual, this often meant so-called 'controlled' drinking, while, at the social level, public health strategies were developed to manage the social impacts of alcohol consumption — for example, separating drinking and drinkers from driving, and changing the drinking environment to reduce the incidence of alcohol-fuelled violence. Prevention and early intervention were considered to be essential, but if drinking to unsafe levels was a problem for some individuals then, perhaps, an environment could be created or modified that reduced these dangers and encouraged the safer consumption of alcohol. Changes to the physical environment could include, for example, the provision of adequate, well-spaced seating, availability of taxis and public transport, entertainment and the provision of water and hot snacks. These ideas reflected a shift from viewing alcoholism as essentially a private health issue to understanding problem drinking to be a matter of public health, and meant 'extending intervention to areas such as education and domestic violence prevention'.[10] In effect, the target group for regulatory measures was increased from alcoholics to all drinkers of alcohol.

★   ★   ★

185

Australia tended to follow the rest of the world in all these major trends, but there were also local variations in problems and remedies shaped by a number of contextual factors. In the early days of European settlement, for example, dealing with alcohol problems was exacerbated by the difficulty of instituting effective controls when at a considerable distance from the ultimate sources of governmental authority, the role of spirits in the naval heritage, and the difficulty of either transporting beer or establishing locally reliable sources of it. As the colonists moved away from Sydney, intermittent supply and physical isolation added new dimensions to binge drinking, which had already begun to be a problem in the industrialising cities of England.

Prior to industrialisation, binge drinking was common to all classes in European society and generally was not seen as a serious offence.[11] Moreover, in many European countries in the pre-modern era, and even up to the mid-nineteenth century, the word 'alcohol' was used to denote distilled spirits, and fermented drinks such as beer and wine were seen as being relatively harmless.[12] With industrialisation came an increasingly mechanised and systematic way of working and living, which included urbanisation. In these urban settings, problems relating to excessive alcohol use became more publicly pressing. Drinking had to be compartmentalised to fit into a new way of life where there was a clear delineation between work and leisure time. In pre-industrial societies, work and home life often overlapped and workloads were usually dictated by the seasons. However, industrial work demanded set work hours and efficiency standards set by market forces, while the development and introduction of machinery made the workplace more dangerous. Under these new circumstances, drinking on the job created both a safety hazard and a threat to new standards of efficiency, so drinking increasingly became an after-hours practice.[13] Also, with increasing formality in the workplace, practices such as drinking alcohol and smoking tobacco became to be seen as slovenly, especially in service industries.[14] When drinking on the weekend began to impinge on industrial working life — the 'Saint Monday' phenomenon referred to employees taking Monday off because of a hangover from drinking all weekend[15] — some employers started to actively support temperance. The South Australian mining town of Moonta was a dry town; and in Western Australia, a pioneering landowning family, the Parkers, established Dangin as an alcohol-free township east of York. In Queensland, the owner of the Silver Spur mine near Stanthorpe, a staunch teetotaller, made it obligatory for all workers and their families to abstain from drinking alcohol.[16]

According to later socialist pamphleteers, many of whom advocated teetotalism, the 'thrifty and industrious abstainer' was a boon to industry, not only because there would be more willing and healthy workers available but because the teetotaller and his family could live on a smaller wage than the drinker and so 'the practice of total abstinence by the workers will result in a fall of wages'.[17] Thus, teetotalism would have the paradoxical effect of degrading one's fellow workers by losing their income if it was not accompanied by removing the capitalist system of exploitation. According to the activist and teetotaller Russell Smart, the non-socialist temperance advocate believed that 'the creation of a community of total abstainers is the one thing necessary to remove the poverty and degradation of the nation'.[18] For many socialists, on the other hand, poverty was the cause of drink. The labour movement in nineteenth-century Australia was often divided between heavy drinkers and total abstainers. The latter, who regarded alcohol as the 'opium of the working class', were the most radical politically. A prime example was the militant Queensland socialist William Lane, who eventually left Australia to set up his utopian community, New Australia, in Paraguay. Total abstinence was a key part of Lane's utopian vision; but it was a counsel to perfection not shared by all the participants. Others in the labour movement in Australia approached the problem of alcohol differently, advocating that the state should control alcohol, to the extent of owning hotels, as a first step to nationalisation and possible prohibition. In Queensland, the radical reformist 1915–19 Labor government of T. J. Ryan established a number of state hotels, along with other enterprises including sawmills and butcher shops. As a linguistic legacy of government-owned public houses, Queensland still has the State Hotel in Babinda.[19] When the hotel opened in May 1917, the Brisbane *Courier* noted: 'The Home Secretary [William Huxham] has performed the notable function of declaring the State groggery at Babinda open for public business. Whether this deed was done by pulling the first cork, or drawing the first beer, or ejecting the first tipsy man we are not told.'[20] Despite not having a monopoly the hotel netted profits for every year of state ownership.[21]

In the increasingly modern world, alcohol was a new kind of problem, not just from a moral point of view, or not as a cause of seasonal social disruption, but as a threat to good order. In the new colony of New South Wales, the chaplains complained about the

The State Hotel, Babinda. Along with other state-owned enterprises, state-owned hotels in Queensland were aimed at preventing price gouging by the liquor industry. They were built to last — this one still stands today. (State Library of Queensland, no. 191213)

John Coakley Lettsom's (1744–1815) Moral and Physical Thermometer shows 'Botany Bay' as the second worst consequence of intemperance, exceeded only by 'Gallows'.

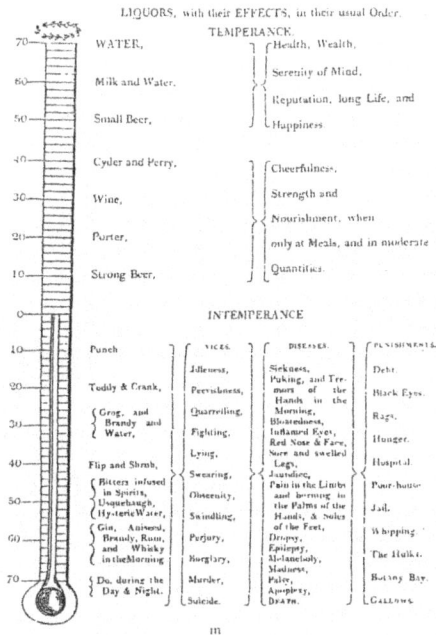

LIQUORS, with their EFFECTS, in their usual Order.

TEMPERANCE.

70	WATER,	⎫ Health, Wealth,
60	Milk and Water,	⎪ Serenity of Mind,
50	Small Beer,	⎬ Reputation, long Life, and ⎭ Happiness
40	Cyder and Perry,	⎫ Cheerfulness,
30	Wine,	⎪ Strength and ⎪ Nourishment, when
20	Porter,	⎬ only at Meals, and in moderate
10	Strong Beer,	⎭ Quantities.
0		

INTEMPERANCE

		VICES.	DISEASES.	PUNISHMENTS.
10	Punch	Idleness,	Sickness,	Debt.
20	Toddy & Crank,	Peevishness,	Puking, and Tremors of the Hands in the	Black Eyes.
30	Grog, and Brandy and Water,	Quarreling, Fighting,	Morning, Bloatedness, Inflamed Eyes,	Rags.
40	Flip and Shrub,	Lying, Swearing,	Red Nose & Face, Sore and swelled Legs, Jaundice,	Hunger. Hospital.
50	Bitters infused in Spirits, Usquebaugh, Hysteric Water,	Obscenity, Swindling,	Pain in the Limbs and burning in the Palms of the Hands, & Soles of the Feet,	Poor-house. Jail.
60	Gin, Aniseed, Brandy, Rum, and Whisky in the Morning,	Perjury, Burglary,	Dropsy, Epilepsy, Melancholy, Madness,	Whipping The Hulks.
70	Do. during the Day & Night.	Murder, Suicide.	Palsy, Apoplexy, DEATH.	Botany Bay. GALLOWS

III

degradation that drunkenness caused, but the governors' concerns — even those who were themselves heavy drinkers — were more utilitarian. When men were drunk, the necessary work of building a sustainable settlement was left undone. The dislocating effects of the economic, social and technological changes accompanying industrialisation and modernisation helped to either create or exacerbate alcohol problems, particularly for those classes already likely to come under the eye of the law, thereby increasing their chances of being transported to Botany Bay. The clear connection in the mind of British authorities between alcohol abuse in Britain and the colony in Botany Bay is illustrated in the physician John Lettsom's *Moral and Physical Thermometer*, an illustration published in the late eighteenth century as a warning of alcohol's harmful consequences. Botany Bay was portrayed as the second worst punitive consequence of gin drinking — one grade worse than the hulks and only one grade better than the gallows.[22]

By the time Europeans were setting out to occupy Australia, Britain was a modernising state and alcohol abuse was a problem with the potential to create significant social harms. Nevertheless, at the time, individuals themselves were seen as the source of these social harms. Alcohol abuse was viewed as a moral problem — of weak will and sometimes of vice. In the eighteenth century, the word 'moral' also connoted the emotional and the psychological, and so, at best, a person with an alcohol problem could be seen as someone with a mental deficiency or emotional problem, and deserving of some compassion.[23] Medically, the term 'moral treatment' often meant a residential treatment combining care and strict routine for the purposes of 'retraining' the individual with the problem.[24] Nevertheless, this 'moral' model often conceptualised alcohol abuse as the product of free choice rather than the drinker being in the grip of an addiction, which suited a penal society where behavioural anomalies and mental problems were closely associated with criminality and were generally managed in a punitive manner.[25]

In the eighteenth century, the colony in Australia took its ideas about alcohol and its control directly from Britain, but from the nineteenth century on ideas about managing alcohol problems, most notably the gradual medicalisation of alcohol misuse, were imported not only from Britain but also Europe and the United States. A considerable number of minority groups throughout the nineteenth century, especially the temperance movement, believed that alcohol itself and its ready availability were the causes of the problem and that the solution was its removal. They were sympathetic to the plight of the drunkard and blamed the industry for encouraging the weak to fall. Nevertheless, large sections of the general public and some medical thinkers continued to hold a moral view about alcohol use and alcohol abusers well into the twentieth century. Although it is not dominant, this view continues into the twenty-first century among some sections of the public and a minority of health professionals.[26]

★　★　★

Increasingly, alcohol is being understood as a problem because it is a type of drug. While this seems obvious, the idea is not generally well accepted at a popular and political level. To return to the example of the 2003 New South Wales alcohol summit, a discrete drug summit had been held four years earlier, thereby treating alcohol as fundamentally different from other drugs. Nevertheless, many discussions at the alcohol summit did refer to alcohol as a dangerous drug. In terms of contemporary medical thought, alcohol is covered by the World Health Organization's definition of a drug, being 'a chemical entity used non-medically, self-administered for its psycho-active effect'.[27] Biologically, alcohol is a depressant, which at low levels of consumption lowers inhibitions and at higher levels of consumption impairs perception, coordination and concentration, reducing the ability to make sound judgments and to respond to the environment.[28] It is the most widely used, and most commonly misused, substance in Australia.[29]

Despite this, the levels of both legal and cultural acceptance of alcohol in Australia are so high that it is either not seen as a drug at all, or, if it is, it is seen as less dangerous than other psychoactive substances — even though, compared to any other drug, alcohol has the potential to cause the most widespread variety of damage to both the body and the mind.[30] The social classification of drugs is not related to the actual harmfulness of the drug being classified.[31] This raises difficulties for public policy. One of the essential components of the ethical framework of liberal democracy — preventing a tyranny of the majority — is the so-called harm principle: 'The law ought to respect the rights of people to make their own moral decisions so long as those decisions do not involve harm to others or prevent others from making their own autonomous decisions.'[32] The widespread cultural acceptance of alcohol, however, directly pits democratic

191

opinion against expert opinion — the uninformed majority against an informed elite. From a moral point of view, the 'harm principle' necessitates some ultimate appeal to expertise and the facts; otherwise, an uninformed majority opinion could harm the fate of minorities.

Historically, excessive consumption has been seen as the main contributor to direct and indirect alcohol harms. In Australia in 2008, public concern about increasing levels of binge drinking reached to the highest level, with newly elected Prime Minister Kevin Rudd announcing the introduction of a $53 million national program to address an 'epidemic in binge drinking' among young people. The government response had been prompted in part by the release of a national survey indicating that one in five sixteen and seventeen year olds were binge drinking in any given week, and a further 170,000 Australians between the ages of twelve and seventeen were drinking to dangerous levels.[33] About $20 million was to be spent on warning young people of the dangers of binge drinking, which in the short term included violence, unwilling or unprotected sex, car accidents and alcohol poisoning, as well as the long-term possibilities of brain and liver damage. The problem was compounded, according to Australian National Council on Drugs chairman John Herron, by the fact that many Australians considered drinking and drug use by young people as a normal activity or a 'rite of passage to adulthood'.[34]

As the 'Saint Monday' phenomenon attests, recently industrialised Britain was already acquainted with binge drinking in the nineteenth century. In Australia, however, physical and social isolation further exacerbated the problem with binge drinking becoming a feature of frontier life. In outback areas, isolation, distance from settlements and the ensuing lack of a regular supply of alcohol meant that heavy drinking tended to be done in spurts or 'binges'. A 'work and burst' ethic developed, whereby men doing hard work on the frontier would head to a nearby town after being paid and spend their earnings on a sustained drinking bout.[35] Such binge drinking had dangerous short-term consequences brought about by the lowered inhibition induced by a high burst of alcohol intake. In terms of what is currently known about binge drinking, these drinking bouts would have precipitated a range of immediate harms, including high levels of violence, accidents, sexual indiscretions or assaults and, in the cases of men who were unhappy or overwhelmed by frontier life or other troubles, increased rates of suicide.[36] Heavy drinking was also common among town dwellers, but mainly consisted of regular drinking, the behavioural consequences of which were usually spread across the week and thus generally acceptable.

Many commentators believed that the increased presence of women would 'civilise' Australian society as the frontier areas became more settled and gender ratios began to even out in both town and country. Often, no doubt, it did. Nevertheless, in many instances these changes also meant that alcohol abuse had new consequences: domestic violence or neglect. By the mid-nineteenth century, issues of physical violence or threats of violence, along with neglect or poverty caused by an addicted family member using household money to buy alcohol, became one of the major concerns of temperance campaigners.[37] Although it does not necessarily follow that the concerns of any public campaign closely mirror the concerns of society at large, the high number of women who supported the abstinence campaign for this reason suggests that issues of alcohol-related domestic violence, neglect or poverty were experienced by a relatively large number of households.

Did moves to restrict the sale of alcohol have the unintended effect of increasing binge drinking? For example, did later laws imposing six o'clock closing of hotels across many states in Australia, initiated and promoted by temperance campaigners, sometimes result in a slight decrease in drinking levels across the board but at the cost of bringing

The six o'clock swill outside the Auburn Hotel in 1952. In 1951, a NSW Royal Commission into liquor licensing found that publicans favoured six o'clock closing because they made more profit selling alcohol quickly in a short period of time and saved on the labour costs associated with closing later. (NSW Police Forensic Archive, Justice and Peace Museum, Historic Houses Trust)

together the cultures of regular drinking and binge drinking? Dire pictures are often painted of the 'six o'clock swill' — how it transformed heritage pub architecture into functional, but risible, drinking holes, and its uncivilising promotion of rowdy and uncouth behaviour of men seeking to maximise their drinking within the allotted time.[38] But these graphic depictions of the six o'clock swill were more favoured by propagandists for extended drinking hours than by those opposing them. The influence of the six o'clock swill on Australia's national drinking habits needs to be kept in perspective. Per capita consumption of beer declined by just over 4 per cent in the five years after the introduction of six o'clock closing compared to the five previous years, which had seen a spike in beer consumption.[39]

Measures such as early closing appear to have had localised rather than society-wide effects on alcohol consumption. Although we might see drinking alcohol as a matter of individual choice, unless one brews or distil one's own drink, it is also a market transaction subject to the forces of supply and demand. Early closing affects supply in a particular place at a particular time, not the overall supply, as take-home sales, for example, are not restricted. It was precisely this kind of local effect that many supporters of early closing intended, including the middle-class moderates. Seasoned temperance campaigners may have wished for a greater social transformation, but significant society-wide changes in patterns of alcohol consumption seem to reflect changing patterns of economic prosperity and decline.

Prior to the introduction of early closing laws, bars in Australia were open from five or six o'clock in the morning until eleven or half-past eleven at night.[40] Various early-closing laws were introduced in the Australian states either during or shortly after World War I. Though six o'clock closing was introduced in South Australia in March 1916, it was never universally adopted. By the end of that year, six o'clock closing had been introduced to New South Wales, Victoria and Tasmania.[41] Western Australia changed to nine o'clock closing, and Queensland did not change its closing hours until 1923, when it adopted eight o'clock closing. That early closing was adopted in the two most populous states explains some of its historical prominence, but also tends to undermine any claims about any widespread social effects. A sense of wartime sacrifice played its part, but so too did the argument for more consistent closing times for businesses across the board — six o'clock being the time set for the closing of shops under the Early Closing Acts in most Australian states.[42] As an alternative to their local option strategy, aimed at creating dry communities one by one, temperance campaigners threw their strategic support behind the harmonising of closing times as a quicker way of restricting alcohol consumption in the community. It was 'a scandal that a civilised — not to say Christian — country,' claimed the Methodist *Spectator*, 'should close shops for the sale of bread, and keep open places for the sale of intoxicants until eleven'.[43] In fact, for some time prior to this, the temperance movement had been campaigning for 'the more modest target of ten o'clock closing'.[44] In the eyes of temperance campaigners aiming to protect families and create happy homes, the most dangerous time for families was straight after whatever hour a hotel closed. Thus, according to Anglican Archbishop Francis Bertie Boyce, the president of the NSW Alliance, which promoted early closing: 'It is unquestionable that the last hours of the liquor business are the worst and the most perilous. Thousands are in bars and parlours drinking who should be at home with their families.'[45]

The idea that carefully managed closing times could help reduce social harms would re-emerge in the twenty-first century as a reaction to late-night closing and 24-hour trading and the re-emergence of binge drinking as a conspicuous social problem in Australia. The focus today is not so much on domestic violence, but on interpersonal violence and self-harm among the primarily young patrons who drink until the early hours of the morning and then spill out of venues. Though alcohol's role in promoting violence is more widely understood, domestic violence issues have been largely reframed around wider social issues of the abuse of power in gender roles — the effect of patriarchy rather than of a product.

As industrialised nations began their love affair with the motor car, a new alcohol-related harm was created — motor car accidents caused by drink-driving. The idea of a motor vehicle crash being an 'accident' did little to focus concern on reducing the related alcohol harms. Well into the 1960s, many drunks would hop behind the wheel with the attitude that any 'accident' that happened on the way home would be, by definition, simply a case of bad luck. By the end of the century, however, our attitude to drink-driving had changed dramatically, largely because of the effect of drink-driving legislation.

The deadly effects of drink driving as depicted by cartoonist Ian Gall in the *Australian Temperance Advocate*, **May-June 1957.** (Courtesy Drug-Arm)

When talking about vehicle incidents collectively, mention is usually made of a road 'toll', but in individual cases the term 'accident' is still widely used. Nevertheless, in some quarters the idea of the 'accident' is being reconsidered. Trauma researchers, for example, argue that 'motor vehicle crash' should replace 'motor vehicle accident' in the lexicon of traumatologists. 'Crash' encompasses a wider range of potential causes for vehicular crashes than does the term 'accident'. Specifically, a majority of fatal crashes 'are caused by intoxicated, speeding, distracted, or careless drivers and, therefore, are not accidents'.[46] It is argued that properly assigning blame to intoxicated or negligent drivers can help change behaviour, and even help victims to overcome any sense of fatalism and speed their recovery.

Patrons at Sydney's Northern Club Hotel celebrate ten o'clock closing in 1955, an end to the six o'clock swill. Only eight years earlier the electorate had voted overwhelmingly to retain six o'clock closing. (Mitchell Library)

In 1947, the New South Wales electorate voted overwhelmingly to retain six o'clock closing, but by the 1950s and 60s governments and Australian society in general had relaxed their attitudes towards alcohol restrictions. Early closing laws were repealed by state governments across Australia, allowing hotels to close later in the evening. As it slowly emerged from many years of living under emergency war measures into a period of prosperity, post-war Australian society became more liberal on many social issues. Concern over drink-driving was an important exception. In the 1960s, states began to seriously look at passing laws, or strengthening existing laws, to control drivers who had consumed alcohol or other drugs. There was considerable opposition in some quarters, despite evidence that drink-driving had been the cause of carnage on the road for many decades, but by the mid-1970s all states had passed laws with harsher penalties for drink-driving offences.[47]

By the late 1970s, the legal blood alcohol limit for drivers was 0.08 per cent across Australia, except for Victoria where it was 0.05. Blood samples were usually taken to determine compliance with the law. In 1969, New South Wales implemented a breathalyser system, whereby drivers suspected of drink-driving or being involved in an accident could have their blood alcohol level read instantaneously via an instrument that measured the amount of alcohol in the breath. During 1974, the New South Wales government ran a series of mass media advertisements to inform the public about drink-driving laws and depicting drink-drivers as 'slobs'. According to the New South Wales Bureau of Crime Statistics and Research, there was a subsequent drop in drink-driving. No concurrent changes had been

Twenty-five years after its introduction in 1982, random breath testing was estimated to have saved 20,000 lives in New South Wales alone.
(© Newspix/Dennis Manktelow)

detected in policing methods or in general drinking patterns, which suggested that the publicity campaign itself had worked to decrease drink-driving.[48]

In the 1980s, governments implemented random breath testing. Police stopped a sample of all motorists and asked them to breathe into the breathalyser, whether or not they had manifested any signs of driving while under the influence. This caused considerable debate between groups concerned for civil liberties and those concerned for public safety. The first driver was pulled over for a random breath test in New South Wales on 17 December 1982. Twenty-five years and 57.6 million breath tests later, the NSW Police Minister at the time, David Campbell, claimed that random breath tests had saved 20,000 lives. It seems unlikely that the majority of the community still objected to the practice — except, perhaps, the eighty drink-drivers still caught each day in New South Wales.[49]

The need to deal with the range of alcohol's known harms — personal, physiological, social and economic — stimulated interest in the search for a corresponding set of causes of those harms. In Australia, the first cause identified was *supply*, that 'wonderful sea of spirits' on which the early colony seemed to float. Early governors were aware that heavy drinking was largely a result of easy availability, and therefore sought to restrict and control the supply of spirits. Temperance campaigners in the nineteenth century, along with others wishing to increase restrictions upon the liquor industry in the twentieth century, also saw supply as a major factor influencing the degree of alcohol-related problems in Australian society. The only periods showing a significant decrease in drinking rates were the depressions of the 1890s and 1930s and other times of restricted access, confirming the primary role of the economic factor in reducing overall consumption. Drinking rates also declined, although less dramatically, throughout the second half of the nineteenth century in Victoria and New South Wales as European society normalised demographically, to the point where from the 1870s onwards the colonies' alcohol consumption rates were lower than British drinking rates, confirming the influences of social factors such as gender and isolation on rates of alcohol consumption.

As the colony grew, the effect of a more normal ratio of males to females went some way to confirming and countering another identifiable early cause of harmful drinking — the disruption of social networks though social isolation and social dislocation. The Botany Bay colony was not only makeshift and improvised, it was also the product of a society shaken up by major social and economic upheavals. At such times of major change, whether positive or negative, the customary mores of a society often become irrelevant or untenable and the practices surrounding the drinking of alcohol are no exception. Indisputably, drinking patterns increase dramatically at times of great social change, such as the spirits craze that accompanied the industrial revolution in Britain and the patterns of heavy binge drinking during the gold rushes in Australia.[50]

The key influences of social and economic factors on alcohol consumption were not widely acknowledged in the eighteenth and nineteenth centuries. As discussed earlier, religious, moral and legal interpretations of alcohol abuse were more prominent at these times, along with ideas from temperance groups about supply being the problem factor with regard to alcohol. The prevailing belief was that alcohol caused social problems, rather than social problems causing alcohol problems. These ideas generally fell under the 'moral' model of conceptualising alcohol problems. At best, these ideas accepted that degrees of agency and responsibility did exist in the lives of those with alcohol problems; at worst, these ideas were not only moral but also moralising, condemning the abuser to their fate. However, there were equally moral views in the latter half of the nineteenth century that held that alcohol itself and its ready supply created social problems, rather than these being caused by the individual alcoholic. By the late nineteenth century it became more common, especially among temperance advocates, to see alcoholics as victims rather than free agents.[51] This kind of thinking took note of the physical and moral decline of the alcoholic, but placed blame for the problem on alcohol itself and its easy availability. Hence, the term 'moral' could denote concern for both the wellbeing of the victims of alcohol dependence, in that they were at risk of poverty, ill health and the crime that often ensued, and for the social responsibilities of the suppliers of alcohol, chiefly publicans, brewers and distillers. Alcohol consumption was still a moral problem, but it was a problem of social morality, not just personal morality.

Wherever there are harms, moral judgments will closely follow. These days, it is increasingly less common to treat moral weakness as a cause of alcohol abuse. As the nineteenth century progressed, medicine, science and social science were beginning to ask questions about the other causes of alcohol abuse, in what was believed to be a detached, scientific manner. By the latter half of the nineteenth century, scientific and medical ideas were coming from continental Europe and North America, as well as from the British Isles. In Europe and the United States, alcohol abuse, or 'inebriety' as it was then known, began to be seen as a discrete health issue.[52] Medical explanations for alcohol abuse flourished, as did ideas for methods of treatment. In 1849, the term 'alcoholism' was coined by Swedish doctor Magnus Huss, who took a special interest in alcohol problems; it was followed by new terms such as 'dipsomania', and also the term 'narcomania' for those abusing other drugs.[53] From the 1870s onwards, alcohol problems began to be seen as a specialist domain for doctors.[54] Still, the medical model did not entirely exclude previous moral ideas, and medical researchers struggled to balance concerns about personal choice and responsibility for supply as factors in the development of alcoholism, with the involuntary medical

DRUNKENNESS

Or the LIQUOR HABIT positively CURED

by administering **EUCRASY.**

It can be given in a cup of coffee or tea or food without the knowledge of the person taking it. Perfectly harmless, and will effect a permanent and speedy cure. It never fails. Pamphlet containing full particulars and testimonials sent sealed free on application to

THE EUCRASY COY.,

62 HUNTER STREET, SYDNEY;

Or 271 COLLINS STREET, MELBOURNE.

At the end of the nineteenth century, alcohol problems were beginning to be seen as medical, rather than moral problems. This advertisement appeared in *The Bulletin*, March 1900, promising to cure 'the liquor habit'.

consequences that ensued.[55] In one way, science had not removed morality from the picture; it had merely redefined the issues in terms of free will versus determinism.

By the late nineteenth century, medical ideas on alcoholism began to be influenced by eugenics and social Darwinism. In France, a theory of 'moral degeneration' became popular among some doctors and policy-makers, who stipulated that medical problems such as alcoholism were inherited and would become more intense with each generation, hence causing a degeneration of the human race over time.[56] In 1909 in the UK, Dr Caleb Williams Saleeby published the first systematic book on eugenics, *Parenthood and Race Culture*, in which he argued that alcohol consumption was a destructive influence on individuals and their offspring, contending that a 'race poison' was caused by alcohol, among other things, which damaged 'germ tissues, and constituted a danger to future generations'.[57]

Persons with 'defects in mental mechanism, generally congenital, sometimes, more or less acquired' must be prevented from breeding.[58] Saleeby, who had given up his gynaecological practice to dedicate his time to eugenics education, contributed temperance chapters to the *Children's Encyclopaedia* and the monthly *My Magazine* for children of the British Empire, much of it reprinted in the New South Wales Department of Education *School Magazine*.

Eugenics theories were welcomed by many in temperance circles because they appeared to replace moral views with scientific ones. One of the founders of the Eugenics Education Society of Melbourne in 1912, Dr Harvey Sutton, was later professor and director of the School of Public Health and Tropical Medicine at the University of Sydney. His 'scientific' temperance lectures to fifth-year medicine students and Diploma of Education students in the 1940s were preceded by a lecture on heredity and eugenics. He would quote from various scientific authorities to argue that 'the chief enemy of the race' was alcohol, followed by syphilis, mental deficiency, tuberculosis and lead. In his published lectures, he elaborated on the significance of race, maintaining that 'our race today is relatively sober because of the fatal results on less resistant stocks by the extraordinary wave of drunkenness of the eighteenth century (especially the first half)'.[59]

Views such as Professor Harvey's provided an aura of scientism that helped to legitimise the presence of temperance education in Australian schools throughout much of the twentieth century, though it's doubtful that his eugenics views were fully understood or shared by the bulk of faithful campaigners more inspired by a sense of moral and religious duty. For those medical thinkers who subscribed to them, eugenics theories resolved the dilemma of reconciling the conflicting issues of choice and compulsion in alcoholism; individuals were suffering from a hereditary condition. Eugenics theories presented an unsympathetic view of alcohol-related medical problems with an inner logic aimed towards eradicating the sufferer rather than curing the disease. The new emphasis on genetics and race also had implications for the conceptualising of alcoholism, as it was no longer seen as merely a threat to public order but as a threat to the health of 'the race'.

Just as personal morality had to make room for social morality, so too did personal medicine make room for social medicine. Concurrent developments in tropical health in Australia and other European colonies placed a new emphasis on the importance of considering the health of a people as a group over the health of the individual. Colonial powers had to develop a new discipline to deal with relatively unfamiliar health problems, as well as to address anxieties as to the viability of the colonies in unfamiliar and often inhospitable environments.[60] As a result, medical issues were now seen as impacting seriously on the public good. There was a shift from viewing alcohol abuse in terms of private health consequences and public legal and moral consequences to viewing it as also having public health consequences. The private versus public perspectives on alcohol problems were debated over the next decades, but by the 1950s and 60s, there was a renewed public interest in alcoholism as an illness.[61] This 'disease' model of alcohol abuse was most widely promoted by the organisation Alcoholics Anonymous (AA), which began in the United States in the 1930s and was established in Australia in 1945. Currently it remains far and away the most successful agency in the treatment of alcoholism.

AA played a significant role in changing public attitudes towards alcohol abuse at a time when medical attitudes were being changed by practitioners specialising in the treatment of alcohol problems. A major medical work, *The Disease Concept of Alcoholism*, was published in 1960 by American doctor E. M. Jellinek, who sought to define alcoholism as an illness. According to Jellinek, the major problem with dealing with alcohol harms was the fact that by the 1960s alcoholism was seen as 'either an economic, a psychological, a physiological or a sociological problem to the exclusion of the other aspects and no matter how much each type of researcher acknowledges these other aspects, they always come back to their own'.[62] He believed that all of these aspects played a role in alcohol abuse, and developed a classification of five types of alcoholism based on behavioural and social aspects of the drinking problem being classified, the causes of alcoholism in each patient and its various manifestations.[63] At the same time, Jellinek concluded his work by stating that: 'Generally, it may be said not only of the public at large but of the medical profession, industry and labour and all the other sections of public opinion, that their feeling is that the idea that "alcoholism" is an illness "is true, but not really true". This feeling will persist until the disease conception of alcoholism attains to clarity and definitiveness.'[64] Jellinek's aim was to medically classify alcoholism as a disease so that people of all walks of life, including his own colleagues, would acknowledge its extent and seriousness and therefore make a positive response towards it. He attempted to include non-medical aspects of alcohol abuse into his classifications, including factors such as cultural practices and norms; and argued that a lack of accurate knowledge was the reason for alcoholics not being treated seriously or properly by the medical profession. Jellinek's work represented an optimistic view that education and clarity could help in the diagnosis and, hopefully, the successful and non-judgmental treatment of alcoholics.

Just over a decade later, the emphasis shifted again: this time from the definition of alcoholism as a disease to the definition of alcohol as an addictive substance that created 'dependence' in the drinker. In 1976, using Jellinek's classifications as a basis, two medical researchers, Griffith Edwards and Milton Gross, published a highly influential paper on alcohol dependence, preferring the newly coined medical term to the more colloquial term 'addiction'. They developed a list of criteria for dependence by which a doctor could determine whether or not a patient was addicted to alcohol. The paper was significant because it introduced the idea that dependence existed at one end of a spectrum of alcohol use and misuse — from controlled use to dangerous use to dependence — with a sliding scale of harms in between.[65] The article also emphasised that, notwithstanding issues of heredity, *anyone* who drank alcohol to excess was capable of becoming dependent on it as a substance. Edwards and Gross concluded: 'Without withdrawing sympathy from the non-dependent drinker who is experiencing harm, society should be asked to realise that the person who has become dependent on alcohol is certainly ill; and the possibility of contracting this illness awaits anyone who drinks very heavily.'[66]

Edwards and Gross's paper became the basis for the idea that without necessarily being an alcoholic, or alcohol dependent, a person who consumes excessive amounts of alcohol could be doing themselves significant harm. It argued that social, biological and behavioural factors were the basis of the dependence syndrome;[67] and further medicalised the problem of alcohol abuse without denying the influence of non-medical factors (although it acknowledged that the relative roles of these various factors in creating dependence were unclear) and without apportioning blame to the drinker or any other single factor. It also argued that the assessment of dependence had serious implications, as a patient dependent on alcohol would most likely need to become abstinent for recovery of health. The paper became the basis for the classifications of dependence in the Diagnostic and Statistical Manual of Mental Disorders (DSM-IV), published by the American Psychiatric Association. Hence, by the mid-1970s, the idea of alcohol being an addictive substance and alcohol dependence being an illness caused by a variety of factors, both medical and non-medical, which required specific treatment became formalised in medical circles.

Still, the 'disease' model of alcoholism was not fully embraced by the medical profession. Many did not see it as a disease in the same sense as other medical illnesses because of the element of free will supposedly involved, at least prior to addiction. Furthermore, while alcohol abuse has the ability to cause significant medical problems, medical researchers have not been able to isolate a definitive biological cause for the 'disease', as is the case for instance with infectious diseases, nor have they been able to prove that there is an underlying disease or predisposition that makes some people more susceptible to addiction than others.[68] Nevertheless, the disease concept of alcoholism had the profound social effect of removing at least some of the negative stigma and blame from alcohol-dependent patients by presenting them as sufferers of a disease in need of treatment, rather than persons with a weak will or weak morals. It also opened up further debates about the causes of alcohol abuse and, by implication, who should address them and how.

This was taken up from the 1980s onwards, when a renewed public health approach to substance abuse problems became the most prominent method of addressing alcohol abuse in Australia. This approach, focusing on the 'big picture', aimed to bring together prevention, early intervention, harm minimisation, health care, education, community issues and justice issues in a 'whole of community' strategy.[69]

In Australia, alcoholism treatment policy went through various stages. As the earliest ideas on alcohol abuse in colonial Australia were legal and moral ones, and there was a major preoccupation with public order, the earliest response to drunkenness was simply punitive. Public drunkenness was commonly punished by public flogging, imprisonment, forced labour or sentencing to a chain gang.[70] As the convict era passed, imprisonment continued to be the most common way of treating drunkenness. Nevertheless, the problem remained that people became seriously ill or disabled, physically and/or mentally, due to their chronic, heavy use of alcohol. Instead of being imprisoned, chronic 'inebriates' were sent to asylums. Although these institutions had different aims, they were in many ways similar to penal institutions. They were run by administrators, not doctors, whose main role was to keep the patients in good order and away from society. Once the penal period ended, colonists were keen to make Australia more respectable. Many, especially those who had come here of their own free will as settlers, had a strong ethic of individual improvement and were keen that evidence of social distress should not be visible on the streets.[71] However, segregating those with alcohol problems within asylums meant that in the public mind alcoholism became equated with mental illness, further stigmatising the condition.[72]

In the mid-nineteenth century, medical personnel began to take over the administration of asylums. In 1846, there was criticism of the fact that the asylum at Tarban Creek at Hunters Hill in north-western Sydney (which later became the Gladesville Mental Hospital) was run by an administrator rather than a doctor.[73] J. T. Digby, who had run Tarban Creek from its beginnings in 1838, was replaced in 1848 by Dr Francis Campbell.[74] From 1870s onwards, many large, medically run state asylums were established, often in the countryside or on large estates, and there was a definite move away from incarceration towards treating 'habitual inebriates' as patients needing cure. In 1899, a Victorian inquiry into the treatment of 'habitual drunkards' recommended that institutions that offered a specifically tailored medical response, along with strict discipline, were a more appropriate solution than incarceration.[75]

The use of mental asylums for the treatment of alcohol problems became even more entrenched at the turn of the twentieth century. In 1900, an Inebriates Act was passed in New South Wales that allowed those charged repeatedly with alcohol-related offences to be committed to an asylum rather than prison. In 1909, the Act was amended to include those who did not have repeat convictions but could not afford private treatment. In 1912, a new Inebriates Act was passed in New South Wales, which included definitions of crimes that could lead to a conviction: namely, not only drunkenness, but also alcohol-affected assault of a woman, child abuse, attempted suicide and wilful damage to property.[76] This new act took seriously the ideas being promoted by some alcohol reformers that alcohol caused crime and social disruption. It also included the medical model: perpetrators were sent to institutions for treatment, rather than to gaol.[77] This new medical solution did not entirely remove the previous criminal stigma of alcohol-related disruption; instead, doctors had now joined the legal profession in passing judgment. Furthermore, while the new way of assessing the problem was meant to be detached and 'scientific', in practice it included moral judgments as well. Alcoholic behaviour continued to be seen as a threat to public order, especially when exhibited by the poor and homeless.[78] Significantly, in 2008 a revamped version of the Inebriates Act was reestablished in New South Wales.

Until the latter twentieth century, alcohol itself was often used as a medical treatment, and such use was widespread in the period leading up to World War I. Doctors used alcohol as a tonic, as a cure for various conditions such as fever, pneumonia and infections, and also as an anaesthetic.[79] At one stage, the Melbourne Children's Hospital spent more on alcohol than on all other medicines, giving an indication of how entrenched its use was.[80] The extent to which alcohol damage or dependence resulted from medical care is impossible to gauge. In the late nineteenth century, other addictive drugs — for example, opiates — were sometimes used to treat or manage alcohol withdrawal symptoms. This treatment had the potential effect of giving the patient an opiate addiction.

By the 1940s, support for public treatment facilities in Australia had diminished, and a revival of state interest in alcoholism treatment would not return until the 1960s, when attitudes towards alcohol became more liberal.[81] This renewal of interest coincided with the new ideas about the disease model of alcoholism and the sense of optimism that ensued. In 1959, the Langton Clinic in inner Sydney was the first public hospital in Australia devoted completely to alcoholism treatment. It was set up as a voluntary admission hospital, and in the 1970s became a hospital for the treatment of other drug dependence as well.[82] After the establishment of the Langton Clinic, various hospitals around Australia began to open their own alcoholism treatment centres; and during the 1970s halfway houses sprang up, providing a stepping stone between specialised treatment centres and the outside world.

Residential rehabilitation centres or 'therapeutic communities' were also established in Australia in the 1970s. The focus of such communities allowed participants to resolve their general life problems rather than focusing purely on the drug itself, although time spent in a therapeutic community was normally one of supportive abstinence, with the aim of staying abstinent after leaving. As with so many Australian responses to alcohol problems, the major influences for these communities came from Britain and the United States. Therapeutic communities started in the 1940s in England, when psychiatrist Maxwell Jones set up a residential community at Belmont Hospital in Sutton, as an alternative to medical treatment for youth with behavioural problems.[83] In 1958, the first drug-free community was set up in California for rehabilitation of drug users.[84] In Australia, one of the earliest examples of a therapeutic community was The Buttery, housed in an old butter factory on the north coast of New South Wales. It was founded in 1973 by an Anglican Church officer, John McKnight, who set it up as an outreach ministry for young people going to Nimbin for the Aquarius Festival in 1972. The Aquarius Festival was a celebration of alternative music and culture and was expected to include high incidences of drug use. The ministry would care for people who might find themselves in need of assistance during the festival. It was initially a Christian organisation, but expanded to include the twelve-step program used by Alcoholics Anonymous and provided contemporary medical, psychological and social assistance for alcohol and other drug problems. By the 1990s, The Buttery was using a combination of group therapy, education, life skills instruction, stress management, a twelve-step program and self-help.[85]

The twelve-step program used by The Buttery and other residential communities was taken directly from Alcoholics Anonymous. However, mutual help organisations existed prior to the advent of AA, the earliest groups being those influenced by temperance movements, such as The Washingtonians, set up in the 1840s in the United States. The earliest institutions for the exclusive treatment of alcohol problems were private boarding houses set up in the nineteenth century by charitable institutions. These houses provided 'moral treatment', which was an earlier version of the therapeutic community approach.[86] In the eighteenth and nineteenth centuries, the word 'moral', along with its modern meaning, also denoted a person's psychological and emotional state. 'Moral treatment' was therefore an early version of psychological or group therapy.[87] Treatment included input from temperance society members and committees and often included both a pleasant environment and religious instruction.[88] Doctors became involved in treatment on a voluntary or advisory basis, but the institutions themselves were run by non-medical staff.[89] In the next century, when AA spread across the globe and began to penetrate Australia, similar ideas of self-help were espoused, along with an embracing of the disease model of alcoholism.

In the 1970s, the 'controlled drinking' controversy developed, which was centred in the United States but was also of consequence in Australia.[90] This was a behavioural modification method that attempted to train people with alcohol problems to drink moderately. Controversy over this treatment erupted among researchers, with some arguing that controlled drinking was the best viable outcome for a person with an alcohol problem and others arguing that abstinence was the only viable option for such a person. Currently, the medical belief is that alcohol-dependent people should be advised to become abstinent, whereas people who have alcohol problems but are not dependent may possibly be able to learn to drink moderately.[91]

During the 1940s, the medical profession began to develop medication to treat alcoholism. The first was a nausea-inducing drug, disulfiram (trade names Antabuse and Antabus). Such drugs were to be used in conjunction with psychological treatment, but their overall long-term results were marginal.[92] In the 1990s, anti-craving drugs were developed, also to be used in conjunction with psychological treatment; their effectiveness is still being assessed.

There were precursors to pharmacological treatment in the nineteenth century, such as the bi-chloride of gold solution used in the various retreats set up by Dr James Wolfenden in Melbourne in the 1890s, and originally taken from Dr Keeley in the US. Dr Wolfenden administered this treatment in the context of 'religious temperance', a form of 'moral treatment' and pleasant surroundings. He claimed a success rate of 72 per cent for men and 98 per cent for women.[93] These results seem extraordinary; and how such success was measured and how long after treatment abstinence continued is impossible to ascertain. Nevertheless, the development of medications in the twentieth and twenty-first centuries, with their incorporation of psychological interventions, were an extension of the late nineteenth century's practice of combining medical and psychological treatment.

Regardless of the model used to describe and understand alcohol abuse, a recurrent feature of all treatments is their relatively low rate of success. Currently, alcohol dependence is seen as a 'chronic, relapsing disorder', but remarks on the high rate of recidivism in alcohol treatment may be found across the centuries.[94] This feature of alcohol dependence has also meant that trends in responses to alcohol abuse have wavered between optimism and pessimism. Jellinek's disease concept of alcoholism and Edwards and Gross's description of dependence were both developed in a spirit of optimism, and at a time when the welfare state was flourishing in the western world after World War II. Despite the early relative optimism of the post-World War II period, the continuing difficulties faced in treating alcoholism have led to a greater focus on prevention and big-picture methods of controlling and reducing alcohol problems.[95] Alcoholics Anonymous and its offshoot, Narcotics Anonymous, are still the most successful long-term agencies in producing recovery from addiction. Years ago, Dr Joe Santamaria (a brother of B.A. 'Bob' Santamaria) had famously written this referral for a haughty Toorak matriarch with a major booze problem: 'I prescribe large doses of Alcoholics Anonymous for this reluctant debutante!' The address on the front of the envelope was the Central Office of AA in Victoria.

Speaking at a Sydney Conference in 2008, Stephen Post, of Case Western University in Cleveland, Ohio, said that 'the reason that sobriety rates were higher among those who followed the twelve step program of Alcoholics Anonymous was that AA is based on alcoholics helping each other. Similarly, depression rates among sufferers of multiple sclerosis fell among those who made a brief 'compassionate' phone call to others suffering from the same condition.[96] It seems that with regard to alcohol, we are always going back to the drawing board, cataloguing its manifold harms, searching for their causes, and exploring options for eliminating, or at least alleviating, them. Like the blind men in the Hindu myth who try to describe an elephant, each age and generation seem able to describe with authority only that part of the problem that it has in hand at the time.

CHAPTER 6

A Taste of Discrimination

In 1838, a mere fifty years after the founding of the colony in New South Wales, the first law was passed prohibiting the supply of alcohol to Aborigines. Similar laws were passed in other states,[1] making alcohol consumption illegal for Aboriginal people, those of mixed descent and Pacific Islanders and Polynesians in Queensland. The only exception was a small minority of people who had been granted special citizenship rights.[2] Prohibition based on race was clear discrimination. As Maggie Brady recounts: 'It was humiliating, a shame job, not to be able to go into a pub and buy a beer alongside white people, or to have a policeman smelling your breath to see if you had been drinking.'[3] In the early twentieth century, civil rights leaders such as William Harris in Western Australia campaigned not only for suffrage for Aboriginal people but also for the right to enter a public house. Without that right, he argued, Aborigines were 'virtually excluded from a district's social life and the opportunity for contacts leading to employment'.[4] During the 1960s, state governments across Australia began to give Aboriginal people the legal right to drink alcohol. In 1967, a referendum was passed by which the white Australian population agreed to allow Aboriginal people to be counted as Australian citizens and, therefore, to be given full citizenship rights, including the right to vote and to drink alcohol. Unfortunately, the association of 'drinking rights' with citizenship has had a long-term negative impact on Aboriginal drinking culture, becoming one of the factors that led to a significant increase in drinking rates and subsequent problems of domestic violence and child abuse in Aboriginal communities.[5]

Arguably, it wasn't alcohol itself but the combined effects of alcohol and European civilisation that devastated many Aboriginal communities. Contrary to the accepted belief that Aboriginal people had no alcohol prior to the British colonisation of Australia, many early governmental papers and private travel journals describe how

Charlie Perkins (second from the right) and his Freedom Riders visited the Burlington Hotel, in Haymarket, Sydney in March 1965 and drank beer without incident. Because Aboriginal people had long been denied the right to vote and the right to drink alcohol, 'drinking rights' became associated with citizenship. (Ted Golding/Fairfaxphotos)

fermented drinks and other drugs were a part of the pre-colonisation Aboriginal diet and culture. For instance, a drink made from the sap of a gum tree in Tasmania (*Eucalyptus gunnii*) was described by G. A. Robinson, Protector of Aborigines in Tasmania in the 1820s and 1830s, as an intoxicant.[6] In western Queensland, a fermented drink was made from bauhinia blossoms (a tropical plant) and wild honey. The process was described in the writings of a white settler woman in 1933:

> From the honey-filled blossoms the blacks make a semi-intoxicating drink. When the bauhinias for miles around come into bloom the gins [sic] pick the blossoms off in coolamonfuls. These are pounded, and the sweet golden liquid drained off into a larger, deeper coolamon [a vessel made of wood or bark for carrying water], then mixed with sugar-bag or ant honey and set aside to ferment, a process which takes eight or ten days.[7]

The pituri plant, a desert shrub whose leaves contain a high level of nicotine, about four times as high as that of tobacco leaves,[8] was traded widely across the Australian continent pre-colonisation and used both as a social drug and to stave off hunger.[9] The dried leaves were mixed with ash and chewed, or kept behind the ear when not being chewed, acting as the equivalent of a nicotine patch.[10] Traditionally, pituri was used only by mature people and was distributed by tribal members who held the legal authority to do so.[11] While it's not known exactly how many tribes used intoxicants and pituri, their use was geographically widespread, suggesting that many tribes had at least come across one or both substances, while others were regular users. Many Aboriginal people, therefore, may not have been as naïve users of alcohol as was often assumed by the British.

Nevertheless, both the strength and quantity of the imported alcohol was greater than local intoxicants, making it possible to become drunk more quickly and more often. More importantly, the fact that the production and distribution of European alcohol was not under Aboriginal control meant that the tribes no longer had the authority and ability to regulate the use of the potentially addictive substances available to them.[12]

Controlling Aboriginal people's access to all addictive substances, even those they had traditionally used themselves, seemed important to the European newcomers in the nineteenth and early twentieth centuries. In the Channel Country of Queensland, colonisers, knowing that pituri was highly prized (and also highly addictive, considering its nicotine content), collected it and used it as payment for itinerant Aboriginal farm workers. Thus, a substance previously under Aboriginal control was appropriated by colonisers to exploit Aboriginal people. Pituri continued to be used for payment by many settlers in the area until it was replaced by government tobacco rations.[13] Tobacco was used as payment to Aborigines engaged in pastoral work in Queensland and elsewhere, or handed out as rations in settlements and missions across Australia, up until the 1960s, when Aboriginal people were introduced to the cash economy through equal pay for stock-workers and access to the social security payments.[14] One result of this practice was that by 2002 the Aboriginal population had almost double the level of tobacco use as the non-Aboriginal population in Australia (56 per cent of Aboriginal men and 46 per cent of Aboriginal women as opposed to 27 per cent of non-Aboriginal men and 20 per cent of non-Aboriginal women).[15]

The figures for contemporary alcohol use by Aboriginal people are quite different. Across Australia, 15 per cent of Aboriginal people have never drunk alcohol, which is similar to the figure of 13 per cent for non-Aboriginal people. Also, there are fewer Aboriginal regular drinkers in Australia (33 per cent) than non-Aboriginal regular drinkers (45 per cent). The rates are much higher, however, for people who have stopped drinking, with 22 per cent of Aboriginal people being ex-drinkers as opposed to 9 per cent of non-Aboriginal people. Within the group of regular drinkers, 68 per cent of Aboriginal regular drinkers drink at hazardous levels (meaning an average of more than four standard drinks a day for a man and more than two for a woman), as opposed to 11 per cent of non-Aboriginal regular drinkers. Overall, 22 per cent of the whole Aboriginal population drinks at hazardous levels.[16] When polled on substance abuse within their communities, 66 per cent of Indigenous respondents nominated alcohol as the drug that caused most deaths, and 55 per cent nominated alcohol as the drug causing the most serious concern or worry for Indigenous people generally. A third of those concerned about alcohol in their communities reported violence as their major worry with respect to alcohol abuse.[17] Ten per cent of Aboriginal deaths are due to alcohol, as opposed to 3 per cent non-Aboriginal deaths.[18] In the 1991 Report of the Royal Commission into Aboriginal Deaths in Custody, alcohol abuse was identified as a major cause of the high rate of Aboriginal incarceration in Australia and a contributing factor in a number of deaths that occurred in custody during the period investigated.[19]

The figures above suggest that the overall Aboriginal population is split between a high number of total abstainers, who have either never drunk alcohol or who are ex-drinkers, and a high number of heavy drinkers. In the past, genetic theories have been used to explain the high incidence of problem drinking in the Aboriginal population; however, as yet scientists have found no alcohol-related genetic differences between Aboriginal and non-Aboriginal people.[20] Both eliminate alcohol through the liver at the same rate (10 grams of pure alcohol per hour).[21] The only alcohol-related genetic differences, to date, have been found in Asian populations.

About 50 per cent of Japanese people, and a similar proportion of other Asian nationalities, have an inactive form of the enzyme aldehyde dehydrogenase, which normally breaks down alcohol. When these people drink alcohol, they experience instant nausea and become flushed in the face; an unpleasant effect that acts as a protective factor against alcohol abuse.[22] As Aboriginal people show no such genetic response to alcohol, it is hard to deny the traumatic effect of colonisation as a significant contributing factor to the population's high incidence of alcohol problems. Similar drinking patterns have been seen in other indigenous populations that have had comparable historical experiences with colonisation and alcohol, such as various Pacific populations and the indigenous people of North America.[23]

Augustus Earl (1783–1838) painted these contrasting portraits of Bungaree, the 'King of the Aborigines', perhaps hinting at the cause of his demise at the age of 30. In the latter work, Bungaree's wife, Cora Gooseberry, is shown with her trademark clay pipe. She often sat with her family outside the Cricketer's Arms Hotel in Pitt Street, Sydney. The owner of the hotel allowed her to sleep in his hotels. She lived to be 75 years old. (National Library of Australia)

★   ★   ★

During the early decades of colonisation, giving alcohol to Aborigines was not illegal. The British supplied European alcohol as payment for work, for sexual services and to provide themselves with entertainment by making Aboriginal people drunk and then encouraging them to fight.[24] With time, and as a response to public order issues, various colonial governments made it illegal to supply alcohol to Aborigines and for Aborigines to consume alcohol (although in some instances employers were given government permission to pay Aboriginal workers in alcohol.),[25] so Aboriginal people relied on 'go-getters', or so-called 'bullockies', to buy grog for them, or it was sold to them illegally from the back of the pub.[26] This illegality may have contributed to heavy drinking, especially binge drinking, in Aboriginal communities as alcohol would be obtained at unpredictable intervals and needed to be consumed surreptitiously and quickly for the drinkers to avoid being prosecuted and jailed.[27]

Arguably, the drinking of alcohol was sometimes, if not often, an act of defiance against the authorities who made it illegal to drink.[28] However, in the post-prohibition era, alienation and hopelessness became greater factors in alcohol abuse. Without land, which is the basis of the Aboriginal economy and also of identity and religion, many Aboriginal people have found it difficult to sustain strong and meaningful communities. Richard Trudgen, author of *Why Warriors Lie Down and Die*, had this to say about the situation of the Yolngu people of Arnhem Land in 2000:

> These days, receiving welfare is the central Yolngu
> economic activity. Welfare leads to a level of
> dependence that is crippling and creates loss of roles,
> loss of mastery and, above all, hopelessness. And

221

hopelessness in turn translates into destructive social
behaviour — neglect of responsibility, drug abuse,
violence, self-abuse, homicide, incest and suicide.[29]

The last group of Aboriginal people to be given their full citizenship
rights, including the right to buy and drink alcohol, were the people of
the Kimberley region of Western Australia in 1971, although some had
been granted citizenship rights after World War II. Additionally, in the
Kimberley region, mandatory payment of wages for pastoral work
wasn't introduced until the late 1950s, and equal wages with whites
until the 1960s. By the late sixties and early seventies, pastoral job
opportunities were decreasing as fences, set water holes, roads and aerial
mustering meant less need for itinerant manual labour. Aboriginal
people in the Kimberley moved away from pastoral stations, which were
on their traditional lands, to town and fringe settlements.[30] Alcohol
became legally available to Kimberley Aborigines at a time of great and
often traumatic changes. Currently, the majority of Aboriginal drinkers
in the Kimberley drink at harmful levels.[31]

The dispossession that brought about such a state of
powerlessness in Aboriginal communities was a product of the
expansion of the frontier across the continent, which persisted well
into the twentieth century. A study of the Diamond Well Mission (a
fictitious name given to a northern Australian Aboriginal
community) provides an illustration of how alcohol was introduced
into remote communities. At the time of the study (1984), Diamond
Well had existed as a community for about eighty years. It consisted
of a population of about 300 Aboriginal people and between twenty
and thirty white people, mainly government-employed workers. The
community began during the 1910s to the 1930s, when Aboriginal
people started to migrate from surrounding areas to settle near a
permanent water soak — previously only travelled to for rituals, or
used as a temporary settlement during times of drought — in

response to pastoral encroachment on their lands. At the same time, a railway line was being built through the desert and the railway authorities tapped water from the soak. Contact was made between the Aboriginal groups living there and the railway workers.[32] The railway workers brought in alcohol, although they were banned from drinking while working on the project, and began to exchange booze with Aboriginal people, although this too was illegal.[33] In this way, covert supplies of alcohol became part of the soak community's economy. Over time, the Aboriginal people living at the soak became less able to remain independent and government rations and basic medical care were introduced, which encouraged more local Aboriginal people to move there from their traditional lands. The United Aborigines Mission (UAM) came to the soak in 1933 and built a church hall, mission house and children's dormitories in the 1940s.[34] An attempt was made to convert the population to Christianity by segregating and indoctrinating the children and suppressing traditional ceremonies, although they continued clandestinely. In 1952, the mission at the soak was closed down.[35] The population was unable to hunt and gather because much of their land had been taken up by pastoral leases. There had also been nuclear testing, making sections of the country a serious health hazard. The population became dependent on welfare. The state government purchased a nearby pastoral property and leased it to the Lutherans, who set up the mission referred to as Diamond Well in the 1984 report, and the soak population moved unwillingly to the new mission. After several decades, the running of the community was handed over to the government, still under white administration and therefore perpetuating the problem of dependence.[36] Over the decades, serious drinking problems have escalated in the Diamond Well community.

In other remote areas of Australia, mining rather than pastoralism affected local Indigenous populations and led to the introduction of alcohol. One example of such a situation is Yirrkala in north-east Arnhem Land. Yirrkala was originally set up in 1935 as a Methodist mission, in response to the dispossession caused by the taking of Aboriginal land by pastoralists. Previously, North East Arnhem Land was quite isolated, with very little contact with white people, although regular trade had taken place for centuries with the Maccassans from Indonesia.[37] However, as the Northern Territory become more fully colonised, the government began to interfere with trade between Maccassans and Yolngu people, until that trade was no longer possible.[38] Along with the loss of traditional trading opportunities and lands, the local people had to adjust to the new lifestyle of living on a mission and a new religion, although the Yirrkala missionaries didn't ban Aboriginal ceremonies and people that converted to Christianity also continued with their original religious rituals.[39] The Yirrkala mission, therefore, became a place of relative safety and religious freedom, albeit one where a dispossessed population lived a radically different lifestyle from the traditional one they had known until very recently.

In 1963, the land between Yirrkala and Nhulunby (previously known as Gove) was excised by the Commonwealth government and granted to the Nabalco mining company, and in the late 1960s and early 1970s the bauxite mine and town of Gove were developed. The Yolngu people of the region protested against the loss of their land by sending a Bark Petition to the Commonwealth Parliament in 1963 requesting land rights, and later challenged the mine in court also on the basis of land rights. However, in 1971 the court ruled against the challenge and mining operations continued.[40] Along with objections to the mine itself, people were aware of the destructive social effects of the mine's influence. In the early 1980s, a series of documentary films, the Yirrkala Film Project, were made about various aspects of life in Yirrkala. One of the films, which focuses on religious practice, both old and new, shows a Yolgnu

Christian youth worker talking to the local Christian youth group. 'Our old people were wise,' he says. 'They warned us long before anything really changed, pointing out about land rights and about drink coming into the town of Nhulunby, all the buildings, and they said to us, "There will be a town and grog and all the other things white men will bring. Are you going to mix up in that or turn your back to our culture?"'[41]

The Yirrkala people were well aware of the potential social, as well as environmental, impact of the mine, including the influx of alcohol that would ensue. Perhaps their insight came from hearing of the experiences of other Aboriginal communities. Yet despite taking proactive steps to avoid such problems, they were ultimately prevented from success.

Although initially illegal, European alcohol became part of the way of life for the Yolngu of Yirrkala, as it had for other Indigenous communities. And with the end of prohibition for Aboriginal people, remote communities began to set up 'canteens' for the sale of alcohol. In many cases these were established under missionary administration, and later under local government as missions began to be taken over by shire councils. The Diamond Well Mission provides an example of how the process worked. Aboriginal people of the state in which Diamond Well is situated were granted legal drinking rights on 1 April 1965. The missionaries running the community needed to decide how to tackle the issue of supply[42] and so conducted a local opinion poll about whether or not alcohol should be made available for purchase on the mission. According to the missionaries, the idea was popular and an application was made for a licence. It was granted in 1968 and a canteen opened in 1969.

One of the aims of the missionaries was to encourage 'civilised' drinking habits by controlling how much alcohol, namely beer, each person could purchase.[43] Prior to the canteen being opened, alcohol was obtained by community members hiring a taxi or using an

225

available car to go to the nearest town to buy port. This was quite an expensive feat, requiring considerable organisation.[44] It also meant that as alcohol supply was irregular, relatively strong alcohol was purchased and binge drinking rather than regular, moderate usage was common. The missionaries were also keen to maintain control over the community by providing it with the things that residents would otherwise be able to obtain outside of it. A quote from a Lutheran magazine discussing the issue of canteens put forward the following argument: 'If a church wants to retain absolute control of an Aboriginal community, and it can only do so with the assistance of considerable funds, it must be prepared to provide all the services common to the local community.'[45] A canteen was established at Diamond Well and a small amount of beer was made available for purchase by each adult on a regular basis. The canteen was set up by a $20,000 loan, which was paid off in the first four years of its opening.[46] All further profits went towards a community cooperative fund. The canteen was also used as a recreation hall, becoming both a focal point of the community and a source of funding for community projects. Consequently, the legitimate, regular supply of alcohol became vital to community wellbeing.[47]

Canteens or community-run licensed clubs were established in many Aboriginal communities, with their proceeds often becoming an important source of funding for community council projects. The controversial nature of the dependence on these funds is related to the mixed results of the canteens themselves. The main question is whether they have achieved their aims, especially whether they have decreased drinking-related harms, or, instead, have promoted an increase in problem and addictive drinking. Although meant to provide a safe drinking environment, canteens have not stopped alcohol being brought into communities from other sources, and studies have shown that they have been associated with an increase in heavy drinking culture. Recent research in Cape York communities indicated that the presence of canteens decreases the number of abstainers and moderate drinkers in a community as heavy drinking becomes normalised and social life is focused on the canteen.[48] A study of seven of the eight Northern Territory communities with licensed clubs in 1994 and 1995 showed that all but one had significantly higher alcohol consumption rates than the national average. (The average rate for females was 183 per cent higher than the Northern Territory average, which was already 32 per cent higher than the national average. The average rate for men was 76 per cent higher than the Northern Territory average, which was already 42 per cent higher than national average.[49]) In Cape York, where canteens are common, alcohol consumption rates were found to be the highest in the world.[50] The presence of a canteen in Indigenous communities does not help to decrease drinking rates, and is most often associated with an increase, as well as creating dependence on the proceeds from the sale of alcohol in those communities.

Away from the atmosphere of the canteen, communal drinking in remote Aboriginal communities is also done in supposedly 'safe drinking camps' or drinking circles. Drinkers obtain alcohol from a variety of sources and join a drinking camp for days or a week, sometimes longer. Drinking is continuous and the aim is to become and remain completely drunk for the duration of the stay.[51] These camps are usually away from the main settlement and from other kinds of camps, such as hunting camps or camps where there are children present. They are supposedly governed by strict set of rules, such as not allowing under-aged people to participate and not interfering with nearby camps; and non-drunks are meant to be present as those drinking are considered not responsible for their own actions or safety.[52] The aim of the drinking camp is to allow alcoholic excess and binge drinking while minimising the negative impact of excessive drinking on the community. In practice, there is usually an adverse impact on the community, both in the short term as drinkers return to the community drunk and unsupervised, and also in the longer term through illness and early death. Between 1972 and 1982, alcohol was the direct cause of 30 per cent of deaths in Diamond Well, and between 1976 and 1982 there were 111 alcohol-related hospitalisations in a population of 300.[53]

Drinking alcohol creates a great deal of havoc in Indigenous communities, no matter how 'controlled' its context. This does not mean that Aboriginal communities or individual Aboriginal people are always unable to manage alcohol in the communities. It seems to suggest that these communities face many of the same challenges that faced the early settlers in Sydney Cove. But while those early settlers were able to bring institutions of law, medicine and administration familiar to them and developed over centuries to bear on the problems of dealing with alcohol in their communities, Aboriginal communities have had many of their own traditions destroyed or weakened and have been expected, almost overnight, either to create new institutions or adapt to those not of their choosing or under their control.

At one level, the problems facing the control or prohibition of alcohol in Indigenous communities are the same as elsewhere. After a period of initial success, consumers simply find other means to fulfil their wants. The demand for alcohol is rooted in stressful environmental conditions that influence individuals to choose to take up drink, but also in the addictive nature of alcohol which subverts an individual's ability to choose otherwise. At a deeper level, however, Aboriginal communities face a unique problem when trying to deal with alcohol abuse. According to anthropologists, 'demand sharing' is a strong part of Aboriginal society: people in kin relationships feel a pressure to share their possessions. According to the Indigenous leader Noel Pearson, director of the Cape York Institute, many abusive drinkers are bastardising Aboriginal cultural values and destroying whole communities: 'It's not barramundi or wild honey that is shared; it is money for drinking, drug-taking and gambling. Unconditional welfare plus addictions demand sharing; you have all the ingredients for social disintegration and the abandonment of responsibility.'[54] A major source of the problem, as Pearson sees it, is the weakening of traditional authority and social responsibility in Aboriginal communities through dependence on unconditional welfare. The recipient of this government largesse can pay for food, shelter and necessities, 'but, increasingly, as addictions grow, the money is allocated to grog, drugs and gambling'.[55]

Drinking circles did not become the zones of safety they were envisaged to be. Pearson argues that, over time, they no longer served any useful purpose, with drinkers manipulating the non-drinkers to feed, house and clothe them.[56] Younger men and women joined the drinking circle, leaving it to the older people — mainly women — to keep the community fed. The perverted sense of an individual 'right to drink' is not only underwritten by a communal obligation to share resources, it is also actively destroying the minds and bodies of a generation who should be shouldering the burdens of leadership and responsibility in their communities.

Group drinking is also practised in urban areas, although the context is quite different. Public group drinking often takes place between Aboriginal people from disparate backgrounds who find themselves displaced in towns or cities. Just as the pub in rural areas may be a forum in which strangers can meet, urban street drinking in communities such as Redfern and surrounding suburbs provides a place for poor, displaced Aboriginal people to meet and feel a sense of community. The song *Charcoal Lane*[57] by Aboriginal singer and songwriter Archie Roach vividly depicts the practice of street drinking as a way to stave off loneliness and provide a sense of camaraderie and short-lived euphoria in the midst of hopelessness and poverty.

Some argue that Aboriginal drinking styles were learnt from the 'work and bust' drinking habits of white rural workers.[58] Others maintain that drinking habits evolved out of the specific needs of Aboriginal communities, especially the need for empowerment.[59] To return to the Diamond Well community, researchers found that heavy group drinking was not solely a social or indulgent experience, but one that also brought about a sense of transformation and empowerment in the drinker:

> Drinkers have told us that when they are drunk they feel different from when they are sober. They feel themselves to have a greater facility with English and so are able to demonstrate that they belong to a world and discourse which is that in which decisions are made about the control and allocation of goods and services. Moreover, they feel that they can approach a European Australian as an equal in verbal interactions, not hindered by a lack of knowledge of the spoken word …

The researchers continued:

> Drinkers have also told us that the drinking experience is one in which they become bold and audacious in their interactions with Whites and are prepared to state the nature of past injustices and demand restitution. When matters of current concern are considered to be the product of unjust dealings, then the drinker may demand that a European Australian right wrongs. Drinkers in their transformed

state of forcefulness and linguistic facility establish
their non-compliance with European directives. If
necessary a drinker will back his requests or resistance
with threats of violence or make an actual assault.
Coupled with assaults on persons are attacks on
European Australian property.[60]

Hence, the state of inebriation may be used to enable a feeling of
empowerment in situations where real power is minimal. Inebriation,
along with the 'right to drink', to purchase alcohol and to enter a pub,
are used as a means of asserting freedom and power. However, in many
if not most regards the power and freedom expressed are illusory and
are mitigated by actual social and economic powerlessness.

Many Aboriginal communities today are polarised into two groups
— those who place an emphasis on 'drinking rights', and those who
believe drinking alcohol is a damaging influence on communities and
stifles revolutionary possibilities.[61] In many instances, the decision *not*
to drink is an expression of actual empowerment. One example of
someone making such a decision was Wenten Rubuntja, an
Aboriginal artist and land rights campaigner and Arrernte man from
the Hermannsburg Lutheran Mission in Central Australia. In his
memoir, Rubuntja explained that he had been a very heavy drinker,
but after a particularly bad drinking spell, and also after being inspired
by the land rights movement of the 1970s, he decided to stop
drinking alcohol and smoking cigarettes:

> I was a proper madman from drink — I used to live in
> the pub. I used to do painting in the beer garden …
> Then one night I there long Stuart Arms. I drink a lot
> and my ideas was a little bit collapsed … When I sat
> down, I saw the ground turning — coloured and
> spinning — like something had turned it around.

> Then I smashed this *ngkwarle* [grog] — I broke
> the three bottles. And I scratched this two
> Marlboro and throwem away. Righto. Me been just
> walk back. That was from 1976. Then I been just
> give up. Just finish. Then land rights start, then I
> just been see-em lands rights start. Then I been
> work for country.[62]

Another famous artist from Hermannsburg, Albert Namatjira, born a generation before Rubuntja, did not have the opportunity to use land rights or even universal drinking rights to express a sense of empowerment. Namatjira, who was born in 1902 and died in 1959, was awarded citizenship status in 1957 because of his prominence as an artist. He was, therefore, able to drink legally, but as drinking was still prohibited for other Aboriginal people, when he supplied alcohol to a fellow Arrernte person in 1958 he was arrested and jailed for six months. He died a year later. The right to drink alcohol was a 'privilege' of Namatjira's citizenship, but not something that he could legally share with his countrymen, neither as an expression of freedom nor of empowerment.

Advocates who believe alcohol to be a negative influence which should be eliminated or minimised have explored several alternatives. One of these alternatives used in Arnhem Land is kava, a mildly intoxicating substance from the Pacific Islands. It is prepared from the kava plant and normally served from a common receptacle. In the early 1980s, Indigenous community representatives visited Fiji and introduced kava on their return. It was seen as a peaceful alternative to alcohol because it does not cause rowdy behaviour. In an interview with Yirrkala youth at a Christian fellowship meeting in 1982, filmed as part of the Yirrkala Film Project, the following comments were made about kava:

Alcohol is terrible. When people drink it they come back drunk and terrorise people — their wives and other relatives — but this kava that we've changed to drinking now ... When we have a kava session the boys get together without causing trouble ... Everybody drinks it, not like grog where one person takes off on his own ... This is a good social drink, because we can talk sensibly and think clearly. Talk openly to each other at work, youth work and so on and that's good ... Before we drank grog all night and now we're on kava and when you wake up you still feel the same person, you don't feel tired, you don't have a hangover, even when you drink for twenty-four hours, you're still the same in mind and body. Yes! Praise the Lord![63]

The fact that kava does not cause rowdiness, promotes sociability and doesn't result in the same level of hangover as alcohol made it an attractive option. However, it also began to be abused. A study of kava use in a western Arnhem Land community in 2000 showed that it was used in seven types of social context: 'ceremonial and celebratory gatherings; drinking in tribal leaders' circles; household groups; card games; close companions and friends; people drinking alone; and people who earn a regular income and who also spend money regularly to buy kava.'[64] In 1989–90, 4.9 kilograms of kava powder was arriving into the community on a weekly basis; in 1990–91, 28.5 kilograms arrived and the number of drinkers increased from thirty-four to eighty-three.[65] Increased availability meant increased use, with the heaviest use by those drinking it alone.[66] Kava was banned in the Northern Territory in 1998 under the Kava Management Act;[67] nevertheless, it has become a familiar feature of Arnhem Land cultural practice.

Another alternative to alcohol use is Christian evangelism. These two alternatives sometimes coalesced, as in the example of the

233

Yirrkala youth group that used both religious instruction and kava in tandem. In the early 1980s, there was an evangelical Christian revival in places such as Yirrkala and its outstations, in Diamond Well and other remote Aboriginal communities. Evangelical Christianity provided people with an alternative method of empowerment, namely through access to a higher power.[68] In Diamond Well, Aboriginal-initiated revivals occurred in December 1981 and again in March 1982. Many heavy drinkers gave up alcohol as part of their new religious commitment. In April 1982, the revival movement was involved in a decision to stop beer imports to settlements, and a dry area was set up near the settlement. The settlement became peaceful for a while, but binge drinking bouts began again in mid-1983. By late 1983, drinking had returned to pre-revival levels.[69] The enthusiasm of these revivals worked to stop harmful drinking in the short run, but could not sustain any long-term change.

Another empowering alternative, which developed in the 1980s in remote Aboriginal communities, was the homelands or outstation movement. Most people living on missions and settlements originally came from surrounding areas and were still situated relatively close to their clan lands. Many settlements that originally began as missions began to take on an additional role as resource centres for Aboriginal people who were moving back onto their traditional land. In Yirrkala, for example, the Madarrpa clan received encouragement from one of the youth group leaders to consider moving back to their clan lands, on the northern shores of Blue Mud Bay. The leader emphasised how everybody knew where their traditional lands were and how they should consider moving back there, saying 'that's where our real life is'.[70] The remoteness of many of the clan lands, in some cases being several hundred kilometres away from the main settlement, meant that alcohol either was not in regular supply or was banned entirely. Moving back to remote areas meant traditional skills and culture were maintained and a degree of self-reliance regained. Often a leading 'auntie' would stop drinking and the rest of the clan would follow suit. Nevertheless, people living on their homelands were still dependent on the main settlement to a certain degree — for instance, in the case of supplies such as petrol or for complex medical care. Therefore some continued to have access to alcohol, although less frequently.

Drawing on aspects of culture to tackle substance addiction was an important part of the first Indigenous alcohol intervention project in Australia at Bennelong's Haven, a drug and alcohol rehabilitation centre in Kempsey, New South Wales. The program was set up in 1974 by Val Bryant, an ex-drinker who had been through the Alcoholics Anonymous program. As she put it: 'I never saw any Aboriginals at AA meetings but I knew it could be the greatest thing for them.' Aboriginal people and AA both are 'basically spiritual', Bryant argued. 'It's simply a matter of channelling it in the right direction.'[71] In the 1980s, other abstinence approaches were introduced that drew on life-skills counselling and vocational training as an alternative to AA's spiritual approach. Nevertheless, the sheer difficulty of controlling drinking in environments where alcohol is abundant has led many Indigenous community members and service providers to share the belief that 'abstinence is the only way for Indigenous people to conquer addictions'.[72]

As well as abstinence, many other strategies of prevention have been employed in recent decades, including primary health care, health promotion, alcohol counsellors, alcohol and drug education, peer support and training, and sporting and recreation activities. Strategies of harm minimisation have been used in the form of acute intervention services designed to prevent people hurting themselves and others, including night patrols and sobering up shelters.[73]

The creation of wet canteens and dry areas have also been used in some areas, with the aim of establishing some measure of community control over the availability of alcohol. The results have been mixed. In 2002, the Queensland government introduced a Meeting Challenges,

Making Choices program as a response to the Cape York Justice Study into alcohol, substance abuse and violence in Indigenous communities.[74] Part of the strategy was to establish community justice groups, consisting of Indigenous elders and others, who were to create alcohol management plans in a partnership between their communities and government agencies. The community justice group had statutory authority to control alcohol by deciding, for example, whether beer, wine or spirits would be allowed, what strengths would be allowable, and how and when alcohol could be purchased. Some communities established dry areas where all drinking was prohibited, others banned takeaway purchases, some prohibited the sale of wine or spirits, others required all drinks to be less than 4 per cent alcohol. Each community, in effect, developed its own combination of controls suited to its own situation. The results, although initially very encouraging, have been equivocal. According to research based on Flying Doctor Service statistics, there was clear evidence of a reduction in serious injury rates in the first two years after the introduction of alcohol management plans.[75] However, in late 2007 the Queensland government admitted that the program was failing in three key areas: offences against the person, serious assaults and hospital admissions.[76] According to Indigenous leaders, the alcohol management plans were poorly managed by the state government, with too much emphasis being placed on the reduction of supply without adequately addressing how to reduce demand. Some claimed that the program wasn't backed up by adequate policing or the provision of services to address the root causes of substance abuse in remote communities. Chris Sara, the executive director of the Indigenous Education Leadership Institute, claimed that the root cause of alcohol abuse in Aboriginal communities was the 'second-rate services fostered by government bureaucracies and service providers who would not stand for the same conditions in a white community'.[77] According to Aboriginal community leader Sam Watson, 'chronic overcrowding in houses, inadequate education facilities and massive unemployment all fuelled the alcohol abuse which exacerbated community violence'.[78] Noel Pearson agreed that the alcohol plans had been poorly managed, with the government failing to address demand-reduction strategies like addict treatment centres and the loopholes exploited by sly-groggers. 'The other part of the solution is Aboriginal people and leaders facing up to problems in the community and, to date, we have not done that,' Pearson argued. He did not see the possibility of prohibition as an unfair law imposed by whites on blacks. 'When you add grog into a kinship system, it becomes a very ugly, dangerous thing.'[79]

Some oppose prohibition on practical grounds: it does nothing to reduce demand and leads to an increase in sly-grogging, encouraging dangerous grog runs through crocodile-infested waters, unsafe home-brewing and distilling, and the relocation of drinkers from dry communities to other towns with a subsequent disruption in the social networks of both communities. In 2007, after tough new restrictions on all takeaway alcohol sales except light beer were introduced in the remote Fitzroy Crossing community in Western Australia, up to a quarter of the population flooded into the nearby towns of Derby, Halls Creek and Broome. One hundred and eighty Fitzroy Crossing residents travelled 450 kilometres to the resort town of Broome to binge on full-strength beer and cask wine and had nowhere to live.[80] The lesson seems to be that while alcohol restrictions can improve health and safety conditions in some communities, the problem is only transferred elsewhere.

While such practical issues challenge the efficacy of prohibition strategies, others oppose prohibition on ethical grounds. From a human rights perspective is it appropriate to apply restrictions to only one section of the Australian population?[81] Strictly speaking, the restrictions imposed by alcohol management plans normally apply to everyone in the geographical area, Aboriginal and non-Aboriginal, although some exemptions have been granted by communities to high-end resorts in their vicinity.

Within communities themselves there is a division between community members who believe in so-called 'drinking rights' and members who believe either in community control or complete prohibition. One example of the effects of this polarisation is a riot that took place on Mornington Island. In late 2003, the community justice group, an elected Aboriginal council organisation, agreed to implement the alcohol restrictions being introduced around Queensland Aboriginal communities in response to the high levels of alcohol-related illness, violence, rape, assault and death. Changes were made to the community's canteen sales policy so that individuals could only purchase one can of beer per day, which was opened before it was handed over so as to avoid buyers giving it away or bartering it later on. According to one community member who supported drinking rights: 'How undignified is that? When you push people into a corner without communicating with them appropriately and you treat people like dogs, then dogs bite back ... We want to revert back to the Mornington Island Council's initial plans, which allows a six-pack takeaway and a dozen on Friday. How bad is that?'[82]

Reportedly, the Mornington Island settlement quietened down considerably as a result of the tighter regulations. However, in response to the new rules, violence also broke out, with a group of young people breaking into the canteen to steal beer, assaulting the manager and later attacking police with rocks.[83] The community justice group was voted out and a new group was elected who rejected the legality of the new regulations. The Queensland Minister for Aboriginal and Torres Strait Island Affairs, who was ultimately in control of the new regulations, was unwilling to back down, as the new policy was to stay in place for twelve months until a review was undertaken. The community became split between people who supported the new regulations and wanted to restrict alcohol use and

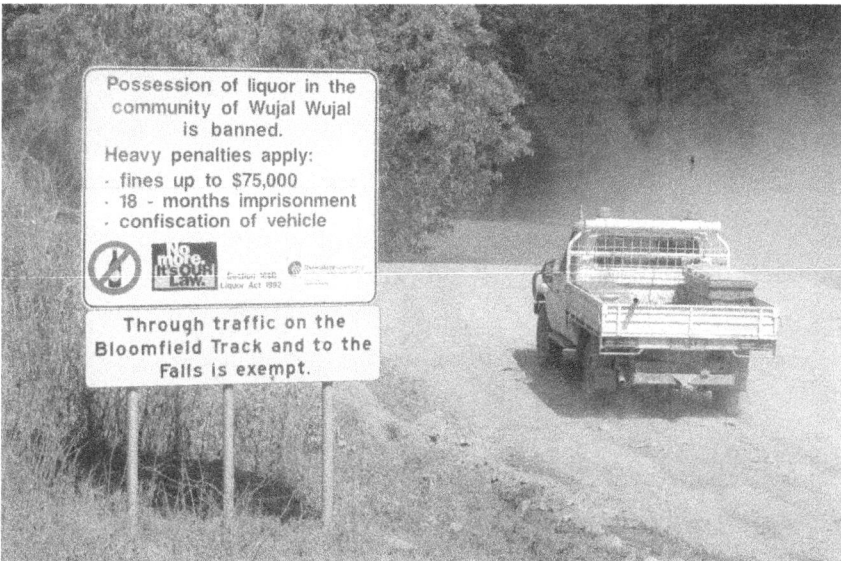

Sign on the outskirts of the Wujal Wujal community in Queensland in 2004. Some Indigenous communities have been allowed to apply their own alcohol restrictions, reflecting the wishes of the majority of their community. (© Newspix/Giulio Saggin)

alcohol-related suffering, and those who opposed them and wanted to defend their 'right' to drink regardless of the consequences. No doubt, history and the indignity of a prohibition imposed for racial reasons played some part in this conflict. Many Indigenous Australians viewed the dismantling of alcohol restriction in the 1960s as 'tantamount to gaining citizenship rights, despite the fact that citizenship rights, such as access to welfare benefits and the right to vote, were granted separately'. Conflating drinking rights with citizenship has led to the right to drink 'being viewed by some as a human prerogative, and is a sticking point in the debate about paternalism versus self-determination in Aboriginal health policy'.[84]

Another significant ethical issue arising in regard to Indigenous community control of alcohol has been the conflict of interest that often arises when communities become dependent on income from wet canteens. An important aim of the Meeting Challenges, Making Choices program introduced by the Queensland government in 2002 was to disconnect alcohol sales from Indigenous community councils, instead passing authority for alcohol-related decisions on to community liquor licensing boards. However, with profits from alcohol sales still flowing to community councils, there remains a significant 'conflict of interest with the council's efforts in improving the health and well-being of the community it serves'.[85]

A similar conflict of interest issue arose from the decision in late 2003 by Imparja Television, a commercial Aboriginal television station that broadcasts from Alice Springs, to revoke its ban on the advertising of alcohol. Imparja, derived from an Arrernte word meaning 'footprints', began broadcasting in the late 1980s and reaches a large number of remote Indigenous communities.[86] Its brief is to promote and maintain Aboriginal law and culture.[87] From the outset, Imparja made a decision not to allow alcohol advertising on the station and therefore forgo large sums of revenue for the sake of avoiding the glamorisation and encouragement of heavy drinking in Aboriginal communities.[88] To the dismay of many Aboriginal community leaders, the ban was lifted on 16 December 2003 and a twelve-month trial started from 1 January 2004.[89] The decision was a business one, made on the basis that the people who watched Imparja watched other channels that advertised alcohol and were, therefore, still being affected by alcohol advertising. Imparja decided to accept the revenue from alcohol advertising and to contribute 30 per cent of the revenue to providing substance-abuse education programs.[90] According to one reporter: 'In many remote Indigenous communities, money from alcohol sales helps to pay for local services. These settlements face a stark choice — the grog that destroys families also generates jobs. The Imparja decision sends communities struggling with this dilemma a dangerous message — a good cause justifies dancing with the devil of drink.'[91]

Such conflicts of interest are only one way in which economic forces influence the consumption of alcohol among Indigenous communities. The demand for alcohol is directly affected by the ready supply of money, in the form of welfare payments, to purchase it. According to Noel Pearson, 'dysfunctional Aboriginal behaviour is financially supported by government funding'.[92] Passive welfare payments are 'money for nothing' which corrode a recipient's sense of personal and social responsibility. In a thoroughly individualistic society, there would be natural limits to a person's self-destructive and anti-social behaviour — they would run out of money. In kinship systems, however, with strong obligations towards reciprocity, the anti-social few continually drain resources from the rest of the community. Pearson advocates that support for individuals be re-linked to acceptable social norms of behaviour, such as not being violent, caring for one's children and maintaining one's home.

Pearson has his critics, some of whom imply that he wants a return to the paternalism of the mission system. Pearson sees himself as a genuine communitarian who wants communities to be able to be in charge of their own destinies, with the power and authority to control violent individuals in their midst. In 2007, he reached an agreement with the new federal Labor government of Kevin Rudd and the Queensland state Labor government of Anna Bligh to pilot the introduction of Family Responsibility Commissions in Cape York communities. These commissions, comprising a magistrate and eminent members of the community, would be empowered to mandate obligations to ensure children attend school, to keep children free from neglect, to abide by laws concerning violence, alcohol and drugs, and abide by public housing tenancy agreements. If an individual was unable to do this then that individual's welfare payments could be redirected to a responsible adult to ensure that obligations were met. Essentially, the aim of the program is to ensure that 'local Indigenous authority is rebuilt, the essential expenses of children are met, welfare payments are not spent on grog and gambling, parents take increased responsibility for their children and positive social norms are restored with regard to issues such as education and alcohol abuse'.[93] Pearson argues that the personal and social traumas that affect Aboriginal people are not sufficient to explain the decaying sense of social responsibility in many Indigenous communities; these factors have been ever-present. Increasing problems with substance abuse are more likely due to an increase in five risk factors that Pearson identifies from the work of Swedish psychiatrist Nils Bejerot: availability of the addictive substance; money to acquire the substance; time to use the substance; example of use of the substance in the immediate environment; and a permissive ideology in relation to the use of the substance.[94] These are the conditions, Pearson argues, that the passive welfare system has created in many Indigenous communities.

Pearson's cause has not been helped by other recent, heavy-handed government attempts to link social responsibility to funding. In one case in 2005, funding for a petrol bowser at the township of Mulan in the Kimberley district in Western Australia was to be dependent on parents making sure their children washed their faces. In another case in western New South Wales, improved housing, including airconditioning, was to be linked to school attendance. These seem like crude cases of social engineering. It is clear that Pearson proposes increased levels of Indigenous engagement and ownership of the process as a key factor contributing to the success of his idea. Still, as he acknowledges, 'We are entering uncharted waters with these reforms.'[95]

Like Governor Arthur Phillip and the European governors and administrators who followed him, Indigenous communities face, in their own specific ways, the similarly daunting task of balancing freedoms and harms. The use of alcohol by most Australians can provide a means to meeting strangers, entertaining guests, celebrating religious ceremonies, signifying social status, or protesting oppression. It can mark distinctions of taste, social class and gender, social and cultural identities. Nevertheless, alcohol is far from discriminating in its effects, and calls for restrictions on its availability have been one way all communities have sought to reduce its harm.

CHAPTER 7

The Limits of Tolerance

The English philosopher John Stuart Mill (1806–73) was a keen observer of society and economics. Heavily influenced in his outlook by his father, James Mill, and his godfather, Jeremy Bentham, the younger Mill was attuned to the utilitarian temper of the times. He suffered in his childhood from a precocious brilliance that so stunted his emotional growth — so he related in his autobiography — that he suffered a nervous breakdown at the age of twenty-one. Aided by generous dosages of William Wordsworth's poetry, he recovered his emotional senses and, after a stint as a clerk in the East India Company and a brief career as a politician, he began to write on a variety of social philosophical subjects, including utilitarianism, representative government and the rights of women. He is perhaps most often quoted today by advocates of freedom in thought and lifestyle, and for his views on the limits to the authority of society over the individual, expressed in his essay 'On Liberty'.[1] Mill contended that in a society that derives its existence from the will of the people expressed through representative government there is an obligation on lawmakers to 'respect the rights of people to make their own moral decisions so long as they do not involve harm to others or to prevent others from making their own autonomous decisions'.[2] This argument has become a cornerstone of the ethical framework of political and legal thought in liberal democracies. According to Mill:

> A person cannot rightfully be compelled to do or forbear because it will be better for him to do so, because it would make him happier, because in the opinion of others to so would be wise, or even right. These are good reasons for remonstrating with him, or reasoning with him, or persuading him, but not for compelling him, or visiting him with woe in case he do otherwise ... Over himself, over his own body and mind the individual is sovereign in his own body.[3]

Often, Mill is misquoted as an advocate of a hands-off, live-and-let-live approach to moral issues such as free speech and the drinking of alcohol. Certainly, as a product of the Enlightenment, a child of reason rather than religion, Mill was a strong advocate of the notion that there must exist a realm of interests that rightly belong to the individual and which must not be encroached upon by society. Nevertheless, Mill himself was at pains to make it clear that he was not advocating a hands-off approach in all matters; it was moral compulsion he was against, not moral influence. We may use whatever means possible to influence our neighbours to lead a moral life — education, persuasion, even disapproval and social exclusion — so long as we do not compel them or punish them 'with woe'.

In a nuanced way, Mill applied this principle of liberty to the drunkard — he had no particular sympathy for such a person, but he upheld that person's right to drink. Familiar with the early temperance movement, Mill viewed as misguided those who agitated in support for extending the prohibition of the sale of alcohol to their communities:

> Under the name of preventing intemperance the people
> of one English colony, and of nearly half the United
> States, have been interdicted by law from making any
> use whatever of fermented drinks, except for medical
> purposes: for prohibition of their sale is in fact, as it is
> intended to be, prohibition of their use.[4]

Those who supported these laws claimed a right to protect their 'social rights'; that is, the right to protect themselves from any behaviour of others which, in Mill's own words, 'impedes my right to free moral and intellectual development, by surrounding my path with dangers, and by weakening and demoralizing society, from which I have a right to claim mutual aid and intercourse'.[5] For Mill, however, this punitive attitude 'ascribes to all mankind a vested interest in each other's moral, intellectual, and even physical perfection, to be defined by each claimant according to his own standard',[6] and he regarded the over-reaching into the lives of individuals in the name of the common good as repugnant. Mill did not deny that society had an interest in people's behaviour, but only in their social behaviour, not their individual behaviour; that is, only in that behaviour which would directly, not indirectly, injure others. Such direct injury, by its nature social, could be socially sanctioned, but not the individual behaviour that may have indirectly caused it. Although he was appalled at the damage drinking caused to others, both directly through violence and indirectly by neglect of duties to family and society, he advocated the direct sanctioning of these crimes rather than making drinking itself illegal:

> If, for example, a man, through intemperance or
> extravagance, becomes unable to pay his debts, or, having

undertaken the moral responsibility of a family, becomes
from the same cause incapable of supporting or educating
them, he is deservedly reprobated, and might be justly
punished; but it is for the breach of duty to his family or
creditors, not for the extravagance. If the resources which
ought to have been devoted to them, had been diverted
from them for the most prudent investment, the moral
culpability would have been the same.[7]

In fact, as a utilitarian, Mill favoured severer penalties for those who
re-offended under the influence of alcohol, as they had had ample
time to mend their ways. He also favoured regulatory measures that
would ameliorate anticipated harms. In many ways we can view Mill's
position as both descriptive and prescriptive — it usefully
demonstrates the balancing act between toleration and regulation that
has typified the story of alcohol in Australia; at the same time, it
presents one possible vision of what we ought to do in the future.

In the first decade of the twenty-first century, there are signs that the
body politic in Australia, as elsewhere in the west, may be reaching its
limit of tolerance with regard to alcohol consumption; that fine
balance between freedom and regulation in liberal democracy may be
coming to an end. It is sometimes said that the one thing we learn
from history is that we learn nothing from history. Each era repeats
the mistakes of the past. Certainly, many of the arguments currently
put forward for either liberalising or restricting access to alcohol were
anticipated by Mill.

Distinguishing between individual and social habits, and pinning
down when an activity becomes a social harm in the sense of directly
affecting the interests of others, has become crucial in determining
rights of access to publicly funded health care. It has also, most
spectacularly, led to the relative demise of tobacco in Australia. How

will alcohol consumption be influenced by the new politics of health, which seeks to trade the freedom to choose in lifestyle matters with increasing restrictions of choice in future access to health and other social services?

As in the past, current public concerns about alcohol consumption tend to focus on highly visible instances of public drunkenness. At the moral if not the practical level, the battle against drink-driving has been convincingly won; few now defend or excuse it. Indeed, random breath testing of motorists and laws against drink-driving are prime examples of legislation actually changing attitudes and behaviour. Being involved in a traffic accident while inebriated is no longer seen as a case of bad luck, but of personal culpability. Zero tolerance of alcohol use has become the norm for some workers, such as taxi drivers, bus drivers, police officers and airline pilots. Public figures caught with a breathalyser reading over the legal limit can undergo significant public shaming, sometimes to the extent of destroying a political or sporting career. For celebrities, a bout of uncontrolled public drunkenness routinely leads to a public confession of an abuse problem and voluntary commitment to a treatment program. There is also very little public acceptance of another product of alcohol abuse — domestic violence. It still occurs, but is no longer excused. Such social disapproval, however, cannot work in a vacuum, and domestic violence remains a problem for those who are socially isolated, either as individuals trapped in restrictive domestic arrangements, or within groups isolated by barriers of class, ethnicity or geography. For similar reasons, the prospect of being caught by a random breath test is often a poor deterrent in rural areas, where the procedure is not cost-effective and therefore is much less prevalent.

The focus of moral concern has shifted to other forms of public disruption caused by alcohol consumption. Binge drinking is again a topical issue, especially in relation to teenagers. In 2008, Prime Minister Kevin Rudd announced a $53 million program to combat binge drinking among younger people, with $20 million committed to advertising, and threats to withdraw funding from sporting and community clubs that did not enforce strict codes of conduct. Binge drinking significantly increases personal vulnerability, since binge drinkers are at high risk of violence, sexual assault, injury and death by misadventure and suicide. One worrying indicator of a new level of cultural acceptance of binge drinking was a Melbourne radio station competition in 2004 that involved two young women filming themselves drinking twenty cocktails in twenty different Las Vegas casinos. Ironically, the competition was sponsored by Australian Unity, a health insurer![8] By 2008, it was reported that New South Wales government statistics indicated that about 520,000 people across the state regularly drank themselves into oblivion.[9] Australia-wide, 168,000 (one in ten) young people between the ages of twelve and seventeen reported binge drinking in any given week.[10]

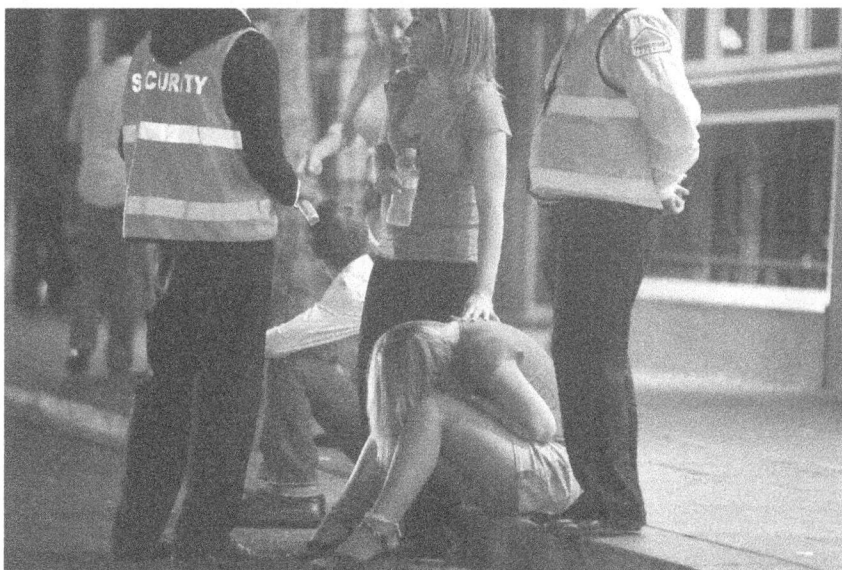

Saturday evening in the Sydney CBD, 2008. Binge drinking, particularly among younger women, has become a concern in recent times with the Rudd government in 2008 announcing a $53 million program to combat it. (© Newspix/Brad Hunter)

249

While Australian attitudes to drinking alcohol in public have changed, and large sections of the population drink openly and in moderation in parks, cafés and at sporting events, public drunkenness has increasingly become ghettoised, with an increase in subcultural drinking and ensuing violence. In some contexts, drinking is not only permitted, it forms an essential part of the social experience — be it watching sport, clubbing, schoolies week (and now even mini-schoolies week in September) or just hanging out with one's mates, male or female.

Binge drinking is prevalent among young people partly for the same reasons that it developed in Indigenous communities at a time when alcohol was illegal: to avoid being prosecuted, drinkers can only obtain alcohol at unpredictable intervals and it needs to be consumed surreptitiously and quickly. National Health and Medical Council figures indicate that one in five male and female students aged between sixteen and seventeen years old regularly binge drink (drinking at levels leading to intoxication).[11] In Victoria, as elsewhere in Australia, it has been claimed that home delivery of alcohol by unlicensed operators has fuelled underage drinking.[12] In 2007, the premier of Queensland, Anna Bligh, announced tougher alcohol laws aimed at parents who provide excessive supplies of alcohol to their children. The move was prompted by the report of Youth Violence Taskforce, formed after a Brisbane teen was kicked to death outside a party, and the announcement came two weeks after $2000 worth of beer and spirits had been seized from two seventeen year olds and an eighteen year old on their way to a mini-schoolies week on North Stradbroke Island in Queensland.[13] In New South Wales, it was estimated that 99,500 young men drank themselves into a stupor over the 2007–08 holiday break. Many hit the bottle so hard that they risked what medical experts have called 'holiday heart' — an acute injury resulting from the toxic effects of alcohol overstimulating the heart.[14]

One component of the binge drinking problem may be a 'spirits craze' among the young, especially teenage girls. Though distillers strongly disagree that their products are responsible for any increase in under-age drinking, in 2006 the National Drug and Alcohol Research Centre found that more than 40 per cent of twelve to fifteen year olds first tried alcohol in a commercially made pre-mixed drink — also called RTDs (ready-to-drink spirits) or alcopops (spirits or beer mixed with fruit juices). By 2008, the percentage of school students between twelve and seventeen who chose pre-mixed spirits over other alcoholic drinks, including beer and unmixed spirits, had doubled since 2001. Over half of all twelve- to seventeen-year-old female drinkers chose pre-mixed spirits.[15] Security guards have even suggested that pre-mixed drinks are a factor in increased violence around licensed venues. According to one security firm director, 'It's because young fellas are drinking pre-mix drinks, vodka drinks, those drinks made from Jaegermeister and Red Bull [Jaegerbombs]. They can't taste the alcohol and drink and drink and drink.'[16] In 2008, it was reported that sales of ready-to-drink products such as Jaegerbombs, with higher alcohol content and often mixed with caffeine, guarana and energy drinks, had grown in three years from nothing to $700 million and now made up a quarter of the total $2.5 billion market. Sales were set to grow by 25 per cent annually — double the growth rate of the total ready-to-drink market.[17] Also in 2008, a study by the Australian consumer group Choice found that eighteen year olds preferred alcopops, ranking them twice as appealing as beer and three times tastier than wine. They also found that one in four could not taste the alcohol in the drinks, and that over half those tested did not realise that a Vodka Mudshake Original Chocolate drink, which contains 4 per cent spirits, was in fact alcoholic.[18]

The hidden taste factor as an intentional attractant for young drinkers was dramatically confirmed by an industry insider, Mat

Baxter, a marketing executive for the vodka-based pre-mixed drink Absolut Cut — a vodka and citrus mix. In comments in a trade magazine, which were later elaborated upon in *The Age*, he confirmed that the market was booming for high-strength pre-mixed drinks that 'get young people drunk faster' and that cheap sugary drinks packaged in bright colours were the best way to start people drinking early in adulthood. According to Baxter, the RTD market in Australia is designed for the young binge drinker on a budget. 'It is one of the few drinks where you don't necessarily know you're drinking alcohol and that's a conscious effort to make those drinks more appealing to young people.' Masking the alcohol taste was important, he said, because, 'when you're young your palate is tuned for sugary drinks'.[19]

In 2008, the average age at which individuals first tried drugs, including alcohol and cannabis, was around twelve to thirteen years, down from seventeen to nineteen years in the 1970s and 1980s.

A bottle of Smirnoff Ice next to two schooners of beer. The alcohol content of the Smirnoff Ice equals that of the two schooners put together.
(© Newspix/Kristi Miller)

According to reports in New South Wales, children as young as ten had been admitted to programs for alcohol abuse.[20] In 2006, in a submission to a senate inquiry, Bundaberg Rum — which uses a talking polar bear in its advertisements, presumably appealing to younger drinkers — denied that under-age drinking was on the rise and that the increasing popularity of RTDs had anything to do with it. They asked for a further reduction in the excise on pre-mixed alcoholic drinks, claiming that their products were being 'unfairly discriminated' against.[21] In 2008, the alcohol industry was surprised by the new Rudd Labor government's decision to increase the excise on pre-mixed drinks to help curb teenage binge drinking. The government based its response on Australian Institute of Health and Welfare statistics that showed 'a quarter of teenagers, particularly young girls, put themselves at risk of alcohol-related harm at least once a month' and a significant increase between 2000 (14 per cent) and 2004 (60 per cent) in young girls aged fifteen to seventeen reporting drinking alcopops in their last drinking session.[22]

The industry conceded the increased popularity of RTDs across the board, but did not accept that they caused binge drinking among young people, citing the steady state of overall consumption patterns reported by the Australian Institute of Health and Welfare. Nevertheless, those figures indicated that more than 26 per cent of young people between the ages of fourteen and nineteen had put themselves at risk of alcohol-related harm in the short term at least once of month during the previous twelve months. The percentage of young women (fourteen to nineteen years) doing so was higher (28.3 per cent) than the percentage of young men (24.5 per cent).[23] Furthermore, health researchers point out that the alcohol industry generates most of its profits from binge drinking: 'Conservatively estimated, two-thirds of all alcohol consumed in Australia (and 90 per cent of that consumed by young men) is consumed in ways that put drinkers' and others' health at risk.'[24]

Another cause of increased public concern about alcohol has been its increased availability, a product of a growing number of licensed premises and extended opening times. In a far cry from the era of six o'clock closing, many bars and pubs are open to the wee hours of the morning, and some for twenty-four hours. Advocates who supported increasing the number of licensed venues and liberalising opening hours argued that these measures would help change a pub culture into a café culture and drinking would be 'tapered and regulated'.[25] Ireland tried this approach in the 1990s, and the result was 'an explosion in alcohol consumption, nearly 50 per cent up over the past decade'.[26] Ireland started restricting opening times again when liberalisation created not a café culture but 'a late-night battlefield of drunkenness and its attendant dangers'.[27] Experiencing similar problems in 2005, the Queensland government of Peter Beattie also brought closing hours forward again.

There is an incontrovertible link between longer trading hours and increased violence. In May 2008, in inner Sydney 12 per cent of hotels accounted for almost 60 per cent of all assaults on hotel premises; in Newcastle 8 per cent of licensed premises accounted for nearly 80 per cent of all assaults on licensed premises; and in Wollongong 6 per cent of licensed premises accounted for 67 per cent of all on-premises assaults. All these hotels had extended hours. The NSW police commissioner, Andrew Scipione, a teetotaller, called for twenty-four hour hotel trading hours to be axed. He said that Sydney was 'drowning in alcohol', and also called for a lower tax for low-alcohol drinks and for community-based 'sobering up' centres.[28]

Drinking has long been a feature of Australian sporting life, but it has recently become a particular issue in some sports. The National Rugby League (NRL), for example, has belatedly recognised that drinking is a serious problem among its players. One survey found that nearly two-thirds of top NRL players believed there was a culture of binge drinking in rugby league. Ironically, the health and fitness regimes that clubs have instituted to protect their expensive investment in players may have contributed to the problem. According to David Gallop, the chief executive of the NRL: 'Alcohol is not a new problem but the opportunity to drink is more limited now than in the previous generations, which increases the dangers of one-off binges.'[29]

Tommy Simpson from South Sydney remembers the hard days of the past. He had his first taste of alcohol in 1972 at fourteen years of age. He appreciated the warm fire in the belly — it gave the shy boy courage to ask girls for a dance. He felt strong and confident. But it also led to strife — pushing and shoving and fights. By the time Tommy achieved his dream of becoming a first-grade footballer for the South Sydney Rabbitohs in 1978, he had become a serious binge drinker. He was asked to leave the club after an unpleasant incident,

The unbeaten Australian Schoolboys Rugby team that toured Great Britain in 1977/78 celebrate with a few cans of Fosters. Reportedly, some of them were not yet old enough to vote at the time. (© Newspix/News Ltd)

which to this day he refuses to talk about. He moved to another club, the Eastern Suburbs Roosters. As Garry Linnell wrote: 'Tommy Simpson and football's culture of heavy binge drinking are a match made in heaven. There's a brawl in the social club. Then, on a trip to Coolangatta he crash tackles a woman outside a hotel. Simpson is arrested, then taken to the airport and another club says they don't want him back.'[30] There are other clubs and other incidents. Simpson loses teeth, has his jaw broken; he smashes into trucks and telephone poles while driving. He can't remember much of his life during this time. Eventually, Simpson got his act together and has been off the booze for over twenty-five years. He now does his best to warn others of the dangers facing elite sports stars. He addresses the NRL rookie camp, candidly sharing his past experiences.

The same problem of binge drinking applies to other football codes, including rugby union and Australian rules football. Earlier, we saw how the 'work and bust' pattern of consuming alcohol heavily on limited occasions was a factor in binge drinking among rural workers and Indigenous drinkers who were subject to community alcohol restrictions. It is tempting to think that gender is also a factor, but this does not explain the increase in binge drinking among current footballers compared to footballers of the past. Another culprit most often mentioned is the high level of disposable income available to the modern sports professional. This would seem consistent with the earlier analysis that wealth rather than gender influenced alcohol consumption levels in the nineteenth century.

During the 2008 season, the booze culture in the Australian Football League (AFL) and especially at the Collingwood Magpies was highlighted with a vengeance. It was revealed that, despite earlier denials made to Collingwood's president Eddie McGuire, coach Mick Malthouse, club captain Scott Burns, and to their teammates, key players Heath Shaw and Alan Didak were both in Shaw's ute when he ploughed into two cars parked in the leafy, Melbourne upper-class suburb of Kew. Shaw, who had a blood alcohol reading of 0.144 (almost three times over the legal limit), lied to protect Didak, who the previous year had to consent to a total nightclub and alcohol ban after his binge-drinking session with notorious Melbourne 'underworld figure' and convicted killer Wayne Hudson. For lying, Heath Shaw and Alan Didak were suspended for the rest of the 2008 season (they had to train with the team as usual) and fined $10,000 and $5,000 respectively. Heath Shaw's injured elder brother Rhyce Shaw, who had been 'drinking excessively' with the duo, was suspended for two matches, fined $5,000 and was traded to Sydney for 2009.

Earlier in 2008, the Collingwood football club had lost more than $4 million in sponsorship from the Transport Accident Commission when another player, Sharrod Wellingham, was caught drink-driving. After the fiasco with Shaw and Didak, not only did Eddie McGuire's presidency seem compromised, but Victorian Labor Premier, John Brumby, a Collingwood fan, said on the record that he thought 'something is wrong with the club's culture.'[31]

The NRL club South Sydney, which in 2007 boasted two high-profile co-owners — movie star Russell Crowe and, until he pulled out mid-year, the financier, Peter Holmes a Court. Had Holmes a Court had his way, not only would the club prohibit profiting from poker machines, but all Rabbitohs players would have had to sign up to a zero alcohol clause for the entire season. Giving the large financial investment clubs make in their playing staff, perhaps it is only a matter of time before such a radical idea is trialled for a season by one of the football codes.

Binge drinking is not a problem faced by footballers alone. Commenting on the assault and grievous bodily harm charges laid against national swimming champion Nick D'Arcy after he floored another swimming champion during a drinking session in early 2008, Tommy Simpson pointed out: 'It's not drinking that's the problem. It's binge drinking. A lot of athletes and swimmers, they

"I'VE NEVER FELT BETTER IN MY LIFE," *says* VIC HEY

the popular Rugby League Footballer

Football is a great game, and Sheaf Stout is the finest drink to renew one's energy — whether after a strenuous match or a hard day's work. The rich barley malt in Sheaf Stout builds body and muscle, and ensures perfect fitness always.

SINCE I COMMENCED A COURSE OF

TOOTH'S SHEAF STOUT

IN THREE SIZES: BOTTLES—HALF BOTTLES—BABY BOTTLES

Perfect fitness in a baby bottle? Advertisements like this are not allowed today. Under the Alcohol Beverage Advertising Code signed up to by major brewers, distillers, and winemakers, alcohol advertising must not depict alcohol consumption as contributing to sporting success or having therapeutic benefits. (ANU Archives Program) don't drink or touch a drop for months when they're in training. And then they go out, it's full-on and they wonder why the trouble starts.'[32] Olympic gold medallist Kieren Perkins confirmed this: 'Culturally there is an attitude, "let's get hammered".'[33]

For many male consumers, perhaps still under the thrall of 'the shout', the amount of beer consumed in one session seems important. Some Queensland hoteliers have claimed that they are obliging the desire to keep drinking without getting drunk by selling beer in 250 ml pots, rather than the standard 285 ml pot (which happens to be equivalent to a standard drink). In June 2006, Queensland Hotel Association chief executive Justin O'Connor was reported as saying that: 'The move to smaller pots was because of the pressure on hotels to clamp down on binge drinking.'[34]

The fag-smoking, beer-swilling Aussie is a dying breed. Australia now has 'the lowest rate of smoking in the industrialised world and we come a mere twenty-third in the rankings of alcohol consumption'.[35] Though it fights hard to the bitter end, tobacco has lost its battle for public hearts and minds — not because of any re-ascendant wowserism, but on the basis of utilitarian liberal principles. The evidence mounted until everyone could see the truth: smoking is considerably harmful. As it turned out, the industry knew this all along. Using John Stuart Mill's criteria, the harms done by tobacco to the smoker are not an issue; so long as smokers are aware of those harms, they can choose to live, or in this case die, with them. In effect, the lengths the tobacco industry went to to deny that smoking was harmful only helped to dig itself into a bigger hole. Even while the industry hotly contested the notion of 'passive smoking', restrictions were being put in place, on sound liberal principals, to respect the decision of those who had chosen not to smoke, enabling them to avoid suffering tobacco's many ill effects and inconveniences.

Ultimately, the tobacco industry became the focus of an abolitionist movement, intent on ridding society forever of an addictive and harmful substance. That may still seem far off and ultimately impossible within the bounds of liberalism; nevertheless, in the twenty-first century, consumers buying a new car are more likely to ask 'Where's the cup holder?' than 'Where's the ashtray?' For a considerable time in Australia's history smoking was regarded as more acceptable than drinking because it did not lead to disruptive behavioural changes. There is some irony, then, in the fact that the exclusion of smokers from workplaces and public spaces has led to considerable social disruption, as smokers are required to seek out spaces further afield to indulge their addiction.

The challenges facing the alcohol industry are somewhat different. While it was once assumed that only heavy smoking resulted in harms to self and others, it is now understood that

Will booze go the way of tobacco? The fag-smoking, beer-swilling Aussie is a dying breed. Australia now has the lowest rate of smoking in the industrialised world, and we only rank twenty-third in alcohol consumption. (© Newspix/Danny Aarons)

smoking can be harmful even at relatively low levels. Alcohol use at low levels is neither a health nor a social problem for regular users. Also, there is no second-hand drinking as there is second-hand smoking. Although it has often been argued that many social harms are triggered by alcohol abuse, Mill's argument still holds true: inflicting harm directly on others and indirectly through neglect of one's duty to family and other responsibilities are best punished as social shortcomings in themselves. But Mill also suggested that reason must pay attention to circumstances and consequences; in which case, there may be good reasons to regulate a trade which, if carried out in a laissez-faire manner, could result in social disruption. There seems little doubt that the alcohol industry is next in the firing line. Leading figures in the UK medical establishment, such as the high-profile TV presenter Lord Robert Winston, have gone on record saying that 'alcohol is the biggest medical problem we face — probably bigger than smoking'.[36]

As a restricted substance, alcohol cannot be legally sold to children under a certain age; yet for many years it was being freely advertised at all times of day, particularly via electronic media. Tobacco lost this battle first; its cause not helped by brazen marketing attempts to hook people up to smoking early. Once direct advertising was scaled down in the electronic media, attention was turned to the proliferation of billboard advertising that promoted tobacco and alcohol consumption. Many of those opposed to these ubiquitous campaigns did not have the funds to counter with positive messages and advertising promoting the health issues, and in the late 1970s some activists decided to take matters into their own hands by applying a kind of moral jiujitsu, turning the force of the opponent back upon themselves. The group BUGA UP (Billboard Utilising Graffitists Against Unhealthy Promotions) became widely known for their bold and direct campaigns attacking billboard advertising.

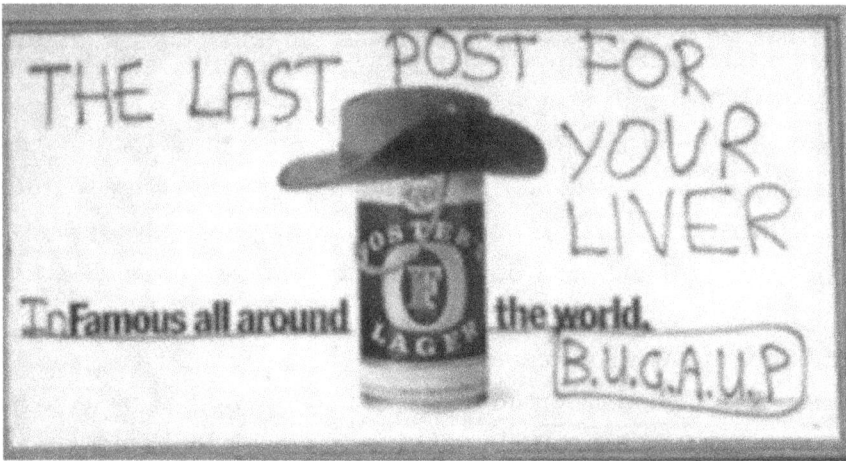

After a successful graffiti campaign in the 1980s against big tobacco, BUGA UP turned its focus to the alcohol industry. (Source: www.bugaup.org)

BUGA UP began in Australia in October 1979 as a movement, rather than a group or organisation, comprising three graffitists in inner Sydney. The movement grew but never had an official 'structure' or membership. Any member of the public could 'buga up' a billboard if they felt so inclined. In the beginning, BUGA UP specifically targeted tobacco and alcohol billboards on government property, claiming that it was hypocritical for the government to promote these products while also trying to deal with the suffering they caused. By 1981, the movement had 'improved' thousands of billboards, creatively defacing them to give a message opposite to that intended. Only twenty-one of the defacements resulted in arrests, with a mere thirteen convictions for damage and 'injury' to the billboards. Public attitudes to tobacco were changing, aided by the increasingly absurd contradictions of so-called product distancing, such as naming cigarettes after pristine natural settings, or tobacco companies sponsoring sporting events when the negative impacts of smoking on health were becoming more widely known.

Alcohol marketing today is essentially self-regulated. According to the industry code, marketing should not detract from moderate, responsible consumption, nor should it have strong appeal to children.[37] Under the Alcohol Beverages Advertising Code, advertisements must 'not depict the consumption or presence of alcohol beverages as a cause of, or contributing to the achievement of ... sexual or other success'.[38] Research has found, however, that panels of independent experts and non-experts are more likely to judge that ads are breaching the code than are members of the Advertising Standards Board.[39] Some claim that it is a case of 'the fox guarding the hen house', and government regulation may have to replace industry self-regulation in order to tackle Australia's binge drinking culture.[40] The Alcohol Beverages Advertising Code fails in constraining alcohol promotion that regularly exploits sexuality and sporting heroes. In a 2007 ad, surfer Koby Abberton wades ashore, drains a bottle of beer, looks at a bikini-clad blonde and exclaims, 'Nothing goes down like a Bondi Blonde'. Although the ad breaks the Advertising Code's rules, it received little effective censure. The brewery responsible for Bondi Blonde, ad man John Singleton's company Bluetongue Brewery, was not a signatory to the code and the ad had been distributed as a 'movie' via YouTube on the internet.[41]

The use of sport as a vehicle for promoting alcohol, and the fact that some sporting competitions are still designed around brands of alcohol, are seen by many in the community as an outrage. In 2008, Michael George O'Brien, a 57-year-old professional from Newtown, commented in a letter to the *Sydney Morning Herald* in response to a proposal by Family First senator Steve Fielding to ban alcohol advertising before 9 p.m.:

> When I was a child, television advertising told me how
> urbane, sophisticated and cool I would be if I smoked this
> or that brand of cigarette. I began smoking at an early age.

On those rare occasions when I now watch commercial television, I see advertisements espousing the manifold virtues of this or that form of alcohol (especially beer and rum); mateship, sophistication, horseplay and good times. These ads are often on at times when children are likely to be watching. Just as those cigarette ads did not show the damaged lungs, stressed hearts and impacted arteries associated with that habit, ads for alcohol these days don't mention the misery and social upheaval alcohol abuse is causing in our society.[42]

In 2008, sporting bodies were quick to offer support for Prime Minister Kevin Rudd's anti-binge drinking program, but as one commentator put it: 'Try finding a national sporting contest that doesn't owe allegiance to the bottle.'[43] The alcohol industry spends $130 million a year on television advertising, mostly placed in prime-time slots or around live sporting events.[44] Foster's, Lion Nathan and Diageo account for 80 per cent of the sponsorship of sport in Australia, investing about $50 million annually. Sponsoring live sport enables them to take advantage of exemptions that allow alcohol adverting to be shown during televised sporting events when children are watching.[45]

Anna E. Blainey, who has researched historic temperance movements, doubts that banning advertising would affect drinking rates, pointing out that 'as we grow up we see a lot more drinking in real life than we do in advertisements with children regularly seeing adults around them enjoying drinking or even bragging about it'.[46] If advertising was a major cause of drinking, she argues, then prohibition of alcohol or other drugs would work a lot better than it has: if a substance is banned it certainly won't be advertised. Both the advertising industry and the alcohol industry accept that advertising influences behaviour — that is why the one gets paid and the other willingly pays. Advertisers know exactly how many people in different demographic groups are exposed to their ads; it is one factor in determining the pricing of advertisements and helping clients to select the timing and forms of media suitable for their target consumers. Anticipating a backlash to the widespread advertising of alcohol, particularly on television, the alcohol industry is shifting its focus from traditional advertising to internet viral marketing, sponsorship events, promotions and giveaways. Indeed, when assessing the influence of advertising, the focus on television advertising alone can be misleading, with radio programs having a disproportionately large youth audience. Overseas studies have also indicated that pre-adolescents' intention to drink is heavily influenced by magazine advertising and the presence of alcohol at sporting and music venues.[47]

Students buy Tooheys beer for a chance to have part of their university HECS fees paid, March 2004. The Alcohol Beverage Advertising Code does not cover point of sale material. (© Newspix/Brett Faulkner)

Advertising industry executives accept the fact that if they are doing their jobs more people will be using their products. That is why, according to a spokeswoman for Diageo, the world's largest alcohol company, its marketing code stipulates that a minimum of 80 per cent of people reached by their ads must be legal age drinkers, adding: 'Of course a ban [on television ads before 9p.m.] would have an impact, but we would support it … We feel we are targeting people who are of legal drinking age and above anyway.'[48]

Increased commitment to responsible drinking by companies such as Diageo has no doubt been influenced in part by research, particularly in the US, indicating that a substantial proportion of alcohol advertising appears in media for which the audience is youth-oriented; that is, composed disproportionately of persons aged twelve to twenty years. Radio is the main source of such advertising, but also magazines. In 2001 and 2002, alcohol companies in the US spent $590.4 million to place magazine ads. A later study on adolescent exposure to these ads indicated that under-age youth saw 45 per cent more beer and ale ads, 12 per cent more distilled spirits ads and 65 per cent more low-alcohol refresher advertising (sweet-flavoured alcoholic beverages, alcopops and alcoholic lemonades), and 69 per cent fewer wine ads, than persons over twenty-one (the legal age for drinking in the US).[49] In Australia, the legal drinking age is eighteen, but the figures are still relevant. Just as concerns for road safety are not confined to illegal under-age drivers, concerns about excessive alcohol consumption among young people in Australia are not confined to under-age drinking but cover the drinking behaviour of those under eighteen and those between eighteen and twenty-five years of age.

The consumption of alcohol has long been seen as both a private and a public health issue. This idea took on new meaning in the late twentieth and early twenty-first centuries with an explosion of concern for, and interest in, health and fitness. Among members of the public, health concerns related to alcohol no longer focus primarily on the disease of alcoholism; rather, they reflect general concerns about health, fitness and wellbeing. Alcohol is seen as part of the general problem of maintaining a work–life balance. Even the ritual of a few drinks after work on Friday night has reportedly 'fallen victim to longer working hours, stress, fatigue and family responsibilities'.[50] Alcohol and tobacco are no longer the only consumables in the firing line — so too are soft drinks, junk food and even coffee.[51]

Until recently, federal and state governments have committed money to address health issues in specific health contexts through public health and education programs, but have remained reticent about creating wider public media campaigns that directly confront alcohol consumption and misuse. This reluctance is notable given the number of successful public health campaigns that have been and are still being waged directly against tobacco consumption. These campaigns focused directly on health issues, pointing out that smoking is an undeniable health hazard. Public campaigns against alcohol, however, focus on drink-driving, with the worthy aim of reducing the road toll — the major cause of alcohol-related deaths — but with seemingly little effect on the young. (Also, the number of drug-affected drivers has overtaken the number of drink-drivers, according to world-first roadside drug testing in Victoria.)[52] This marked difference between the high-impact smoking ads and the low-impact drinking ads (other than road-safety ads) could result in a 'boiled frog syndrome' — a somewhat macabre metaphor that observes that a frog placed into boiling water will immediately jump out; while a frog placed into cold water that is slowly boiled will end up being cooked. One possible unintended effect of the neglect of high-impact electronic media advertising of alcohol health issues may be that these health issues slowly creep up on individuals without them noticing, at great cost, ultimately, to themselves and the public health system. Cynics argue that governments have been simply outflanked by the alcohol industry, with both state and federal governments developing 'partnerships' with the industry 'to change drinking culture and reduce alcohol-related problems, resulting in "regulatory capture" with governments increasingly accepting the industry's diagnosis, and preferred remedies, for the problem'.[53] Some segments of the industry even talk about promoting the existence of a so-called 'sustainable drinking culture' by 'changing the negative aspects of Australia's drinking culture'.[54]

There are some in the alcohol industry who would argue that offence is the best defence. For its part, the wine industry in Australia has been willing to hop on board the health train, rather than ending up squashed on the tracks. Strategically, the industry has intentionally sought to distance itself from brewers and distillers by actively promoting the consumption of wine in moderation and 'in its proper social context;'[55] a stance that the wine producers have consistently supported since the early 1980s. Others in the alcohol industry have simply chosen the path of contradiction, asserting the positive health benefits of drinking alcohol and the relative health risks of abstinence. In 2006, for example, Lion Nathan's website informed us that: 'When enjoyed in moderation, beer confers a number of healthful attributes on drinkers. It's reassuring to know that the risk of heart disease can be reduced through a moderate regular approach to beer drinking as part of sensible diet and exercise lifestyle.'[56] By 2008, Lion Nathan's claims were less specific, if not more modest: 'There is an increasing body of opinion that suggests that our beverages, when enjoyed in moderation, can confer significant health benefits.'[57]

Claims as to alcohol's efficacy go back a long way. According to the New Testament, 'A little wine is good for digestion.'[58] The wine industry, in particular, has seized upon research indicating the benefits of anti-oxidants, taken in regular, small doses. But everyone wants a piece of the action. A medical conference in Scotland in 2005 was told that malt whisky, with its high levels of anti-oxidants, can 'beat' the threat of cancer.[59] The liquor industry generally is pleased to suggest that drinking not only protects you against cancer and heart disease, it can make you a better thinker. One study conducted by the Australian National University claimed that drinking an average of two alcoholic drinks per day improved your verbal skills, memory and speed of thinking, and showed that moderate drinkers outperformed abstainers and heavy drinkers.[60] Despite these claims of a health benefit from alcohol taken in relatively small amounts, the medical consensus remains that excessive alcohol consumption increases the risk of a number of cancers, particularly in smokers.

Perhaps there is some acknowledgment of the importance of the harm principle to public discussion in a liberal democracy when the Australian Brewers' Foundation provides funds for independent research on the health and social impacts of alcohol.[61] In 1996, their advisory committee reviewed about thirty published papers from around the world on the link between alcohol and heart disease. They found that people who drank beer in moderation lived longer and were less likely to have heart disease problems than abstainers. The link applies to any alcoholic beverage, but, echoing the past virtues of 'Beer Street', the committee suggested that 'Beer can be regarded as the drink of moderation because it has half the alcohol content of wine'.[62] According to the study, 'consumption of no more than four glasses of beer a day for men and two for women is considered moderate'.[63] While this may be moderate if averaged over twenty-four hours, the consumption of these amounts within a short period of time could have unhappy consequences for individual drinkers, depending on their physiological characteristics and circumstances. In fact, until 2007, the National Health and Medical Research Council guidelines defined 'low-risk' drinking as an average of four standard drinks per day and not more than six standard drinks in any one day for men, and two standard drinks per day and not more than four per day for women. The guidelines also recommended one or two alcohol-free days a week, and weekly limits of twenty-eight standards drink for men and fourteen standard drinks for women. However, new draft guidelines produced in 2007 have abandoned weekly limits and redefined 'low-risk' drinking, based on the evidence that: 'There is no clear level of drinking below which alcohol-related accidents and injuries do not occur, or below which there is no reduction in the length or quality of life due to alcohol-related diseases.'[64]

To put it simply, both short-term and long-term risks are related to the amount of alcohol consumed. The draft revised guidelines suggest that 'low-risk' drinking for both men and women is no more than two standard drinks or less in any one day. They also recommend 'not drinking' as the safest option for pregnant women and for all those under eighteen years.

The guidelines have been attacked by the alcohol industry as 'unrealistic'.[65] The Winemakers' Federation of Australia even momentarily hopped off the health bandwagon and described the guidelines as 'culturally irrelevant'.[66] Professor John Currie, chair of the NHMRC Alcohol Guidelines Committee responded that: 'The responsible consumption of alcohol is a health issue, not a cultural issue. People make their own choices — it's not our role to tell them how to behave.'[67] It appears that the alcohol industry wants the level of health risks to be determined democratically rather than scientifically. Even specialists in alcohol treatment claimed that the proposed levels were 'unrealistic' and 'failed the credibility test'. According to Paul Haber, head of addiction medicine at Sydney University, the new guidelines went to being 'the least generous in the world at a single bound'.[68] Alex Wodak, chairman of the alcohol working party of the Royal College of Physicians, who helped devise earlier guidelines, also claimed that 'very few Australian males ... would think a maximum of two drinks is reasonable'.[69] There seems a clear inference from these critics that recommendations based on scientific assessments of immediate and long-term risks ought to be modified if they are culturally unpalatable.

Many health campaigners who questioned the notions of 'moderate drinking' would be glad of the new emphasis on 'low-risk' drinking and the implication that *all* other levels of drinking are, to a degree, risky. They have also questioned the notion of 'standard' drinks, viewing such terminology as being, at best, only mildly helpful and, at worst, misleading. There is widespread confusion, for example, between the recommended daily alcohol consumption for health and legal driving limits. A weekly average for males of twenty-eight standard drinks sounds very convenient; there are twenty-four stubbies in a 'slab'. Unfortunately, unless it is a stubbie of mid-strength beer, each stubbie or can is more than a standard drink. Generally, customers are not sold, and often do not buy, 'standard' drinks. Women in particular are consuming far more alcohol than they realise, as they are more likely to be drinking wine. The average quantity of wine equivalent to a standard drink is only 100 millilitres. Some blame the use of large wine glasses in restaurants and at home, but research has shown that when asked to pour a standard drink of wine, consumers estimated poorly, pouring a drink that was anything from 10 per cent to 100 per cent more than a standard drink.[70] For hard-pressed policy makers, concepts such as standard drinks and moderate drinking may have seemed a useful political compromise between the interests of health authorities and the alcohol industry. In practice, however, this compromise seems to heavily favour the alcohol industry at the expense of a relatively unknowledgeable public. And while the NHMRC guidelines are intended as advice as to what is low-risk, moderately risky and high-risk drinking, and are definitely not designed to promote alcohol consumption, they can be used to add legitimacy to industry claims, such as Lion Nathan's 'When enjoyed in moderation, beer confers a number of healthful attributes on drinkers'.

Alcohol's alleged 'health benefits' can be seen as another symptom of an industry fighting a rearguard defence against the most potent form of moral attack in a liberal society — the documenting of demonstrable harms. Even in the light of the apparent cardiovascular benefits from consuming very limited amounts of alcohol, the chairman of the Australian Brewers' Foundation, Professor Kwong Lee Dow, did not advise abstainers to start drinking. 'Health authorities and educators,' he said, 'need to acknowledge the role of alcohol in our society and develop policies that minimise the potential for physical, social and emotional harms that result from its use.'[71] In recent years, assessments of the studies linking moderate drinking to heart benefits have become increasingly nuanced, confirming that previous studies have often been misunderstood. According to Robert Ali, chairman of the addiction medicine chapter of the Australasian College of Physicians, alcohol's oft-cited protective effects are 'overstated, misunderstood and misrepresented'.[72] Any benefits — which are slight and seem only to apply to middle-aged men who drink low volumes — are on a finely balanced seesaw. Drink just two standard alcoholic drinks a day and you get the benefit; drink more and you start to lose the benefit. As evidenced by the autopsies of alcoholics, heavy drinking does clear the arteries, 'but what is the use of clean arteries at the cost of damage to major organs'.[73]

Medical researchers and alcohol companies have hugely different motivations when publishing the findings on their research. Medical researchers may be trying to assess health and other risks and find a 'safe' level of alcohol consumption, however problematic that concept may be and however many changes there may be over time to what constitutes 'safe' drinking. In contrast, alcohol companies are trying to encourage people to feel safe about consuming their product.

The bad news remains that 'alcohol causes 1.8 million deaths globally each year through trauma, injury, accidents and disease'.[74] In

Australia, alcohol kills at least 3000 people a year and causes more than 70,000 hospitalisations at a cost of $7.5 billion. Late in 2005, the Australian Drug Foundation called for health warnings to be placed on alcohol products and advertisements, 'both to inform consumers and balance the one-sided view put by industry advertising'.[75] Companies exporting to the US had already put some warnings on their labels to meet legislative requirements there.

The highly visible and non-selective nature of random breath testing has been a strong deterrent to drinking and driving.[76] Like any industry, brewers, distillers and vintners seek ever-increasing sales of their product, but with the introduction of random breath testing members of the public became aware that being caught driving while under the influence was an increased risk. Government and industry not only created the notion of the so-called 'standard drink'; they also now began to advise the public as to how much could be consumed of various beverages, and over what time frame, while still remaining under the legal driving limit. Random breath testing also led to a significant change in the type of beer consumed, particularly at social functions, with an increasing uptake of light and mid-strength drinks.

Social responsibility itself never sells beer, and is rarely a theme in beer commercials. Advertising campaigns for new light and mid-strength beers were carefully constructed to reinforce the notion that lower-alcohol beers could allow drinkers to 'stay a little bit longer', reinforcing traditional notions of drinking and mateship. A larrikin sense of irresponsibility has been preserved as a core part of the message — as seen in recent light beer advertisements from Hahn. In one, its male protagonist spoils a romantic moment by dive-bombing into a hot tub. In another, in the middle of a romantic tryst on the Grand Canal in Venice, he drags a fish into the gondola. The message is clear: it might be light beer, but it's still strong enough to make men do silly things.

For brewers, the initial serious challenge in producing lighter beers was filling the flavour gap, but technology came to the rescue, along with a renewed interest in boutique beers and the role of taste in marketing beer — a long-forgotten victim of the dominance of regionalism as the factor in beer consumption. Light beers have certainly done their job, and they regularly appear at social functions as a choice for drinkers. (Fear of litigation by event organisers if low-strength alternatives were not provided might also be a factor.) Consuming light beer, however, tends to reduce those pleasures of drinking derived from the effects of alcohol. That is perhaps why the real success story has been in the mid-strength market. In 2006, Foster's chief claimed that drinking patterns were changing, particularly in the humid climates of Queensland and Western Australia, where quantity consumed was important and mid-strength had emerged as the beer of choice. (Ironically, due to the diuretic and dehydrating effects of drinking alcohol, it is unlikely that drinkers' thirsts would, in fact, be relieved.) It is not surprising, then, that in 2007, Foster's was forced to introduce a mid-strength version of that icon of heavy beer drinking — VB. It was fully dressed up in a gold can to mimic XXXX Gold, Lion Nathan's highly successful mid-strength product. One real advantage these mid-strengths beers have over both heavier and lighter beers is that one can usually equals one standard drink, in theory making it easier for drinkers to calculate their levels of consumption. On the down side, mid-strength beers are often provided at hotels, restaurants and events as the light beer alternative, replacing genuine light beers which have even lower alcohol content.

One outcome of the shift to lower-strength beers is that the breweries can sell more product; that is, more units of beverage. Not only can individuals drink more of the product, due to Australia's tax system it is also cheaper. Not surprisingly, low-alcohol beer currently accounts for 40 per cent of all beer consumed in Australia.[77] Australian scientists have also been working on a low-alcohol wine in response to demands from the wine industry and drinkers. Australian wines have higher sugar content than overseas wines, which results in higher alcohol levels. Sakki Pretorius of the Australian Wine Research Institute confirmed that the motivation from the industry side was to increase sales. People will drink more wine, not less — a frank and fearless admission, no doubt pleasing to shareholders.[78] The very concept of 'light' wine, however, can be seen as a serious concession by an industry looking anxiously over its shoulder.

If the idea of light wine catches on to the same degree as mid-strength beer has, what will it say about where Australian society has come to after its long journey under the influence? Has the harm principle at last become sexy and saleable, or is it simply a fact that most Australians more clearly understand that individual freedoms need to be balanced by social responsibility? Light beer has become a consumer solution to the balancing act between individual freedom and social responsibility, perhaps a new symbol of Australian values 'lite'. It is worth considering the near fetishistic role light beer has played in the alcohol restrictions put in place in communities such as Palm Island in Queensland or Fitzroy Crossing in the Kimberleys in Western Australia, where there are bans on all takeaway alcohol except light beer.

But is light beer really the key to a sustainable drinking culture? Can the balance between freedom and responsibility be so easily commodified? Unless it involves some level of intoxication, is any drinking culture really sustainable as a drinking culture? The drug effect is a large part of the attraction of alcohol. As the National Health and Medical Research Council draft guidelines on alcohol consumption inform us: 'In lay terms, intoxication is a subjective feeling, the experience of a substantial effect of alcohol on mood, brain function, and psychomotor function. However, there are marked variations in the amount of alcohol different people need to consume in order to experience intoxication.'[79] Hasn't mood change been the ultimate purpose of drinking for the majority of Australians throughout our history?

Currently, the real battleground for working out a genuinely Australian solution to the perennial problem of balancing freedom with responsibility is in our Indigenous communities. Here the stakes are high: finding a solution to alcohol abuse is a matter of life and death to the individuals and the communities concerned. It is a morally challenging task, because in meeting that challenge each community will be given a chance to express who they are, what they value, and who and what they care about and for. Indigenous leader Noel Pearson's 'third way politics', with its rhetoric of personal responsibility and mutual obligation and its deep distaste for passive welfare, sometimes makes him appear to be a neo-liberal advocate of universal individual rights and an opponent of community consensus and community self-determination. At the same time, his advocacy of strong community control of antisocial behaviours suggests that he is deeply communitarian. Universalists and communitarians see the world in different ways, the former founding their values on a detached critical morality based on principles applicable to all individuals, and the latter basing morality on a deep involvement in a tradition. Pearson is not a universalist and he refuses to equate drinking rights with citizenship rights. His more substantive understanding of citizenship puts him in the communitarian camp. But if Pearson is a communitarian, he is clearly not a straightforwardly conservative one, or at least not a traditionalist. He seems intent on exploring new arrangements that express a collective commitment to fostering individual social responsibility.

In approaching the issue of alcohol abuse, Indigenous leaders such as Pearson completely reject the idea of harm minimisation. Pearson knows from experience that such measures do not work in an environment where alcohol is freely available. To those involved in alcohol treatment, he appears to advocate 'zero tolerance, the illness model of alcohol and blurring of the distinction between alcohol dependence and alcohol abuse'.[80] He even entertains the possibility of prohibition in some circumstances. It is highly unlikely that Pearson would complain that the new NHMRC draft guidelines for low-risk drinking are out of touch or culturally irrelevant, or that he would be fazed if very few males in any Australian community thought a maximum of two drinks was reasonable. In the end, the experience with Alcohol Management Plans in Queensland showed that merely fiddling with supply was not solving the problem. Pearson focuses on directly ameliorating the harms that alcohol abuse and dependency cause. In this respect, he is one of the few current Australian leaders on the same wavelength as John Stuart Mill. It is the social behaviour of drunks and its effects on others in the community that concerns Pearson, and he wishes to deal directly with the problems that alcohol is causing in Indigenous communities. Like Mill, Pearson is appalled by the damage to others caused by drinking alcohol, both directly through violence and sexual abuse and indirectly by neglect of family and society. His proposal for a Family Responsibility Commission goes directly to the heart of the matter, intervening not in a person's drinking or their right to drink, but in their neglect of their duties towards others, and thereby ensuring that funds are diverted to the care of others and away from alcohol. For Pearson, the consequences of such direct engagement would be a rebuilding of local Indigenous authority, ensuring that the essential expenses and educational needs of children are met, and that welfare payments are not spent on grog. Stronger local communities would be better equipped to deal with sly-grogging and the financial resources of those communities would not be drained by addictions.

There is little doubt that the majority of Australians have, knowingly or not, come to accept the classic utilitarian position of that great architect of western liberty John Stuart Mill. With regard to the use and misuse of alcohol in Australia, individual freedom needs to be balanced with social responsibility and not harming others. Speaking metaphorically, it's all about learning to live with fire without promoting pyromania. Is it possible that Noel Pearson's direct approach to dealing with the harms caused by alcohol will ultimately prove to be a more genuinely liberal approach than our collective experiments with drinking rights, harm minimisation and 'a sustainable culture of drinking'? As Pearson notes, 'We are entering uncharted waters.'[81] If his proposals work out as planned when trialled in Cape York communities in the near future, it will be an occasion of momentous import in Australia's long history under the influence of alcohol, perhaps undoing much of the damage that flowed from that fateful day in 1770 when Captain James Cook set foot on what he called Possession Island at the tip of Cape York, claiming the land from there to south of New South Wales for Britain and, unwittingly, launching it upon a sea of spirits.

CHEERS!

Afterword

Since finishing the main part of this book, public concern about the use and misuse of alcohol in Australia has continued apace. While we await the results of developments in Cape York, there are signs that sensible alcohol restrictions are working in Indigenous communities elsewhere. In 2008, when the liquor licensees in Halls Creek in the Kimberley's agreed to restrict sales of full-strength beer to thirty cans per person per day for two weeks the number of assaults in the community were halved.[1] Others may have not learned the lesson so well. Bra boy surf gang leader Koby Abberton, star of John Singleton's Bluetongue brewery internet beer ads, designed to circumvent alcohol advertising codes, was jailed in Hawaii for the assault of an off-duty police officer outside a nightclub.[2]

Many critics of the federal government's measures to address the binge-drinking problem among young people have questioned the effectiveness of the increase in excises on pre-mixed spirit drinks, labelling it a stunt and a revenue raiser.[3] Within months of the introduction of the increased excises the distilling industry was claiming that their own surveys of liquor shop owners were indicating that sales of pre-mixed drinks had decreased while sales of spirits had increased. The Rudd government countered that such increases were seasonal and expected, coinciding with the onset of winter. Figures quoted in February 2009 by the federal Health Minister, Helen Roxon, indicated that the measures were working far beyond original expectations, with alcopop sales falling by 40 per cent and overall spirits sales falling almost 10 per cent, seemingly disproving opponent's claims that the measures were merely revenue raisers.[4]

Perhaps the most significant indication that sales of pre-mixed drinks were declining was the move in early 2009 by Diageo, the world's largest alcohol company, to get around the negative impact of increased excises by introducing beer-based pre-mixed drinks to the Australian market. Such drinks were already available in overseas markets. Was this a move away from Gin Lane and back to Beer Street? Not really. The new Smirnoff Platinum drinks are colourless, and have a citrus taste, and while they are not as sweet as other alcopops, they still contain six per cent alcohol. Because the excise on beer is less than that on spirits, it is also a cheaper drink. Diageo's introduction of these drinks to Australia can be seen, on the one hand, as a grudging admission by the alcohol industry that the Rudd government's strategy was working. On the other hand, the move exposed a widely perceived weakness in the government's approach — that it was targeting particular beverages and particular drinkers, rather than the alcohol content itself.

Critics of the federal government's move to target alcopops tend to favour volumetric taxation. Beverages, they argue, ought to be taxed according to their alcohol content rather than their type. It is an idea strongly supported by both anti-alcohol campaigners and the distilling industry — the former arguing for consistency and the latter for fairness. Distillers claim that breweries, and in particular winemakers, receive favourable treatment under the present arrangements. Although volumetric taxation does seem logical, drinkers consume alcoholic beverages not units of alcohol, and the type of alcohol consumed varies according to gender and age of the drinker. Figures clearly show, for example, that pre-mixed spirits in a can are the preferred drink of over 60 per cent of both male and female drinkers between fourteen and nineteen years of age.[5] What is clear is the fact that increased taxes alone will not prevent alcohol harms. Education and changes to drinking environments must be combined with economic influences to reduce the multiple harms and damages caused by alcohol.

Alcohol-fuelled violence has become the focus of concern especially in New South Wales, where the Commissioner of Police, Andrew Scipione, a teetotaller and evangelical Christian, points out that extremely violent cities like Los Angeles have fewer alcohol-related assaults than cities like Newcastle and Sydney.[6] Clearly Australia faces a huge problem that urgently needs to be addressed. There is a good reason for New South Wales to be the focus on new initiatives to foster responsible alcohol consumption. Of the six hundred or so 24-hour drinking licences around Australia, 60 per cent of them are located in New South Wales, the vast majority in Sydney and Newcastle.

Faced with the reality that more than 40,000 drinkers are admitted to New South Wales hospitals each year with alcohol-related injuries and illnesses, the government of that state has been exploring a number of new measures, including a freeze on new 24-hour licences, the banning of glasses, and 2 am lockouts in violent and high-risk pubs, as well as calling for increased restrictions on alcohol advertising. According to a federal government report, quoted by the NSW health minister John Della Bosca, partial bans on alcohol advertising would reduce drinking by 16 per cent, road fatalities by 10 per cent, and the yearly social costs of alcohol abuse by

$2.45 billion and road accidents by $310 billion. A total ban on alcohol advertising in Australia was predicted to reduce drinking by 25 per cent, road fatalities by 30 per cent, the yearly social costs of alcohol abuse by $3.86 billion and road accidents by $960 billion.[7]

While these may seem like drastic measures to some, since 2000 the biggest increase in alcohol-related hospital admissions has been among 18 to 24 year-olds, with an overall increase of 130 per cent. Female admissions in that age group had increased by 200 per cent.[8] It is not surprising, then, that whereas advertising bans would have garnered little support in the not so distant past, according to a National Drug Strategy Household Survey released in November 2008, more than 72 per cent of respondents over 14 years of age currently support a ban on all alcohol advertising before 9.30 pm, and more than half supported banning alcohol sponsorship of sporting events.[9]

Sometime in the near future, 2008 and 2009 may be viewed as watershed years as far as alcohol and sport are concerned. High-profile athletes in all football codes, cricket, netball and swimming became front page news for alcohol-fuelled misdemeanours. Frustrated by the amount of attention devoted to incidents involving his high-profile players, Brisbane Bronco's rugby league club chief executive Bruno Cullen, whose team is sponsored by XXXX, Bundaberg Rum and Wyndham Estate wines, complained that relatively little corresponding attention had been given to other sports. He cited the fact that the Queensland Firebirds netball captain Peta Stephens, for example, had allegedly returned a .066 blood alcohol reading after being pulled over by police at 6 am after a night on the town.[10]

A study reported in the international journal *Addiction* in 2008 found that players from teams receiving alcohol industry sponsorship drank more heavily than those who did not. Of 1279 athletes surveyed, over half received sponsorship that included free drinks or discounted alcoholic drinks. Even free uniforms were enough to encourage players to drink the sponsor's product. More than half the players reported drinking at levels defined by the World Health Organization as hazardous, that is, more than six standard drinks in one sitting.[11]

As has been evidenced in this book, the relationship between alcohol and sport is pivotal to our culture. It is not surprising that all the major sports codes in Australia have seen the writing on the wall and signed up to be part of the Rudd government's $53 million dollar national alcohol code for sports. The strategy includes advertising, community initiatives and preventative education. The National Rugby League (NRL), the Australian Football League (AFL), Netball Australia, the Football Federation of Australia (soccer), the Australian Rugby Union and Cricket Australia have all supported a uniform code, which asks players to behave in a dignified and professional manner when drinking and not to put themselves or others at risk of injury or social harm. According to Andrew Demetriou, head of the AFL, promoting a responsible alcohol environment helps 'ensure our clubs are family-friendly environments.' He takes pride in the leading role that Aussie Rules players are taking in 'driving the responsible alcohol message', citing in particular the 'Just Think' campaign at Geelong, where AFL players led a campaign to promote a responsible alcohol attitude in response to problems at local nightclubs.[12] David Gallop, head of the NRL, who in 2009 weathered a storm of alcohol-fuelled controversy, agrees that if sport addresses its own issues it can play a lead role in changing attitudes. Abuse of alcohol, he says, is 'never someone else's problem', pointing out that a number of NRL players play a key role in spelling out the dangers of alcohol abuse and the distinction between responsible and irresponsible drinking. Yet, he adds, 'It is naïve to suggest that young people will never make mistakes but it is important to do all we can to prevent them being made.'[13]

Coupled with recent government moves to break the nexus between alcohol and sport, these are, perhaps, encouraging signs. Australians are now reflecting seriously on the use and misuse of alcohol and are moving beyond the divisive national stereotypes of boozers and wowsers toward a new era of social responsibility.

Endnotes

INTRODUCTION

1 'Shock drink ads air for schoolies', *The Australian*, 22–23 November 2008, p. 3.
2 'Shock ads on binge drinking', *Daily Telegraph*, 22 November 2008, p. 15.
3 'Teen booze binge', *Daily Telegraph*, 12 November 2008, p. 14.
4 Sonja Koremans, 'Absolut cuts pre-mixed drink from market', *B & T*, 31 July 2007, viewed at www.bandt.com.au/news/34/0c04eb34.asp, accessed 5 May 2008.
5 Australian Institute of Health and Welfare, *2007 National Drug Household Survey; First Results*, Drug Statistics Series No. 20, AIHW, Canberra.
6 '$56bn cost of drink and drugs', *The Australian,* 9 April 2008.
7 'Trouble in the Territory: The Darwin Revolution of 1918–1919', *Two Hundred Years*, Issue No. 9, Bay Books, Kensington, 1987, pp. 200–202.
8 Michael Symons, *One Continuous Picnic: A History of Eating in Australia*, Duck Press, Adelaide,1982, p. 59.
9 'Old believer not easily dismissed', *The Australian*, 31 October 2002, p. 13.
10 *Dinner for One*, director Heinz Dunkhase, released 31 December 1963 (West Germany), Norddeutscher Rundfunk (NDR).
11 Michael Wilding, *Marcus Clarke, Henry Kendall and Adam Lindsay Gordon* (in press).
12 Ross Fitzgerald and Mark Hearn, *Bligh, Macarthur and the Rum Rebellion*, Kangaroo Press, Sydney, 1988, p. 37.

CHAPTER 1: A GROGGY START

1 David Day and Australian Customs Service, *Smugglers and Sailors: The Customs History of Australia 1788–1901*, AGPS Press, Canberra, 1992, p. 2.
2 Alan Atkinson, *The Europeans in Australia: A History. Vol. 1: The Beginning*, Oxford University Press, Melbourne, 1998, p. 69.

3   Sidney W. Mintz, *Sweetness and Power: The Place of Sugar in Modern History*, Penguin, New York, 1985, p. 170.
4   ibid.
5   Geoffrey Blainey, *A Short History of the World*, Viking, Ringwood, Victoria, 2000, p. 411.
6   Sidney Mintz, op. cit., p. 43.
7   ibid., p. 40.
8   A. E. Dingle, '"The truly magnificent thirst": an historical survey of Australian drinking habits', *Historical Studies*, vol. 19, no. 75, October 1980, p. 235.
9   Alan Atkinson, op. cit., p. 62.
10 ibid., p. 208.
11 ibid., p. 262.
12 ibid., p. 209.
13 John Birmingham, *Leviathan: The Unauthorised Biography of Sydney*, Vintage, Sydney, 2000, p. 31.
14 Alasdair MacIntyre, *After Virtue: A Study in Moral Theory*, 2nd edition, Duckworth, London, 1984, pp. 236–7.
15 ibid., p. 235.
16 ibid., p. 241.
17 M. H. Ellis, *John Macarthur*, Angus & Robertson, Sydney, 1955, pp. 46–47.
18 Sidney Mintz, op. cit., p. 178.
19 G. Austin, *Alcohol in Western Society from Antiquity to 1800: A Chronological History*, ABC-Clio Information Services, Santa Barbara, 1986, p. 298.
20 Sidney Mintz, op. cit., p. 138.
21 ibid., p. 170.
22 E. Malcolm, *'Ireland Sober, Ireland Free': Drink and Temperance in Nineteenth-Century Ireland*, Gill and Macmillan, Dublin, 1986.
23 A. Herman, *The Scottish Enlightenment: The Scots' Invention of the Modern World*, Fourth Estate, London, 2001, p. 183.
24 A. E. Dingle, 'Drink and working-class living standards in Britain, 1870–1914', in D. J. Oddy and D. S. Miller (eds), *The Making of the Modern British Diet*, Croom Helm, London, 1976; F. Braudel, *Capitalism and Material Life 1400–1800*, Harper, pp. 168 and 324.
25 Alan Atkinson, op. cit., p. 87.
26 Keith C. Powell, *Drinking and Alcohol in Colonial Australia 1788–1901 for the Eastern Colonies*, National Campaign Against Drug Abuse, Monograph Series No. 3, AGPS, Canberra, 1988, p. 6.
27 David Day, op. cit., p. 5.
28 *Historical Records of Australia*, series 1, vol. 1, p. 376.
29 M. H. Ellis, op. cit., p. 46.
30 ibid.
31 Cited in Ross Fitzgerald and Mike Hearn, op. cit., p. 25.
32 T. G. Parsons, cited in ibid., p. 26.
33 Cited in ibid., p. 23.
34 David Day, op. cit., p. 3.
35 ibid.

36 Keith C. Powell, op. cit., p. 7.
37 Stuart Macintyre, *A Concise History of Australia*, 2nd edition, Cambridge University Press, Melbourne, 2004, p. 36.
38 Cited in Fitzgerald and Hearn, op. cit., p. 40.
39 ibid., p. 41.
40 Sidney Mintz, op. cit., p. 169.
41 Alan Atkinson, op. cit., p. 42.
42 Cited in Fitzgerald and Hearn, op. cit., p. 43.
43 ibid.
44 Cited in David Day, op. cit., pp. 7 and 9.
45 Cited in Fitzgerald amd Hearn, op. cit., p. 45.
46 David Day, op. cit., p. 10.
47 ibid., p. 11.
48 ibid., p. 12.
49 ibid., p. 13.
50 ibid.
51 M. H. Ellis, op. cit., p. 49.
52 David Day, op. cit., p. 60.
53 Cited in Fitzgerald and Hearn, op. cit., p. 44.
54 ibid., p. 45.
55 David Day, op. cit., p. 16.
56 Fitzgerald and Hearn, op. cit., p. 50.
57 ibid., p. 48.
58 ibid., p. 49.
59 Stuart Macintyre, op. cit., p. 38.
60 David Day, op. cit., p. 26.
61 Michael Duffy, *Man of Honour: John Macarthur: Duellist, Rebel, Founding Father*, Pan Macmillan, Sydney, 2003.
62 Alain de Botton, *Status Anxiety*, Pantheon Books, New York, 2004, p. 108.
63 Fitzgerald and Hearn, op. cit., p. 53.
64 ibid.
65 Alan Atkinson, op. cit., p. 305.
66 David Day, op. cit., p. 61.
67 ibid., p. 52.
68 Cited in ibid., p. 58.
69 ibid., p. 59.
70 ibid, p. 60.
71 Cited in M. H. Ellis, op. cit., p. 309.
72 Cited in Fitzgerald and Hearn, op. cit., p. 91.
73 ibid., pp. 103–104.
74 ibid., p. 107.
75 ibid., p. 110.
76 Jeremy Bentham, *A Plea for the Constitution: Shewing the Enormities Committed, to the oppression of British subjects, innocent as well as guilty; in breach of Magna Charta, the Petition of Right, the Habeas Corpus Act, and the Bill of Rights. As likewise of Several Transportation Acts, in and by the Design, Foundation, and*

Government of the Penal Colony of New South Wales; see Alan Atkinson, 'Jeremy Bentham and the Rum Rebellion', *Journal of the Royal Australian Historical Society*, vol. 64, 1978, pp. 1–3; on the general influence of utilitarian ideas on the empire, see B. Schultz and G. Varouxakis, G. (eds), *Utilitarianism and Empire*, Lexington Books, Lanham, 2005.

77 Alan Atkinson, op. cit., p. 304.
78 Cited in Alan Atkinson, op. cit., p. 304.
79 ibid.
80 ibid., p. 305.
81 Cited in M. H. Ellis, op. cit., p. 405.
82 Cited in Fitzgerald and Hearn, op. cit., p. 123.
83 Alan Atkinson, op. cit., p. 281.
84 ibid.
85 'Trouble in the Territory: The Darwin Revolution of 1918–1919', *Two Hundred Years*, op. cit.
86 Alan Powell, 'Gilruth, John Anderson (1871–1937)', *Australian Dictionary of Biography*, vol. 9, Melbourne University Press, Melbourne, 1983, pp. 17–19.
87 Ernestine Hill, *The Territory*, Angus & Robertson, Sydney, 1951, p. 286.
88 Alan Powell, op. cit.
89 Ernestine Hill, op. cit., p. 287.
90 Alan Powell, op. cit., p. 18.
91 Raffaello Carboni, *The Eureka Stockade*, reprinted 1855; with introduction by Thomas Keneally, Melbourne University Press, Melbourne, 1993, p. 54.
92 ibid., p. 89.
93 ibid., p. 91.
94 ibid., p. 93.
95 Geoffrey Blainey, *The Rush That Never Ended: A History of Australian Mining*, 5th edition, Melbourne University Press, Melbourne, 2003, pp. 55–56.
96 ibid.
97 John Molony, *Eureka*, Melbourne University Press, Melbourne, 2001, pp. 149–50.
98 'Old believer not easily dismissed', *The Australian*, 31 October 2002, p. 13.

CHAPTER 2: A MASS OF IMMOVABLE MEN
1 Cited in Michael Symons, *One Continuous Picnic: A History of Eating in Australia*, Duck Press, Adelaide, 1982, p. 51.
2 Jonathan Dawson, 'Our Beer', in J. Dawson and B. Molloy (eds), *Queensland Images in Film and Television*, University of Queensland Press, St Lucia, 1990, p. 103.
3 ibid., p. 98.
4 Michael Symons, op. cit., p. 119.
5 John Birmingham, *Leviathan: The Unauthorised Biography of Sydney*, Vintage, Sydney, 2000, p. 45.
6 Cited in Michael Symons, op. cit., p. 51.
7 Roland Barthes, *Mythologies*, Paladin, London, 1973, p. 59.
8 Jonathan Dawson, op. cit., p. 94.

9   Andrew McGahan, 'Nor made in Queensland', in R. Sheahan-Bright and S. Glover (eds), *Hot Iron Corrugated Sky: 100 Years of Queensland Writing*, University of Queensland Press, St Lucia, 2002, p. 40.

10 ibid.

11 J. M. Freeland, *The Australian Pub*, Sun Books, Melbourne, 1977, p. 171.

12 *The Bulletin*, 4 May 2005, listed the granting of a licence to Sarah Bird as one of 'the 125 most defining moments in our dramatic history'.

13 C. Wright, *Beyond the Ladies' Lounge: Australia's Female Publicans*, Melbourne University Press, Melbourne, 2001, p. 20.

14 J. M. Freeland, op. cit., p. 171.

15 Cited in Geoffrey Blainey, *A Shorter History of Australia*, William Heinemann, Melbourne, 1994, p. 33.

16 N. G. Butlin, 'Ho, ho, ho and how many bottles of rum?', *Australian Economic Historical Review*, vol. 23, 1983.

17 A. G. L. Shaw, '1788–1819', in F. Crowley (ed), *A New History of Australia*, William Heinemann, Melbourne, 1974.

18 Milton Lewis, *A Rum State: Alcohol and State Policy in Australia*, AGPS, Canberra, 1992, p. 7; citing K. C. Powell, *Drinking and Alcohol in Australia 1788–1901 for the Eastern Colonies*, AGPS, Canberra, 1988, pp. 8–9, 52.

19 Milton Lewis, ibid.; citing W. J. Rorabaugh, *The Alcoholic Republic: An American Tradition*, Oxford University Press, New York, 1979, p. 5.

20 A. E. Dingle, '"The truly magnificent thirst": an historical survey of drinking habits', op. cit., p. 242.

21 Garryowen, *The Chronicles of Early Melbourne 1835–1852, Historical, Anecdotal and Personal*, vol. 2, Fergusson & Mitchell, Melbourne, 1888.

22 *Report of the Royal Commission of the Wine, Spirit, Sale Statute, 1867.*

23 Cited in 'Australian Beer History', www.australianbeers.com/history/history.htm, viewed 19 April 2006.

24 Garryowen, op. cit., p. 559.

25 ibid.

26 Cited in 'Australian Beer History', op. cit.

27 See Brett J. Stubbs, 'Captain Cook's beer: the antiscorbutic use of malt and beer in late 18th century sea voyages', *Asia Pacific Journal of Clinical Nutrition*, vol. 12, no. 2, 2003, pp. 129–137.

28 ibid., p. 129.

29 ibid., p. 135.

30 J. M. Freeland, op. cit., p. 30.

31 K. T. H. Farrer, *A Settlement Amply Supplied: Food Technology in Nineteenth Century Australia*, Melbourne University Press, 1980.

32 Cited in Michael Symons, op. cit., p. 104.

33 M. Bingham, *Cascade: A Taste of History*, The Cascade Brewing Company Ltd, Hobart, 1991; 'History of Cascade Brewery', www.cascadebrewery.com.au/history.html viewed 9 June 2006.

34 'Brewing industry feature', *Food Australia*, vol. 46, no. 4, April 1994, p. 165.

35 K. T. H. Farrer, op. cit., p. 214.

36 Michael Symons, op. cit., p. 105.

37   Brett J. Stubbs, 'City vs. Country: the demise of the brewing industry in country New South Wales c. 1898–1932', *Australian Geographer*, vol. 31, no. 1, 2000, p. 56.
38   T. A. Coghlan, *A Statistical Account of the Seven Colonies of Australasia*, Government Printer, Sydney, 1891.
39   For state comparisons of alcohol consumption, see K. E. Powell, *Drinking and Alcohol in colonial Australia 1785–1901 for the Eastern Colonies*, Monograph Series No. 3, AGPS, Canberra, 1988; A. E. Dingle, op. cit.
40   R. Twopenny, *Town Life in Australia*, Elliot Stock, London, 1883, p. 64.
41   Michael Symons, op. cit., p. 105.
42   ibid.
43   ibid.
44   ibid., pp. 133–134.
45   Michael Symons, op. cit., p. 134.
46   Geoffrey Blainey, op. cit., p. 128.
47   ibid.
48   'Brewing industry feature', p. 162.
49   ibid.
50   Jonathan Dawson, op. cit., p. 102.
51   ibid., p. 98.
52   AAP Australian National News Wire, 28 September 2006.
53   'Alan Bond', www.australianbeers.com, viewed 12 June 2006.
54   'Our Brewery', www.malt-shovel.com.cu/ brewery.asp, viewed 17 June 2006.
55   'Brewing Industry Feature', p. 165.
56   VB website, 'VB Midstrength Lager', www.fosters.com.au/enjoy/ VBmid.htm, viewed 18 June 2007.
57   Lyrics by Barry Humphries, used with permission.
58   *Stateline*, ABC TV, 20 October 2001.
59   Jonathan Dawson, op. cit., p. 103.
60   ibid., p. 102.
61   ibid., p. 103.
62   Russel Ward, *The Australian Legend*, 2nd edition, Oxford University Press, South Melbourne, 1966, p. i.
63   ibid., p. vii.
64   ibid., p. 2.
65   J. S. Blocker, '*Give to the Winds Thy Fears': The Women's Temperance Crusade, 1873–74*, Greenwood Press, Westport Conne, 1985.
66   A. E. Dingle, op. cit., p. 240.
67   *Western Australian Year Book*, 1902–1904, p. 286.
68   ibid., p. 322.
69   *Victoria Year Book*, 1889–1890, p. 78.
70   T. A. Coghlan, op. cit., p. 27.
71   ibid., p. 27.
72   ibid., p. 352.
73   *The Australia Handbook for 1897*, Gordon & Gotch, p. 86.
74   T. A. Coghlan, op. cit., 1897, p. 356.

75   T. A. Coghlan, op. cit., 1886–1887, p. 500.

76   ibid.

77   ibid.

78   ibid.

79   Richard Cashman, *Paradise of Sport: The Rise of Organised Sport in Australia*, Oxford University Press, Melbourne, 1995, p. 23.

80   ibid., p. 24.

81   ibid., p. 23.

82   P. Corris, *Lords of the Ring: A History of Prize Fighting in Australia*, Cassell, Sydney, 1980, pp. 102–3.

83   R. R. Aitken et al., *Mercantile: A Century of Rowing*, Mercantile Rowing Club, Melbourne, 1980, p. 103.

84   Richard Cashman, op. cit., p. 23.

85   R. Stremski, *Kill for Collingwood*, Allen & Unwin, Sydney, 1986, p. 139.

86   Corris, op. cit., p. 84.

87   J. H. Fingleton, *The Immortal Victor Trumper*, Collins, London, 1978, p. 135.

88   Gideon Haig, *The Big Ship: Warwick Armstrong and the Making of Modern Cricket*, Aurum Press, London, 2002, p. 173.

89   ibid.

90   J. Mulvaney and R. Harcourt, *Cricket Walkabout: The Australian Aborigines in England*, MacMillan, Melbourne, 1988, p. 135.

91   M. Lake, 'The Politics of Respectability: Identifying the Masculinist Context', *Historical Studies*, Vol. 22, No. 1, April 1986.

92   C. McConville, 'Rough women, respectable men and social reform: a response to Lake's "masculinism"', *Historical Studies*, vol. 22, no. 88, April 1987.

93   *Report of the Royal Commission of the Wine, Spirit, Sale Statute, 1867,* p. 17.

94   ibid.

95   D. Kirkby, *Barmaids: A History of Women's Work in Pubs*, Cambridge University Press, Melbourne, 1997.

96   *Report of the Board Appointed to Inquire into the Question of the Treatment of Habitual Drunkards*, p. 30.

97   W. M. James Mercer, *Emily Graham: or the Dawning of Light: A Temperance Tale*, James Curtis, Ballarat, 1870.

98   *Union Signal*, 6586.

99   J. Allen, '"Mundane" men: historians, masculinity and masculinism', *Historical Studies*, vol. 22, No. 89, October 1987.

100 K. Peiss, '"Charity girls" and city pleasures: historical notes on working class sexuality, 1880–1920', in A. Snitow et al., *Powers of Desire: The Politics of Sexuality*, Monthly Review Press, New York, 1983.

101 *The Age*, 18 November 2005.

102 *The Age*, 19 May 2006.

103 *The Australian*, 19 June 2006.

104 Rory Gibson, 'A star is born', *Courier-Mail*, Good Life, 3 October 2005, p. 11.

105 ibid.

CHAPTER 3: GLASS DISTINCTIONS

1   K. T. H. Farrer, 'The Rev Dr J. I. Bleasdale and the Medical Society of Victoria', *Journal of the Royal Society of Medicine*, vol. 86, March 1993, p. 166.
2   See 'How we entertained a prince' in Michael Symons, op. cit., pp. 57–59.
3   ibid.
4   A. Herman, *The Scottish Enlightenment: The Scots' Invention of the Modern World*, Fourth Estate, London, 2001, p. 183.
5   Michael Symons, op. cit., p. 38.
6   Robert Mayne, *Understanding Australian Wine*, Australia Wine and Brandy Corporation with Heritage Publications, Sydney, 2nd edition, 1986, p. 31.
7   Michael Symons, op. cit., p. 18.
8   John Beeston, *A Concise History of Australian Wine*, Allen & Unwin, Sydney, 1994, p. 5.
9   ibid., p. 10.
10   D. Dunstan, *Better Than Pommard! A History of Wine in Victoria*, Australian Scholarly Publishing, Melbourne, 1994.
11   Reportedly in 1988 the English wine writer Hugh Johnston tasted a red produced at Camden Park between 1825 and 1870. He found it to be 'of enormous richness'; cited in 'Wine Literature of the World', State Library of South Australia, www.winelit.slsa.sa.gov.au/ ozwater.htm, accessed 20 August 2006, p. 1.
12   K. T. H. Farrer, op. cit., p. 23; 'Wine Literature of the World', State Library of South Australia, www.winelit.slsa.sa.gov.au/ozwater.htm, accessed 20 August 2006, p. 1.
13   John Beeston, op. cit., p. 13.
14   K. T. H. Farrer, op. cit., p. 23; 'Wine Literature of the World', op. cit.
15   John Beeston, op. cit., p. 20.
16   *The Vagabond Papers: Sketches of Melbourne in Light and Shade*, Series III, George Robertson, Melbourne, 1877, p. 101.
17   R. Twopenny, *Town Life in Australia*, Elliot Stock, London, 1883, p. 64.
18   *The Wakefield Companion to South Australian History*, Wakefield Press, Adelaide, 2001.
19   'Gramp, Johann (1819–1903)', *Australian Dictionary of Biography*, vol. 4, Melbourne University Press, Melbourne, 1972, p. 283.
20   John Beeston, op. cit., p. 42.
21   Jaki Ilbery, 'Smith, Samuel (1812–1889)', *Australian Dictionary of Biography*, Vol. 6, Melbourne University Press, Melbourne, 1976, p. 157.
22   D. Dunstan, op. cit., p. 54,
23   John Beeston, op. cit., p. 44.
24   ibid., p. 45.
25   ibid., p. 49.
26   Osmar White, *A Guide and Dictionary to Australian Wine*, Lansdowne Press, Melbourne, 1972, p. 33.
27   'The eccentric genius that was Benno', www.seppelt.com.au/house/ benno.html, accessed 22 June 2007.
28   Claude Lévi-Strauss, *The Savage Mind*, Weidenfeld & Nicolson, London, 1972.

29   This description is based on the process as described by Osmar White, *A Guide and Dictionary to Australian Wine*, Lansdowne, Melbourne, 1972, p. 33.
30   Mayne, op. cit., p. 26.
31   John Beeston, op. cit., p. 119.
32   Robert Mayne, op. cit., p. 24.
33   Osmar White, op. cit., p. 19.
34   Robert Mayne, op. cit., p. 67.
35   Osmar White, op. cit., p. 35.
36   John Beeston, op. cit., p. 202.
37   ibid., p. 203.
38   ibid., p. 217.
39   ibid., p. 223.
40   ibid., p. 230.
41   ibid., p. 230.
42   ibid., p. 231.
43   ibid., p. 230.
44   Robert Mayne, op. cit., p. 83.
45   ibid., p. 83.
46   ibid., p. 85.
47   John Beeston, op. cit., p. 232.
48   'Murray Tyrrell', National Portrait Gallery, www.portrait.gov.au/static/coll_908Murray+Tyrrell.php, accessed 22 June 2007.
49   'The History of Wolf Blass', www.nicks.com.au, accessed 20 August 2006.
50   ibid.
51   John Beeston, op. cit., p. 259.
52   *The Age*, 18 November 2005.
53   Figures taken from the *1998 National Drug Strategy Household Survey*, Australian Institute of Health and Welfare, as quoted in Gary Hulse, Jason White and Gavin Cape (eds), *Management of Alcohol and Drug Problems*, Oxford University Press, Oxford, 2002, p. 11.
54   Pramod Adhikari and Amber Summerill, *1998 National Drug Strategy Household Survey: Detailed Findings*, Australian Institute of Health and Welfare, Canberra, 2000, p. 12.
55   ibid., p. 21.
56   ibid.
57   Hulse, et al., op. cit., p. 311.
58   P. Adhikari and M. Summerill, op. cit., p. 21.
59   ibid., p. 19.
60   Hulse et al., op. cit., p. 311.
61   ibid., p. 10.
62   ibid.
63   Geoffrey Blainey, *Black Kettle and Full Moon: Daily Life in a Vanished Australia*, Viking, Melbourne, 2003, p. 336.
64   ibid.
65   'Intoxication', *The Way We Were*, ABC TV, 21 August 2004.

66   Wayne J. Kelly, *Booze Built Australia*, Queensland Classic Books, Brisbane, 1994, p. 5.
67   David McKnight, *From Hunting to Drinking: The devastating effects of alcohol on an Australian Aboriginal community*, Routledge, London, 2002, p. 194.
68   Wayne J. Kelly, op. cit., p. 5.
69   'Intoxication', *The Way We Were*, op. cit.
70   Pamela Lyon, *What Everybody Knows About Alice: A report on the impact of alcohol abuse on the town of Alice Springs*, Tangentyere Council, Alice Springs, 1990, p. 115.
71   ibid., p. 116.
72   ibid., p. 30.
73   Heuristics has recently been popularised in J. Groopman, *How Doctors Think*, Scribe, Melbourne, 2007.
74   *2001 National Drug Strategy Household Survey*, Australian Institute of Health and Welfare, Canberra, 2001, p. 17.
75   ibid., p. 15.
76   ibid.
77   ibid., spirits consumption measured in litres of pure alcohol.
78   *Apparent Consumption of Alcohol — Australia 2004–05* Australian Bureau of Statistics, Canberra, 2006, p. 142.
79   P. Adhikari and M. Summerill, op. cit., p. 14. Includes the whole population from the age of fourteen upwards.
80   'Stalking the devil in the drink', *Courier-Mail*, 16–17 February 2008, p. 51.
81   John Smart and John Wiggers, *The White Wine Boom: An analysis of liquor preference in Australia*, revised edition, Department of Sociology, University of Newcastle, Australia, 1985, p. 2.
82   'Intoxication', *The Way We Were*, op. cit.
83   Ross Fitzgerald and Harold Thornton, *Labor in Queensland: From the 1880s to 1988*, University of Queensland Press, St Lucia, Queensland, 1989, p. 192.
84   J, Smart and J. Wiggers, op. cit., p. 3.
85   ibid., p. 41.
86   ibid., p. 42.
87   ibid., pp. 32–38.
88   ibid., p. 22.
89   ibid., p. 99.
90   ibid., p. 4.
91   ibid., p. 24.
92   ibid., p. 18.
93   Clara Iaccarino, 'Girls who misbehave even better than boys', *Sun-Herald*, 15 February 2004, p. 35.
94   P. Adhikari and M. Summerill, op. cit., p. 14.
95   ibid.
96   *Don's Party*, Screensound Australia, Canberra, 1976.
97   ibid.
98   ibid.
99   ibid.

CHAPTER 4: A PUB WITH NO BEER

1   A. E. Blainey, 'The prohibition and total abstinence movement in Australia, 1880–1910', in R. Dare (ed), *Food, Power and Community: Essays in the History of Food and Drink*, Wakefield Press, Adelaide, 1999, p. 142.
2   I. Tyrrell, *Woman's World: Woman's Empire: The Woman's Christian Temperance Union in International Perspective, 1880–1930*, University of North Carolina Press, Chapel Hill, 1991, p. 18.
3   Ross Fitzgerald, 'Through a glass darkly', *Courier-Mail*, 18 May 2000, p. 15.
4   A. E. Dingle, '"That truly magnificent thirst": an historical survey of Australian drinking habits', op. cit., pp. 243–244.
5   Cited in William J. Sonnenstuhl, *Working Sober: The Transformation of an Occupational Drinking Culture*, Cornell University Press, New York, 1996. p. 7.
6   L. L. Shiman, *Crusade Against Drink in Victorian England*, Macmillan, Basingstoke, 1988, p. 23.
7   M. Roe, *Quest for Authority in Eastern Australia 1835–1851*, Melbourne University Press, Melbourne, 1965, p. 165.
8   Garryowen, op. cit., p. 535.
9   *Temperance News*, September 1870.
10 L. L. Shiman, op. cit., p. 110.
11 R. Bordin, *Woman and Temperance: The Quest for Power and Liberty*, Temple University Press, Philadelphia, 1981, p. 3.
12 Alan Atkinson, *Camden*, Oxford University Press, Melbourne, 1988, p. 181.
13 *Spectator*, August–September 1882.
14 *White Ribbon Signal* (New South Wales), November 1894.
15 A. Hyslop, 'Temperance, Christianity and Feminism: The Woman's Christian Temperance Union of Victoria, 1887–1987', *Historical Studies*, Vol. 17, No. 66, April 1976, p. 34.
16 P. O'Farrell, *The Catholic Church and Community in Australia: A History*, Thomas Nelson, Melbourne, 1977, p. 283.
17 WCTU of Victoria, *Annual Report*, 1891.
18 *Union Signal*, 3 June 1886.
19 A. Mitchell, 'Temperance and the Liquor Question in Later Nineteenth Century Victoria', MA Thesis, University of Melbourne, 1966, p. 90.
20 *Spectator*, 17 October 1884.
21 A. E. Blainey, op. cit., p. 147.
22 ibid.
23 L. L. Shiman, op. cit., p. 70.
24 *White Ribbon Signal*, March 1905.
25 *Temperance in Australia: The Memorial Volume of the International Temperance Convention 1888*, Melbourne, 1889, p. 247.
26 T. Broadribb, *Manual of Health and Temperance*, Government Printer, Melbourne, 1891.
27 For a history of the colonial local option movements see *Temperance in Australia: The Memorial Volume of the International Temperance Convention 1888*, Melbourne, 1889.

28 John C. Oldmeadow, 'Casey, James Joseph (1831–1913)', *Australian Dictionary of Biography*, vol. 3, Melbourne University Press, 1969, pp. 365–6.

29 A. E. Blainey 'The "Fallen" are Every Mother's Children: The Woman's Christian Temperance Union's Campaigns for Temperance, Women's Suffrage and Sexual Reform in Australia, 1885–1905', PhD Thesis, La Trobe University, 2000, p. 69.

30 B. Harrison, *Drink and the Victorians: The Temperance Question in England, 1815–1872*, Faber, London, 1971, p. 201.

31 For more on this theme see A. E. Blainey, 'The "Fallen" Are Every Mother's Children', op. cit., pp. 105–10.

32 *Alliance Record*, 23 March 1889.

33 *Alliance and Temperance News*, 1 April 1896.

34 *Temperance News*, June 1872.

35 A. Mitchell, 'Temperance and the Liquor Question in Later C19th Victoria', MA Thesis, University of Melbourne, 1966, p. 215.

36 *Southern Cross*, 11 January 1995.

37 *Official Year Book of the Commonwealth of Australia, 1901–1919*, p. 1117.

38 *Alliance Record*, December 1903.

39 J. D. Bollen, 'The temperance party and the Liberal Party in NSW politics, 1900–1914', *Journal of Religious History*, vol. 1, no. 3, June 1961, p. 178.

40 W. H. Wilde, *Courage and Grace: A Biography of Dame Mary Gilmore*, Melbourne University Press, Melbourne, 1988, p. 92.

41 *Temperance in Australia: The Memorial Volume of the International Temperance Convention 1888*, Melbourne, 1889, pp. 114 and 116.

42 *Argus*, 9 September, 1885.

43 *Alliance Record*, July 1884.

44 *Alliance Record*, September 1885.

45 M. Lake, 'The Politics of Respectability: Identifying the Masculinist Context', *Historical Studies*, Vol. 22, No. 86, April 1986, p. 127.

46 *Report of the Royal Commission of the Wine, Spirit, Sale Statute, 1867*, p. 17.

47 E. Windschuttle, 'Women, Class and Temperance: Moral Reform in Eastern Australia, 1832–1857', *Push from the Bush*, No. 3, May 1979, p. 20.

48 See, for example, *Temperance News*, February 1872.

49 *Spectator*, 19 June 1883.

50 B. H. Lee, *One of Australia's Daughters: An Autobiography of Mrs Harrison Lee*, Ideal Publishing Union, London, 1900, p. 74.

51 *Champion*, 16 May 1896.

52 WCTU of Australasia, *Minutes of Triennial Convention*, 1891.

53 J. S. Blocker, *Retreat from Reform: The Prohibition Movement in the United States, 1890–1913*, Greenwood, Westport Conn., 1976, p. 42.

54 A. E. Blainey, 'The "fallen" are every mother's children', op. cit., pp. 111–112.

55 *Alliance Record*, March 1895.

56 D. Kirkby, *Barmaids: A History of Women's Work in Pubs*, Cambridge University Press, Melbourne, 1997, p. 38.

57 A. E. Blainey, 'The "fallen" are every mother's children', op. cit., p. 140.

58 ibid., pp. 138–139.

59 A. E. Blainey, 'The prohibition and total abstinence movement in Australia, 1880–1910', op. cit., pp. 143–146.
60 *Australian Temperance World*, 1 January 1896.
61 WCTU of South Australia, *Annual Report*, 1893.
62 *Alliance Record*, September 1895.
63 B. H. Lee, op. cit., p. 200.
64 *Alliance Record*, 8 March 1890.
65 B. Harrison, 'The rhetoric of reform in modern Britain 1780–1918', in B. Harrison (ed), *Peaceable Kingdom: Stability and Change in Modern Britain*, Clarendon Press, Oxford, 1982, p. 378.
66 *Report of the Board Appointed to Inquire into the Question of the Treatment of Habitual Drunkards, VPP, 1899–1900.*
67 A. E. Blainey, 'The prohibition and total abstinence movement in Australia, 1880–1910', op. cit., p. 145.
68 WCTU of Victoria, *Annual Report*, 1893.
69 *Report of the Board Appointed to Inquire into the Question of the Treatment of Habitual Drunkards, VPP, 1899–1900.*
70 *Official Year Book of the Commonwealth of Australia*, No. 6, 1901–12, pp. 1175–82.
71 *Alliance and Temperance News*, March 1892.
72 *Official Year Book of the Commonwealth of Australia*, 1901–1919, pp. 1112–4.
73 *Alliance Record*, 6 September 1890.
74 *Victorian Year Book*, 1910–1911, p. 399.
75 F. B. Boyce, *The Drink Problem in Australia or the Plagues of Alcohol and the Remedies*, National Temperance League Publication Depot, London, 1893, p. 93.
76 *Alliance Record*, 6 September 1891.
77 F. B. Boyce, op. cit., p. 93.
78 A. E. Dingle, op. cit., pp. 247–249.
79 ibid., p. 234.
80 T. A. Coghlan, *The Wealth and Progress of New South Wales, 1886–87*, Sydney, 1887, p. 501; *Victorian Year-Book, 1908–1909*, p. 178.
81 W. Phillips, '"Six o'clock swill": the introduction of early closing of hotel bars in Australia', *Historical Studies*, vol. 19, no. 75, October 1980, p. 250.
82 ibid.
83 ibid., p. 256.
84 A. E. Dingle, op. cit., p. 246.
85 *WCTU of Australia, Minutes of the Triennial Convention*, 1921.
86 *Official Year Book of the Commonwealth of Australia, 1901–1919*, p. 881.
87 Referenda results are available on the respective parliamentary websites.
88 A. E. Dingle, op. cit., p. 246.

CHAPTER 5: IN HARM'S WAY

1   N. Heather, 'Pleasures and Pains of Our Favourite Drug', in N. Heather, T. J. Peters and T. Stockwell (eds), *International Handbook of Alcohol Dependence and Problems*, John Wiley & Sons, Chichester, 2001, p. 5.

2   *Report of Proceedings of Summit on Alcohol Abuse, Day 1*, Parliament of New South Wales, 2003, p. 6.

3   ibid.

4   *Report of Proceedings of Summit on Alcohol Abuse, Communique*, Parliament of New South Wales, 2003, p. 4.

5   'Alcohol: time to change attitudes', *Sydney Morning Herald*, 30 August 2003, p. 36.

6   John Birmingham, 'Bob, mate, that's what governments are meant to do', *Sydney Morning Herald*, 27 August 2003, p. 13.

7   Betsy Thom, 'A Social and Political History of Alcohol', in N. Heather, T. J. Peters and T. Stockwell (eds), *International Handbook of Alcohol Dependence and Problems*, John Wiley & Sons, Chichester, p. 2001, p. 19.

8   ibid.

9   *Alcoholics Anonymous: The Story of How Many Thousands of Men and Women Have Recovered from Alcoholism*, 4th edition, Alcoholics Anonymous World Services, New York, 2001, p. 59.

10 Betsy Thom, op. cit., p. 16.

11 Jean-Charles Sournia, *A History of Alcoholism*, Basil Blackwell, Oxford, 1990, p. xi.

12 ibid., p. 46.

13 Susanna Barrows and Robin Room, *Drinking: Behaviour and Belief in Modern History*, University of California Press, Berkeley, 1991, p. 418.

14 Geoffrey Blainey, *Black Kettle and Full Moon: Daily Life in a Vanished Australia*, Viking, Melbourne, 2003, p. 315.

15 S. Barrows and R. Room, op. cit., p. 405.

16 Ross Fitzgerald, 'Through a glass darkly', op. cit., p. 15.

17 H. Russell Smart, *Socialism and Drink*, 2nd edition. Manchester, UK, 1895.

18 ibid., p. 4.

19 Ross Fitzgerald, op. cit., p. 15.

20 *Brisbane Courier*, 30 May 1917.

21 Ross Fitzgerald and Harold Thornton, *Labor in Queensland: From the 1880s to 1988*, University of Queensland, St Lucia, 1989, p. 76.

22 S. Barrows and R. Room, op. cit., plate 6.

23 Milton Lewis, *Managing Madness: Psychiatry and Society in Australia 1788–1980*, Australian Government Publishing Service, Canberra, 1988, pp. 8–9.

24 Milton Lewis, *A Rum State: Alcohol and State Policy in Australia*, AGPS, Canberra, 1992, p. 100.

25 Milton Lewis, *Managing Madness* ..., op. cit., p. 1.

26 Gary Hulse, Jason White and Gavin Cape (eds), *Management of Alcohol and Drug Problems*, Oxford University Press, Melbourne, 2002, p. 8.

27 ibid., p. 4.

28 ibid., p. 5.

29 ibid., pp. 11, 22. Figures as at 1998.

30 ibid., p. 35.

31 ibid., p. 4.

32 M. Charlesworth, 'Ethics in Public Life', *Occasional Papers in Applied Ethics*, QUT Program for Applied Ethics and Human Change, 1991, p. 6.
33 'Teenage drink and drug abuse rife', *The Australian*, 25 February 2008, p. 3.
34 ibid.
35 Geoffrey Blainey, op. cit., p. 350.
36 Gary Hulse et al. (eds), op. cit., p. 198.
37 A. E. Blainey, 'The prohibition and total abstinence movement in Australia, 1880–1910', op. cit., p. 144.
38 The architectural effects are discussed in J. M. Freeland, *The Australian Pub*, Sun Books, Melbourne, p. 148ff.; the boisterous atmosphere is recounted in Walter Phillips, '"Six o'clock swill": the introduction of early closing of hotel bars in Australia', op. cit., p. 250.
39 Based on 'Commonwealth per capita drink consumption, 1907–1976 (in gallons)' figures in A. E. Dingle, '"The truly magnificent thirst": an historical survey of Australian drinking habits', op. cit., p. 246.
40 Walter Phillips, op. cit., p. 250.
41 ibid.
42 ibid., p. 252.
43 *Spectator*, Melbourne, 16 June 1916, quoted in Walter Phillips, op. cit., p. 253.
44 Walter Phillips, op. cit., p. 253.
45 *Australian Christian World*, 3 October 1911, quoted in Walter Phillips, p. 254.
46 Alan E. Stewart and Janice Harris Lord, 'Motor vehicle *Crash* versus *Accident*: a change in terminology is necessary', *Journal of Traumatic Stress*, vol. 15, no. 4, August 2002, pp. 333–335.
47 A. P. Diehm, R. F. Seaborn and G. C. Wilson, *Alcohol in Australia: Problems and Programmes*, McGraw-Hill, Sydney, 1978, p. 173.
48 ibid., *p.* 171.
49 'Drink-drive laws save 20,000 lives', *Daily Telegraph* (Sydney), 17 December 2007, p. 9.
50 Dillon, op. cit., pp. 304–05; Geoffrey Blainey, op. cit., p. 350.
51 A. E. Blainey, 'The prohibition and total abstinence movement in Australia, 1880–1910', op. cit., p. 146.
52 E. M. Jellinek, *The Disease Concept of Alcoholism*, Hillhouse Press, New Brunswick, 1960, p. 2.
53 Jean-Charles Sournia, op. cit., p. 46; S. Barrows and R. Room, op. cit., p. 17.
54 S. Barrows and R. Room, op. cit., p. 17.
55 Milton Lewis, *A Rum State ...*, op. cit., p. 98.
56 Jean-Charles Sournia, op. cit., p. 107.
57 Grant Rodwell, '"Persons of lax morality": temperance, eugenics and education in Australia, 1900–1930', *Journal of Australian Studies*, no. 64, 2000, p. 64.
58 ibid., p. 65.
59 ibid.
60 Warwick Anderson, *The Cultivation of Whiteness: Science, Health and Racial Destiny in Australia*, Melbourne University Press, Carlton, Victoria, 2002, p. 102.

61   Milton Lewis, *A Rum State* ..., op. cit., p. 132.
62   E. M. Jellinek, op. cit., p. 13.
63   ibid., pp. 36–41.
64   ibid., p. 185.
65   Gary Hulse et. al. (eds), op. cit., p. 6.
66   Edwards and Gross, op. cit., p. 1061.
67   Gary Hulse et al. (eds), op. cit., p. 6; Edwards and Gross, op. cit., p. 1061.
68   Maggie Brady, *The Grog Book: Strengthening Indigenous Community Action on Alcohol*, Commonwealth Department of Health and Family Services, Canberra, 1998, p. 310.
69   Gary Hulse et al. (eds), op. cit., p. 13.
70   A. P. Diehm et al., op. cit., p. 5.
71   Milton Lewis, *Managing Madness* ..., op. cit., pp. 1–2.
72   A. P. Diehm et al., op. cit., p. 5.
73   Kociumbas, p. 291.
74   ibid.
75   A. E. Blainey, 'The prohibition and total abstinence movement in Australia, 1880–1910', op. cit., p. 145.
76   Milton Lewis, *A Rum State* ..., op. cit., p. 109.
77   ibid.
78   ibid.
79   Geoffrey Blainey, op. cit., pp. 352–353.
80   ibid., p. 353.
81   ibid., p. 118.
82   A. P. Diehm et al., op. cit., p. 220.
83   Wayne Hall, Rosemarie Chen and Barry Evans, *Clients Admitted to 'The Buttery', a Therapeutic Community, 1980–1992*, National Drug and Alcohol Research Centre Technical Report No. 18, National Campaign Against Drug Abuse, University of New South Wales, 1993, p. 2.
84   ibid.
85   WCTU of Australia, Minutes of the Triennial Convention, 1921.
86   S. Barrows and R. Room, op. cit., p. 16.
87   ibid.
88   A. E. Blainey, 'The prohibition and total abstinence movement in Australia, 1880–1910', op. cit., p. 149.
89   S. Barrows and R. Room, op. cit., p. 17.
90   A. E. Blainey, 'The prohibition and total abstinence movement in Australia, 1880–1910', op. cit., p. 149–150.
91   Gary Hulse et al. (eds), op. cit., pp. 69, 191–2.
92   Milton Lewis, *A Rum State* ..., op. cit., pp. 126, 127.
93   A. E. Blainey, 'The prohibition and total abstinence movement in Australia, 1880–1910', op. cit., p. 149.
94   Gary Hulse et. al. (eds), op. cit., p. 192.
95   Milton Lewis, *A Rum State* ..., op. cit., p. 150.
96   Adele Horin, 'Helping others the key to happiness', *Sydney Morning Herald*, 10–11 May 2008, p. 3.

CHAPTER 6: A TASTE OF DISCRIMINATION

1   Western Australia in 1843, Victoria in 1864, South Australia in 1869, Queensland in 1885, Tasmania in 1908 and Australian Capital Territory in 1929.

2   From the 1940s, state goverments issued citizenship or exception certificates to Aboriginal people who agreed to forego their traditional way of life and assimilate into the white community. Many Aboriginal people dismissively referred to the certificates as 'dog licences'.

3   Maggie Brady, op. cit., p. 10.

4   Lois Tilbrook, 'Harris, William (1867–1931)', *Australian Dictionary of Biography*, Vol. 9, Melbourne University Press, 1983, pp. 213–214; Harris was one of seven children of Welsh convict William Harris (alias William Paulet), and his wife Madelaine whose mother was Aboriginal.

5   Gary Hulse, et. al. (eds), p. 313.

6   Maggie Brady, op. cit., p. 1.

7   ibid., p. 3.

8   'Research finds traces of nicotine on the map of Australia', *The University of Sydney News*, 30 November 2000.

9   ibid.

10 ibid.

11 Maggie Brady, op. cit., p. 3.

12 ibid., p. 4.

13 Research finds traces of nicotine on the map of Australia, op. cit.

14 Ministerial Council on Drugs Strategy, *National Drug Strategy: Aboriginal and Torres Strait Islander Peoples Complimentary Action Plan 2003–2006, Action Plan*, Commonwealth of Australia, Canberra, 2003, p. 3; on rationing as social control, see Jim Rowse. *White Flour, White Power: From Rations to Citizenship Control Australian*, Cambridge University Press, Melbourne, 1998.

15 Gary Hulse et al., (eds), op. cit., p. 311.

16 ibid. The Australian National Health and Medical Research Council (NHMRC) definition of hazardous drinking is an average of more than four standard drinks a day for men and more than two standard drinks a day for women (Gary Hulse, et. al. (eds), op. cit., p. 33).

17 W. McLennan and R. Madden, 'The Health and Welfare of Australia's Aboriginal and Torres Strait Islander Peoples', Australian Bureau of Statistics and Australian Institute of Health and Welfare, Canberra, 1997, pp. 46–47.

18 Gary Hulse et al. (eds), op. cit., p. 311.

19 Wayne Hall, Ernest Hunter and Randolph Spargo, 'Alcohol-related problems among Aboriginal drinkers in the Kimberley region of Western Australia', *Addiction*, 88, 1993, pp. 1091–1100, 1098.

20 Maggie Brady and Kingsley Palmer, *Alcohol in the Outback: Two Studies of Drinking*, North Australia Research Unit, Australian National University, Darwin, 1984, p. 31; Gary Hulse et al. (eds), op. cit., p. 313.; according to *Australian Alcohol Guidelines: Health Risks and Benefits*, National Health and Medical Research Council, 2001, p. 5, genetics is not a factor explaining differences in susceptibility to alcohol among Aboriginal Australians and

other groups; in fact, the level of alcohol-related problems varies between
Aboriginal communities due to social and economic factors.

21   A. Eckermann, T. Dowd, E. Chong, L. Nixon, R. Gray and S. Johnson, *Binan
      Goonj: Bridging Cultures on Aboriginal Health*, 2nd edition, Churchill
      Livingston, Sydney, 2006, p. 75.
22   Jean Lennane, *Alcohol The National Hangover: The Social and Personal Costs of
      Drinking in Australia — and What You Can Do About It!*, Allen & Unwin,
      Sydney, 1992, pp. 29–30.
23   Wayne Hall et al., op. cit., pp. 1091–1092.
24   ibid., p. 313.
25   Maggie Bracy, op. cit., p. 8.
26   ibid.
27   Ministerial Council on Drugs Strategy, *Action Plan*, p. 3.
28   McKnight, op. cit., p. 195.
29   Richard Trudgen, *Why Warriors Lie Down and Die: Towards an Understanding of
      Why the Aboriginal People of Arnhem Land Face the Greatest Crisis in Health and
      Education Since European Contact*, Aboriginal Resources and Development
      Services Inc., Darwin, 2000, p. 7.
30   Wayne Hall et al., op. cit., p. 1092.
31   ibid., p. 1091. The Australian National Health and Medical Research Council
      (NHMRC) defines harmful drinking as being over six standard drinks in any
      one day for men and over four standard drinks in any one day for women,
      Gary Hulse et al. (eds), op. cit., p. 33.
32   Brady & Palmer, op. cit., p. 11.
33   ibid., p. 13.
34   ibid., p. 11.
35   ibid.
36   ibid., p. 12.
37   Richard Trudgen, op. cit., pp. 14–15.
38   ibid., p. 27.
39   *We Believe In It — We Know It's True*, Film Australia, Lindfield, 1986,
      videocassette.
40   Heather Goodall, 'Aboriginal Land Rights', in Graeme Davison, John Hirst
      and Stuart Macintyre (eds), *The Oxford Companion to Australian History (revised
      edition)*, Oxford University Press, Oxford, 2001, pp. 5–7, 6.
41   *We Believe In It — We Know It's True*, op. cit.
42   M. Brady and K. Palmer, op. cit., p. 14.
43   ibid., p. 15.
44   ibid., p. 14–15.
45   ibid., p. 15.
46   ibid.
47   ibid., p. 16.
48   Ministerial Council on Drugs Strategy, *National Drug Strategy: Aboriginal and
      Torres Strait Islander Peoples Complementary Action Plan 2003–2006, Background
      Paper*, Commonwealth of Australia, Canberra, 2003, p. 28.
49   ibid.

50   ibid.
51   M. Brady and K. Palmer, op. cit., p. 26.
52   ibid., pp. 24, 26.
53   ibid., p. 64.
54   Noel Pearson, 'Blame game ends here', *The Australian*, 15 December 2007, p. 24.
55   ibid.
56   Cited in A. Eckermann, et al., op. cit., p. 75.
57   *Charcoal Lane* was recorded by Archie Roach in 1990 on Mushroom
       Records.
58   Pamela Lyon, *What Everybody Knows About Alice: A Report on the Impact of
       Alcohol Abuse on the Town of Alice Springs*, Tangentyere Council, Alice Springs,
       1990, pp. 32–3.
59   M. Brady and K. Palmer, op. cit., pp. 75–76.
60   ibid., p. 70.
61   Ministerial Council on Drugs Strategy, *Background Paper*, p. 29.
62   Wenten Rubuntja, with Jenny Green and with contributions from Tim
       Rowse, *The Town Grew Up Dancing: The Life and Art of Wenten Rubuntja*,
       Jukurrpa Books, Alice Springs, Northern Territory, 2002, pp. 105–106.
63   *We Believe In It — We Know It's True*, op. cit.
64   Alan R. Clough, Christopher B. Burns and Ngarrawu Mununggurr, 'Kava in
       Arnhem Land: a review of consumption and its social correlates', *Drug and
       Alcohol Review*, 19, 2000, pp. 319–328, 321.
65   Alan R. Clough et al., op. cit., p. 322.
66   ibid., p. 323.
67   Alan R. Clough, Terrence Guyala, Maymuna Yunupingu and Christopher B.
       Burns, 'Diversity of substance use in eastern Arnhem Land (Australia):
       patterns and recent changes', *Drug and Alcohol Review*, 21, 2002, pp. 349–356,
       351.
68   M. Brady and K. Palmer, op. cit., p. 72.
69   ibid., p. 30.
70   *We Believe In It — We Know It's True*, op. cit.
71   Cited in D. Gray, B. Sputore, A. Stearne, D. Bourbon and P. Strempel,
       Indigenous Drug and Alcohol Projects 1999–2000, National Drug Research
       Institute, Curtin University of Technology, Australian National Council on
       Drugs, 2002, p. 4.
72   ibid., p. 5.
73   ibid., p. 6.
74   T. Fitzgerald, *Cape York Justice Study*, Queensland Government, Brisbane, 2001;
       Queensland Department of Premier and Cabinet, *Meeting Challenges, Making
       Choices: The Queensland Government's response to the Cape York Justice Study*,
       Queensland Government, Brisbane, 2002.
75   S. A. Margolis, V. A. Ypinazar and R. Muller, 'The Impact of Supply
       Reduction through Alcohol Management Plans on Serious Injury in Remote
       Indigenous Communities in Remote Australia: A Ten-Year Analysis Using
       Data From the Royal Flying Doctor Service,' *Alcohol and Alcoholism*, Advanced
       Access, 8 October 2007.

76   'Alcohol management plans fail top end towns', *Courier-Mail*, 20 December 2007, p. 3.
77   ibid.
78   ibid.
79   'Poorly run alcohol plans fated to fail', *Courier-Mail*, 22–23 December 2007, p. 10.
80   'Drink ban town's neighbours have Crossing to bear', *The Australian*, 30 October 2007, p. 8.
81   D. Martin and M. Brady, 'Human Rights, Drinking Rights? Alcohol Policy and Indigenous Australians', *Lancet*, Vol. 364, October 2004, pp. 1282–83.
82   Louise Willis, 'Warnings of violence over alcohol restrictions', PM, *ABC Online*, www.abc.net.au/pm/contents/2003/s1008344.htm
83   ibid.
84   D. Martin and M. Brady, op. cit., p. 1282.
85   ibid.
86   'Imparja covers six states and territories, reaching remote communities in the Northern Territory and the majority of remote areas in South Australia, Queensland and New South Wales with select coverage in both Victoria and Tasmania.', www.imparja.com, accessed 2 February 2008.
87   'ATSIC urges Aboriginal TV station to continue ban on alcohol advertising', ATSIC Media Release, 17 December 2003.
88   Lyon, op. cit., p. 116.
89   Misha Schubert, 'Black TV scraps drink ad ban', *The Australian*, 17 December 2003, p. 3.
90   'Imparja should not advertise alcohol', *The Australian*, 18 December 2003, p. 12.
91   ibid.
92   Noel Pearson, 'Blame game ends here', *The Australian*, 15 December 2007, p. 24.
93   Noel Pearson, 'Sense of obligation a route out of handout hell', *Weekend Australian*, 22–23 December 2007, p. 22.
94   'Agendas of addiction', *Weekend Australian*, 1–2 March 2008, p. 26.
95   Noel Pearson, 'Blame game ends here' op. cit.

CHAPTER 7: THE LIMITS OF TOLERANCE

1   John Stuart Mill, 'On Liberty' in *On Liberty and other Essays*, John Gray (ed), Oxford University Press, Oxford, 1991 (rpt. 1859), pp. 5–127.
2   Max Charlesworth, 'Ethics in Public Life', *Occasional Papers in Applied Ethics*, No. 1, Queensland University of Technology, 1991, p. 6.
3   John Stuart Mill, op. cit., p. 14.
4   ibid., pp. 98–9.
5   ibid., p. 99.
6   ibid., p. 100.
7   John Stuart Mill, op. cit., p. 90.
8   'Radio cocktail contest angers critics', *The Age*, 4 June 2004.
9   'Bingeing a heart risk', *Daily Telegraph* (Sydney), 2 January 2008, p.15.

10   'Teenage drink and drug abuse rife', *The Australian*, 25 February 2008, p. 3.
11   'Stalking the devil in the drink', *Courier-Mail*, 16–17 February 2008, p. 51.
12   'Crack down on alcohol home delivery', AAP, 8.27, 6 May 2005.
13   'Tougher alcohol laws for parents', *Courier-Mail*, 28 November 2007.
14   'Bingeing a heart risk', *Daily Telegraph* (Sydney), 2 January 2008, p. 15.
15   'Stalking the devil in the drink', *Courier-Mail*, 16–17 February 2008, p. 51.
16   'Bouncer copping brunt of pub crowds', *Brisbane Times*, 16 February 2008.
17   Julian Lee, 'Alcohol empire strikes back', *Sydney Morning Herald*, 15–16 March 2008, p. 29.
18   'Teens can't taste liquor in alcopops', *The Australian*, 26 February 2008.
19   'Insider tells of young drinkers being targeted', *The Age*, 6 August 2007.
20   'Illicit drug use, drinking, starting at 12', *Sydney Morning Herald*, 18 December 2007, p. 3.
21   'Pre-mix tax rate criticised', *Courier-Mail*, 7 June 2006.
22   *The Australian*, 28 April 2008, p. 2.
23   Australian Institute of Health and Welfare, *2007 National Drug Household Survey; First Results*, Australian Institute of Health and Welfare, 2007 National Drug Household Survey; First Results, Drug Statistics Series No. 20. Canberra: AIHW.
24   Wayne Hall, 'More alcohol, more often is hardly the solution to a growing problem' opinion, *Sydney Morning Herald*, 20 April 2007.
25   Martin Kettle, 'My name is Britain, and I have a drink problem', *The Guardian*, 13 May 2003.
26   ibid.
27   Ben Atham, 'Land of the Rum Rebellion', *newmatilda.com*, accessed 8 May 2008; *Daily Telegraph*, 28 May 2008, pp. 1–2.
28   ibid.
29   Jacquelin Magnay, 'Drug and alcohol abuse rife, admit stars', *Sydney Morning Herald*, 21 June 2006.
30   'In excess: Does binge drinking in port reflect a wider social problem?', *Daily Telegraph*, (Sydney) 5 April 2008, pp. 75–7.
31   'Drinking, driving, lying — good old Collingwood,' *The Australian*, 6 August 2008, pp. 3–20.
32   'In excess: does binge drinking in port reflect a wider social problem?', *Daily Telegraph*, (Sydney) April 5, 2008, pp. 75–7.
33   ibid.
34   Edmund Burke, 'Shrinking beer glass', *Sunday Mail*, 11 June 2006.
35   Selina Mitchell, 'Aussies run out of puff', *The Australian*, 29 July 2005.
36   'Lord Winston in tirade on drink laws', *The Observer*, 4 September 2005.
37   Richard Midford, 'Australia and Alcohol: Living Down the Legend', *Addiction*, 100, 2005, p. 895.
38   'Sexy booze ads "still flouting standards"', *The Australian*, 15 January 2008, p. 3.
39   S. C. Jones and R. J. Donovon, 'Self regulation of alcohol advertising: is it Working?' *Journal of Public Affairs*, 2, 2002, pp. 153–165; 'Sexy booze ads still "flouting standards"', op. cit.
40   'Family First targets booze ads', *Weekend Australian*, 19–20 January 2008, p. 4.

41 Julian Lee, 'Alcohol empire strikes back', *Sydney Morning Herald*, 15–16 March 2008, p. 29.
42 *Sydney Morning Herald*, 16 February 2008, p. 34.
43 Garry Linell, 'Rudd's plan just a drop in the bucket', *Daily Telegraph*, 11 March 2008, p. 17.
44 Julian Lee, 'Alcohol empire strikes back', op. cit,, p. 30.
45 ibid.
46 Anna E. Blainey, e-mail communication, 20 February 2008.
47 E. Ellickson, R. L. Collins, K. Hambarsoomians and D. F. McCaffrey, 'Does Alcohol Advertising Promote Adolescent Drinking? Results from a Longitudinal Assessment', *Addiction*, 100 (2), February 2005, pp. 235–46.
48 'Alcohol ads on television in senator's sights', *Sydney Morning Herald*, 15 February 2008, p. 2; Diageo is the world's leading premium drinks business whose brands include Smirnoff, Johnnie Walker, Captain Morgan, Baileys, J&B, José Cuervo, Tanqueray, Guinness, Crown Royal, Beaulieu Vineyard and Sterling Vineyards wines, and Bushmills Irish whiskey. They claim that, 'A key component of our strategy is to promote a shared understanding of what it means to drink responsibly.' As part of that strategy they have developed a range of branded advertisements whose core objective is to deliver a responsible consumption message. Different advertisements have been developed for different cultures, including the UK, Thailand, Ireland, Australia, the US, Spain and the Netherlands. In the US, Diageo claims to spend 20 per cent of its broadcast advertising budget on branded responsibility advertisements. www.diageo.com
49 D. H. Jernigan, J. Ostroff, C. Ross, and J. A. O'Hara III, 'Sex difference in adolescent exposure to alcohol advertising in magazines', *Archives of Pediatrics and Adolescent Medicine*, vol. 158 (7) July 2004, pp. 702–704; Center for Disease Control and Prevention, *Morbidity and Mortality Weekly Report*, Vol. 55 (34), September 2006, pp. 937–940.
50 'Closing time', *The Age*, 8 September 2004.
51 'California says "no" to junk-food sales in schools', *The Christian Science Monitor*, 6 September 2005.
52 Rachel Kleinman, 'Drug drivers outstrip drunks', *The Age*, 15 April 2005.
53 Wayne Hall, 'More alcohol, more often is hardly the solution to a growing problem', Opinion, *Sydney Morning Herald*, 20 April 2007, p. 11.
54 Lion Nathan, 'Communities', www.lion-nathan.com/Great-Company/ Our-Responsibilities/Community.aspx. viewed 13 February 2008.
55 John Beeston, op. cit., p. 330.
56 Lion Nathan, 'How much is moderate?', www.lion-nathan.com.au/ all+about+drinks/all+about+beer/, accessed 12 June 2006.
57 Lion Nathan, 'Communities', op. cit.
58 I Timothy 5:23, Jerusalem Bible.
59 ABC Online News, 'Whisky claimed to cut cancer risk', 8 May 2005.
60 'Alcohol helps you think, say scientists', *Courier-Mail*, 3 August 2005.
61 Laudably, this funding has always appeared genuinely to be provided at arm's length. The Australian Brewers' Foundation, for example, provided some

funding to support this research project, and the authors can attest that our academic independence has been respected at all times.

62   *The Mercury*, 12 June 1996, p. 5.
63   ibid.
64   *Australian Alcohol Guidelines for Low-risk Drinking: Draft for Public Consultation*, National Health and Medical Research Council, October 2007.
65   'New drinking rules "unrealistic"', *The Australian*, 29 October 2007, p. 8.
66   ibid.
67   'Alcohol guidelines based on strong evidence', media release, NHMRC, 22 January 2008.
68   'New drinking rules "unrealistic"', op. cit.
69   ibid.
70   'Women "tricked" into drinking', *Courier-Mail*, 2 February 2008.
71   *The Mercury*, 12 June 1996, p. 5.
72   'Singing alcohol's praises out of tune with reality', *Australian Financial Review*, 16 February 2006, p. 67.
73   ibid.
74   ibid.
75   ibid.
76   Midford, op. cit., p. 894.
77   Wayne Hall, 'More alcohol, more often is hardly the solution to a growing problem' , op. cit.
78   ABC News Online, '"Light" wine on the cards', 27 April 2005.
79   *Australian Alcohol Guidelines for Low-risk Drinking: Draft for Public Consultation*, National Health and Medical Research Council, October 2007, p. 19.
80   D. Martin and M. Brady, op. cit., p. 1283.
81   'Sense of obligation in a route out of handout hell', *Weekend Australian*, 22–23 December 2007, p. 22.

AFTERWORD
1   'Halls Creek grog ban halved attacks', *Weekend Australian,* 24–25 January 2009, p. 9.
2   'Bra Boy gets three days in Hawaiian jail', *The Australian,* 22–23 November 2008, p. 3.
3   'Policy on the Rocks. The alcopop tax rise was a rort that wouldn't work', *The Australian*, 6 February 2009, p. 13.
4   Siobhain Ryan, 'New Zealand ministers say no evidence the alcopops tax is effective', *The Australian*, 6 February 2009, p. 7.
5   Australian Institute of Health and Welfare 2008, *2007 National Drug Strategy Household Survey: detailed findings.* Drug statistics series no. 22, AIHW, Canberra, 2008, pp. 32–33.
6   Ross Fitzgerald, 'Drowning in drink', *The Spectator Australia,* 25 October 2008, p. iv.
7   'Alcohol ads must go: Della Bosca', *Sydney Morning Herald,* 5 November 2008, p. 3.
8   ibid.

9   ibid.
10 R. Ironside, 'Club chief questions treatment by media', *Courier-Mail*, 19 September 2008, p. 2.
11 'It's their shout: sponsors on rocks over binge drinking', *Sydney Morning Herald*, 17 November 2008. pp. 1–2.
12 Email communication to authors, 10 April 2009.
13 Email communication to authors, 20 April 2009.

ACKNOWLEDGEMENTS

The authors would like to thank Anna E. Blainey and Christine Rakvin for their assistance on this project and the staff at the Queensland University of Technology Library, Fryer Library at the University of Queensland, John Oxley Library at the State Library of Queensland, National Library of Australia, Mitchell Library at the State Library of NSW, State Library of the Northern Territory, State Library of SA, State Library of WA, State Library of Victoria, the Historic Houses Trust, the National Gallery of Australia, Drug-Arm Queensland, Yalumba Wines, *Courier-Mail*, *The Weekend Australian*, Newspix, Fairfax Photos, Viscopy, and Redback Graphix.

We would also like to acknowledge the help and assistance of Lyndal Moor, Teresa Jordan, Phil Brown, Sandra McLean, Peter and Heather Beattie, Rob Whiddon, Stuart McIntyre, Geoffrey Blainey, Geoffrey Bolton, Brian Kelly, Harold Thornton, Margaret Kennedy, Glynn Davis, Jessica Halloran, Mandy Sayer, David Gallop, Andrew Demetriou, Barry Humphries, Gerry Connolly, Alison Wishart, John Birmingham, Kevin Leamon, Nick Nicholson, Anna Ridley, Alice Livingstone, Catherine Read, John Beeston, Corrine Hills, Bob Blasdall, Jonathan Dawson, Bruce Molloy, Brianna Sinclair, Robert Hill Smith, Christine Rogers, Paula Callan, Catherine Haden, Kate Harbison, Hilary Beaton, Sue Abbey, Tony Hooper, Gail Turnbull, Margaret Miles, Averill James, Gail Paynter, Beth Pinel, Bruce Howard, Robin Smith, Ken Gooding and Michael Callaghan.

We thank the Australian Brewers' Foundation Medical Advisory Committee for providing funds through their competitive grant scheme to cover some of the costs of our research into the use and misuse of alcohol.

Index

www.ingramcontent.com/pod-product-compliance
Lightning Source LLC
Chambersburg PA
CBHW022136020426
42334CB00015B/918